D1524633

CORNELIA HAHN OBERLANDER

Cornelia Hahn

Oberlander

MAKING THE MODERN LANDSCAPE

SUSAN HERRINGTON

"Landscape architecture is the art and the science of the possible"

Cornelia

[signature]

Cornelia

University of Virginia Press | Charlottesville and London

University of Virginia Press
Printed in the United States of America on acid-free paper

First published 2014

9 8 7 6 5 4 3 2 1

Library of Congress Cataloging-in-Publication Data

Herrington, Susan.

Cornelia Hahn Oberlander : making the modern landscape /
Susan Herrington.

pages cm

Includes bibliographical references and index.

ISBN 978-0-8139-3459-4 (cloth : alk. paper)

ISBN 978-0-8139-3536-2 (e-book)

1. Oberlander, Cornelia Hahn. 2. Women landscape architects—
Canada—Biography. 3. Landscape architects—Canada—Biography.
4. Holocaust survivors—Canada—Biography. 5. Jewish women—
Canada—Biography. 6. Harvard University. Graduate School of
Design. I. Title.

SB470.O23H47 2013

712.092—dc23

[B]   2013023350

Illustration Credits: *Figures not otherwise credited here or in the text were provided by Cornelia Hahn Oberlander Landscape Architect.* Bryan Beça, *pages 185 (top and bottom), 191, 196, 198, 212 (top and bottom), 215.* Collection Centre Canadien d'Architecture/Canadian Centre for Architecture, Montréal, *pages 43 (top), 46, 53, 64, 70, 78 (top), 82, 93, 95, 127, 167, 168 (top, middle, and bottom), 169, 203, 204, 206 (top and bottom), 208–9, 214.* © Felice C. Frankel, *page 86 (right).* Getty Images, *page 55.* Courtesy of the Frances Loeb Library, Harvard University Graduate School of Design, *page 25.* Stuart McCall/North Light, *pages 90, 91, 117 (bottom), 131, 162, 221.* Selwyn Pullan, photographer, *pages 38, 66 (bottom), 73, 74, 78 (middle), 78 (bottom), 79, 81 (top and bottom), 89, 110 (top, middle, and bottom), 111 (top and bottom), 113 (top and bottom), 210.* Ezra Stoller/Esto, *pages 130, 133.* University of British Columbia Archives, UBC 1.1/16353, *page 157.* Louis I. Kahn Collection, the University of Pennsylvania and the Pennsylvania Historical and Museum Commission, *page 49.* Walter P. Reuther Library, Wayne State University, *page 43 (bottom).* Courtesy of HM White, New York, N.Y., *page 145.* Turner Wigginton, *pages 66 (top), 86 (left), 87, 94 (top and bottom), 132, 143.*

To Cornelia Hahn Oberlander

OC FASLA FCSLA LMBCSLA

and future landscape architects

CONTENTS

Foreword by Marc Treib ix

Acknowledgments xv

Introduction 1

1 Identity 11

2 Housework 31

3 Human Environment 97

4 Ecological Environment 149

5 Invention 199

Conclusion 219

Notes 227

Bibliography 245

Index 262

Color gallery follows page 96

FOREWORD

Until quite recently it would have been difficult to name a significant landscape architect working in Canada — although as we learn from this book, for more than four decades there has been at least one woman who could claim that accolade. The name we should have known, of course, is Cornelia Hahn Oberlander, who moved to Vancouver in 1953 and has been engaged in active practice there ever since. It has been said that landscape architecture is an invisible profession, given that the public tends to identify trees, shrubs, and flowers as the result of natural processes rather than purposeful design. While the names of a few architects are mentioned periodically in the media, rarely cited is the landscape architect for any particular project — at least not since the time of Frederick Law Olmsted some hundred and fifty years ago. The publication of *Cornelia Hahn Oberlander: Making the Modern Landscape* is therefore a very welcome event, not only in Canada but internationally as well.

Should some few of us have been familiar with any of Cornelia Hahn Oberlander's landscape designs it would probably have been the landmark Robson Square and Provincial Law Courts in Vancouver from the late 1970s. This project comprised a major urban renewal effort that transformed three derelict blocks of Vancouver's downtown into a vital governmental and art center — and most of all a vibrant multiuse public space. That Arthur Erikson's architectural design relied heavily on concrete as his prime building material caused some contention at the time of its realization, but there were few questions raised about the nature or the qualities of the project's landscape design. Through a variety of plantings and scales, Oberlander conjured a range of spaces that varied from the individual and intimate to those reeking of collective public display. Water — in pools and falls — complemented the vegetation, serving double duty by screening street noise and contributing sensual delight. Despite the unquestioned success of Robson Square, the name of the landscape architect hardly became common knowledge.

The Oberlander story begins with her childhood in Germany and gathers drama with the family's escape to England in the 1930s and move thereafter to the United States. With a mother dedicated to both child development and gardening it appears that Oberlander's career as a landscape architect was almost preordained. With graduate studies at Harvard completed in the 1940s she began to work on public housing landscapes in Philadelphia, experience that would in many ways be formative. These projects constituted an initial foray into the making of public landscapes that were squarely directed towards social good, a consideration that would inform her work across six decades of practice.

Oberlander was certainly not alone in this quest for socially responsible design. In her native Germany before the war, the landscape architect Leberecht Migge designed for every level of society, from estates for the wealthy to housing landscapes for the working class. His visions extended as far as proposals for self-sufficient communities independent of the city, an early effort towards ecological planning. Farther north, the Stockholm park system, propelled by the vision of Holger Blom and the design talent of Erik Glemme, embodied the social democratic vision of Sweden in the 1930s. There, park department and society together produced a myriad of green areas small and large intended to serve rather than instruct the populace. During these same years — the era of the Great Depression — American landscape architects such as Garrett Eckbo served in the Farm Security Administration, creating camps for the agricultural workers displaced by drought and foreclosure. Where most of the European landscape architects focused squarely on social good using a naturalistic aesthetic, Eckbo and his colleagues considered social welfare and creative form with equal interest. Seen in hindsight they attempted to apply — somewhat naively, or at least over-optimistically — some of the most advanced form-making ideas to habitation for the lowest stratum of society. Their success was only partial, it must be admitted.

In this sense Cornelia Oberlander is more North American than European. From the get-go she has always considered form to be an, or even *the*, essential element of landscape architecture. After all, form and space, as designed and constructed, are what we perceive. She has held the belief that through the design of form and space one may control — if that is not too strong a term — the perceptions of landscape that lead to enjoyment, instruction, and even revelation.

Oberlander's practice has spanned small and large scales, suburban and urban situations, and somewhat uniquely, wilderness design — if such a term is not an oxymoron. Social and urban concerns conjoined in the 1970s design of Robson Square and its adjoining Provincial Law Courts, the project for which she remains best known. Constructed on three blocks in central Vancouver, this project not only created vital public space — the city's veritable green oasis and activity center — but also played a key role in revitalizing the neighborhood around it. Despite modifications to the original design over the years — unfortunately changes made without Oberlander's consultation — Robson Square maintains its position as Vancouver's most important urban space.

If the urban square was one theater of achievement, no less so were the parks and playgrounds Oberlander designed over the decades. Drawing on child development studies and observations of her own children playing in the postwar years, she designed a series of children's play areas both engaging and challenging. Some of these works shared similarities with Robert Royston's coeval playground designs in California, yet they differed to some degree in their intentions and vehicles. In parks in Palo Alto and Oakland, for example, Royston designed playgrounds embodying carefully defined social programs, but their swoopy forms and constructions were fixed. In contrast, Oberlander adopted and adapted elements of the "adventure playground" first conceived by landscape architects such as Carl-Theodor Sørensen in Denmark and given broader application in Britain thereafter. Oberlander's playgrounds melded shaped elements with construction materials, fixity with fluidity, designs intended to provoke children to respond to the situation and to literally build an alternative environment. Sadly, as in so many of these playgrounds around the world, liability has trumped creativity. As a result the adventure playground has all but become extinct, replaced by trite and standardized play equipment from coast to coast.

From the time of her move to Vancouver, Cornelia Hahn Oberlander has been an avid conservationist and vocal proselytizer for a landscape architecture that takes full cognizance of its ecological situation as both obligation and opportunity. As author and lecturer she has furthered the agenda for these values at both local and national scales — and she has literally practiced what she has preached. Her designs have produced site planning and landscapes that have reduced the energy loads of buildings, with planted roofs that insulate and mitigate storm water runoff while filtering impure water, and have used recycled materials for both economic and moral benefit. While she does not entirely restrict her schemes to local plants, exotics are judiciously chosen to be fully in accord with the conditions in which they must exist. In projects such as the assembly building in Yellowknife, however, the task was more directed to repair rather than invention — and those species already growing on-site were the only logical choice.

There is little doubt about the skill with which Oberlander has designed her landscapes; to this must be added the extensive knowledge of the living and synthetic materials with which she has worked. As with the making of all good landscape architecture, design begins with an understanding of the site, its limits, and its potentials. In Canada these can be extreme given the span of distances and the range of temperatures and soil conditions. A theme that runs throughout Susan Herrington's tale is how Oberlander has continued to inquire and learn, although at some point in their careers most landscape architects believe that the knowledge they possessed is quite enough. The possessor of an iterate curiosity, however, Oberlander continues to ask, continues to collaborate with experts, and continues to observe. She applies new or improved materials — like roofing membranes — when their development represents progress and a better product. She uses plants new to her palette when the climatic or soil condition demands — but employs them in manners that in almost all cases are evident, without question, as having been designed. Neither an unquestioning naturalism nor a fawning historicism has characterized her practice. Oberlander's work rarely disappears into the existing context — although in some extreme instances, disappearance has been the basic concept. One could cite the roof garden — or green roof, if you will — atop Library Square in Vancouver. While inaccessible to the public, the roof is visible from the surrounding towers. Drawing on a river metaphor, Oberlander configured the required plant list as a meandering swath, anchored by masses of ground cover. Here an almost level site was given a visual dimension through apparent design. The polar opposite approach guided the design of a landscape in the far north, where traces of the landscape architect's hand all but disappeared — yet the designer's work configured building, landscape, and the relation between the two.

Of all Oberlander's designs this landscape, although it appears the least interesting in photographs, is probably her most significant in contribution. It is a landscape in the hinterlands of the Northwest Territories. Her first project there was the landscape situating the assembly building for the territory, which had only recently achieved some degree of political autonomy. As an area incredibly sensitive to climate change, as a true wilderness site, it was obvious that the site was going to be seriously affected by the construction of a building of this magnitude and the infrastructure needed to support it. The scrubby flora and the peat bogs that comprise the site would require many, many years to recover should serious damage be done. Under her prompting the access road was rerouted around the existing peat bog and "grafts" of this peat helped repair the inevitable damage from construction. Drawing from the sewing notion of "invisible mending" she proposed to insert native species back into their home landscape.

Cleverest of all was the process by which these new plantings could be produced. The growing season is terminally short at that high latitude, and insufficient for rapid propagation. Nor were there greenhouses in the region. In the field, Oberlander and her colleagues collected seeds, cuttings, and tissue cultures and propagated them in greenhouses in Vancouver — and thereafter returned them to Yellowknife for planting. In photographs the landscape architect's work is barely noticeable, if at all. Yet it is a project of which Oberlander is most proud and from which we can surely learn.

There seems to be a moral to this story, or perhaps several morals. The first is that one must know the site, and must have the tools and understanding to read the site intelligently and to understand how to proceed. "Site" in this case includes the people and the program of use as well as the natural situation. But one cannot assume that a viable solution issues directly from analysis — creativity is required. Most often the primary contribution of the landscape architect is to use material for its form and in configurations that define space. These are consequential. Yet if one thinks locally — on-site — one must also think globally, considering the consequences of this particular landscape in relation to the neighborhood, the city, the region, the earth. Oberlander's work on the University of British Columbia campus, like those in the extreme conditions of the Northwest Territories, demonstrates how form and intelligence are hardly incompatible — in fact, one demands and benefits from the other.

Susan Herrington's years of interviews with Cornelia Hahn Oberlander, the study of her works on-site and in drawings, and her research on the people and places that have formed the context for Oberlander's development and practice have yielded a first study that begins to compensate for years of invisibility. It is a story well told.

Marc Treib
Berkeley, California
April 2013

ACKNOWLEDGMENTS

During the course of my research for *Cornelia Hahn Oberlander: Making the Modern Landscape,* many institutions and organizations gave me assistance. The Social Science and Humanities Research Council of Canada provided the first grant that was essential to realizing the book. I have also been supported by the Canada Council for Arts, which funded much of the visual material. The color plates in this book were made possible by a production grant from the Graham Foundation for Advanced Studies in the Fine Arts. Lastly, a University of British Columbia Killam Faculty Fellowship helped me take precious time off for writing.

I am in debt to numerous individuals who made this assistance possible. I am grateful to Mark Francis, Kenneth Helphand, Joan Iverson Nassauer, and Marc Treib, who wrote letters of support for my initial grants regarding this project. Boyd Zenner at the University of Virginia Press was also an early backer. Their enthusiastic support was instrumental to funding much of the research. For their careful reading of draft versions of my manuscript, I thank my friends and colleagues: Sonja Dümpelmann, Sherry McKay, Michelangelo Sabatino, Marc Treib, and Thaïsa Way, as well as the reviewers for the University of Virginia Press. Their comments and suggestions provided vital insights into my thinking and writing about Oberlander and her work. Likewise, the Women and Modernism in Landscape Architecture colloquium at Harvard University's Graduate School of Design, a lecture at the University of Washington College of Built Environments, and a presentation that I coauthored with Gemma McLintock at the Council of Educators in Landscape Architecture's annual conference provided venues for me to present my ongoing research and receive helpful comments and suggestions.

Also, I am grateful to the archivists and librarians at the Architectural Archives of the University of Pennsylvania, the American Heritage Center at the University of Wyoming, the Canadian Architectural Archives at the University of Calgary, the Canadian Centre for Architecture, the Chestnut Hill Historical Society, the Collections Canada, the Frances Loeb Library Special Collections at Harvard University, the Harvard University Archives, the Library and Archives of Canada, the National Park Service Frederick Law Olmsted National Historic Site, the North Carolina Department of Cultural Resources, the University of British Columbia Archives, the Vancouver Historical Society, and the Walter P. Reuther Library and Archives at Wayne State University. In particular, I thank Renata Guttman, the head of Collection Reference at the Canadian Centre for Architecture, who helped me navigate through the vast amount of material at the Cornelia Hahn Oberlander Archive. I also thank Mary Daniels, the Special Collections librarian at Harvard University's Frances Loeb Library, for helping me wade through the student work, lecture notes, and scrapbooks from the 1940s Graduate School of Design curriculum at Harvard.

Numerous individuals gave me their valuable time for interviews and e-mail exchanges: Beryl Allen, Martin Lewis, Nick Milkovich, Gino Pin, Gundula Proksch, Selwyn Pullan, Bing Thom, Hank White, Elisabeth Whitelaw, Ron Williams, Milton and Fei Wong, Jim Wright, Linda Yorke/Forbes, the owners of Residence X and Residence Y, and of course Cornelia Hahn Oberlander. It is with deep regret that I note Milton Wong's passing during the course of the research for this book. Milton was very passionate about landscape and art, and the work that Oberlander did for his family over the years. His generosity and warmth are missed by many.

I also thank the landscape architecture graduate students at the University of British Columbia who worked with me on the interviews, case studies, and literature reviews: Gemma McLintock, Sarah Rankin, and Megan Vogt. Their hard work and love of laughter made research particularly enjoyable. There are also photographers and graphic designers to thank: Bryan Beça, Tom Fox, Stuart McCall, Selwyn Pullan, and Turner Wigginton. Their discerning eyes provided the chief visual complement to the text. Lastly, I am deeply grateful to Dominic McIver Lopes for his patience and thoughtful criticism throughout the making of this book.

INTRODUCTION

This account of Cornelia Hahn Oberlander's life work also tells a story of modern landscape architecture. Both a biography and a history, I chronicle Oberlander's career as it plays out ahead and alongside the profession's unfolding from World War II to the present in North America. Most people know Oberlander for her award-winning rooftop landscapes and her unwavering promotion of green design, which show no grey patches of ambiguity. But lesser known is that Oberlander has been steadily practicing landscape architecture since 1947. This fact is not always evident when meeting her, for she exudes both the possibilities of youth and the hard-won wisdom that comes with time.

The interplay of history and biography has reciprocal benefits. By situating Oberlander's projects within the historical context of modern landscape architecture's formation, I aim to reveal the systems of beliefs that made them possible, and how in many instances she advanced these beliefs to transform the field. Given that Oberlander's practice has now spanned more than half a century, her oeuvre provides a fertile opportunity for understanding modern landscape architecture. Moreover, she has always maintained that her work "addresses the needs of the times,"[1] and as society's needs have shifted and expanded with time, so too has her career, demonstrating that history conveys human agency — the choices an individual makes — as well as circumstance — the conditions shaping decisions and events. Certainly for Oberlander this is an appropriate way of accounting for her work. She has never viewed herself as the lone artist who is set apart from the world and struggling against it. On the contrary, in talking with Oberlander today you get the sense she is completely aware of the exigencies of the present and of planning for the future.

Likewise, biography contributes to a historical examination. The historian Joseph Ellis describes the important contributions made by biography to history, positing that biography centers the historical quest by giving "a chorus to the cacophony of historical facts" as "it permits us to clothe generalization with palpable and textured evidence."[2] Without a doubt Oberlander's life story has intersected with pivotal moments of the modern period, so her story has much to reveal. Born in Germany in 1921, she experienced as a child the ferment of Weimar art and architecture. She later witnessed the rise of National Socialism. In 1938 Oberlander escaped Nazi persecution with her mother and sister, eventually settling in the United States. After graduating from Smith College's integrated program of architecture and landscape architecture, she was admitted into the Graduate School of Design (GSD) at Harvard University in the second cohort of full-time students to include women since the school's inception.

Exposed to the first wave of modern landscape architects (including Christopher Tunnard, Lester Collins, and Walter Chambers, as well as the former Bauhaus architects Walter Gropius and Marcel Breuer), Oberlander participated in some of the earliest experiments in modern design pedagogy in North America. This educational experience stressed abstraction, the social obligations of design, and the importance of cross-disciplinary collaborations, ideals she would continue to develop throughout her career. After graduation she worked in Philadelphia for the Citizens' Council on City Planning (CCCP), helping to spearhead direct community involvement in the creation of parks and community gardens. She was also deeply influenced by Dan Kiley, whom she assisted in designing public housing with architects Louis Kahn and Oskar Stonorov in the 1950s. This housing was distinguished by a new building typology for the city: a combination of two- and three-story structures and towers set within extensive shared open spaces, a configuration that posed both opportunities and challenges.   In 1953 she married the architect and planner H. Peter Oberlander and moved to Vancouver, where they both influenced the development of the city and their professions, raised a family, and maintained a passionate and intellectual union that lasted until Peter's death in 2008. In the 1950s and 1960s there was a growing appetite for modern design in this relatively young West Coast city, so her move was both well placed and well timed. As one of the few modern landscape architects practicing in Vancouver, Oberlander had many opportunities to realize gardens for private residences designed by modern architects. She continued with her public housing work and also expanded her conception and design of children's play spaces in the late 1960s, demonstrating a new model for play environments at Expo 67 in Montreal.

Starting with Robson Square, Oberlander began working with the architect Arthur Erickson, and over the next thirty years they would realize numerous projects that produced a seamless cohesion between architecture and landscape. Working on Robson Square also advanced Oberlander's technical expertise in bringing natural elements into cities and strengthened her spatial understanding of architecture. During the 1970s, many urban landscapes were defined by windswept concrete plazas, swaths of surface parking, and treeless streets, a condition perceived as largely indifferent to human needs. In response, landscape architects designed numerous urban landscapes providing human experiences with a foil to these harsh urban conditions.

This work was interrelated with the growing environmental movement that had a tremendous effect on landscape architecture and for which Oberlander was an early proponent. By the 1990s her landscapes helped forge a second wave of urban landscapes that integrated plants, water, and other elements into a project's ecological infrastructure. Through her built work, lectures, publications, and the construction process itself, she promoted recycling, native plants, water conservation, and biodiversity. In fact she continues to lead the way in this arena as one of the first landscape architects to practice in Canada's far north.

By using Oberlander's work as a lens to view modern landscape architecture I hope that new knowledge will be revealed concerning its history. For example, a key contribution will be a deeper understanding of a female landscape architect practicing in the mid-twentieth century. In 1994 the landscape historian Heath Schenker argued that most of what we know about the history of landscape architecture has been told through a series of works by "master designers" who have been almost exclusively male.[3] Fifteen years later Thaïsa Way published *Unbound Practice: Women and Landscape Architecture in the Early Twentieth Century,* revealing numerous women who made contributions to the field prior to World War II. Yet, we know very little about the women practicing immediately after the war. Thus a goal of this book is to increase our understanding of a practicing, female landscape architect. This knowledge is important now more than ever before as women are increasingly present in both academic institutions offering degrees in landscape architecture and landscape architecture practice. And as Ellis reminds us, the "secret truth" about biography's appeal is that "we study other lives so we might better live our own . . . it's about me now."[4]

Moreover, Oberlander is not just the mortar between two bricks — Lawrence Halprin and Ian McHarg, for example. Rather her work changes the contours of the foundation upon which subsequent designers have built their careers. In contrast to many landscape architects working in the École des Beaux-Arts tradition, which relied on historical styles and ornamentation, Oberlander consistently employed a modern design vocabulary that stressed abstract forms. Also, many of her projects were public landscapes in an urban setting, rather than exclusively domestic and suburban. Thus her work has helped to expand the type of projects and design vocabulary deemed appropriate for her gender.

Oberlander's work also confronts misconceptions about the history of landscape architecture such as the profession's elaboration of environmental ideals in the 1970s. While environmental advocacy and ecological design during this time period is often attributed to Ian McHarg and others who operated at a regional scale, Oberlander worked at a human scale, advancing the environmental movement by designing urban landscapes that offered direct experiences with natural systems. The landscape architectural theorist Elizabeth K. Meyer has found this in Lawrence Halprin's practice as well. Meyer has suggested, "Halprin's work represented a type of critical practice that gave form to ecological environmental values through the construction of experience."[5] For both Oberlander and Halprin the profession's advocacy of nonhuman nature did not supplant their humanist conception of environment. In fact, the communication of ecological ideas and human experience are powerfully linked. Oberlander would build upon this linkage in her later projects, as features of her work became fully incorporated in the ecological functioning of the building and landscape as one system.

Another goal here is to expand our knowledge of Canadian landscape architecture. The Canadian poet and novelist Margaret Atwood has described the border between the United States and Canada as the longest one-way mirror in the world, with Canadians seeing Americans and Americans looking back at themselves. As the landscape architect Ron Williams has pointed out, the number of professionals practicing in Canada during the course of the twentieth century has been and is still relatively small in relationship to the vast scale of the country.[6] Moreover, the political context of its postwar modernism, particularly in Vancouver, differed from American versions. While there are visual similarities between the design works in both countries, the political structures that supported these forms varied. According to the historian Rhodri Windsor-Liscombe, Vancouver was "a small city literally 'on the margin,' with a limited if liberal cultural identity attuned to the European note in transatlantic modernism."[7] This attunement to European modernism, and its social convictions, is evident in the public housing landscapes that Oberlander designed in Vancouver versus those in Philadelphia.

Oberlander as a Modern Landscape Architect?

A term that I have wrestled with in writing this book is "modern landscape architecture." Given that we are in the second decade of the twenty-first century, can Oberlander still be called a modern landscape architect? Is her current work modern? She maintains that unlike some of her colleagues, she has never been "kissed by postmodernism."[8] Clearly answering this question depends on how you define modern versus postmodern. If modern and postmodern are delineated as styles that follow architectural time periods in the United States, then Oberlander's landscapes from the past twenty-five years could not be deemed modern. Setting aside these chronological definitions in architecture however, and looking to the use of the term in the profession's own history, we may find a definition that speaks to a genealogy of the term "modern" in landscape architecture that is tied to social transformation.

The term "modern" has been primarily associated with the eighteenth century and notions of "progress" and "development."[9] The British antiquarian and politician Horace Walpole captured this meaning in *Essays on Modern Gardening* (1780) with his descriptions of the revolutionary landscape gardens created in Britain during the eighteenth century. These landscape gardens were made possible by advancements in agricultural technology that increased productivity and radically changed the country's socioeconomic and cultural order. Post–World War II North America also witnessed an epoch-defining period when cultural mores, systems of production, and patterns of consumption radically changed. These transformations changed the profession, and it was Garrett Eckbo in *Landscape for Living* (1950) who most lucidly mapped out a postwar version of modern landscape architecture. Marc Treib has pointed out that Eckbo canvassed two important ideas central in this book.[10] First, Eckbo substantiated the connection between abstraction in the plastic arts and the use of abstraction in landscape design. Second, he conceptualized the profession as an agent for social change towards a more egalitarian society.

Oberlander's belief in the social efficacy of landscape architecture and her use of abstraction have been unshakeable dimensions of her practice; thus, I have chosen to call her work modern. It is important to note, however, that as Oberlander gained recognition in the field, the types of clients she addressed extended from residents of public housing to middle-class homeowners to wealthy art collectors and philanthropists. Likewise, her practice, which originally included the design of neighborhood-scaled parks and playgrounds, expanded to encompass large urban projects. Yet, she never lost her conviction to serve all of society and she has continued to work on public housing projects, modest gardens, playgrounds, and landscapes for people with special needs. As she commented in an interview with me in 2010, "Why would I disregard the very reasons why I joined this profession in the first place?"[11]

So how has she been able to maintain these convictions? One answer lies in her belief that equality and human agency are what make the moving parts of democratic life tick, values that she shared with Peter Oberlander. Given her personal history in Germany during the 1930s, Oberlander's conviction that equality and agency lie at the root of a tolerant democratic society is not just a popular sentiment — it is also a belief that she saw tested firsthand. Moreover, these political values are linked to an aesthetic. For Oberlander, the quotidian life needs food, clothing, and shelter; but it needs beauty as well. She believes that beauty "is not separate from social responsibility."[12] Indeed, this contention forms part of Elaine Scarry's theory of beauty and social justice. Scarry posits that beauty leads us not away, but towards social justice.[13] When we observe something beautiful, such as a bird or a face, it makes us pause as we attempt to understand others, which is a crucial step in creating a society based on equal rights.

Research Methods

Analyses of journal articles, books, exhibit catalogs, essays, and newspaper articles on and by Oberlander, combined with reviews of the historical and contemporary literature on modern landscape architecture and architecture, helped me distill the major themes for the book: housing, human environment, ecological environment, and invention. In particular the substantive writing by Marc Treib on modern landscape architecture provided an immeasurable amount of ideas and insights.[14] This reading was also accompanied by repeated site visits to Oberlander's built landscapes. She has been involved with more than five hundred projects since 1947; thus, the thematic structure facilitated the selection of projects and life events to include here.

Using Mark Francis's "A Case Study Method for Landscape Architecture," and with the help of graduate students, I also compiled case studies of Oberlander's major projects. These studies are organized by context, design process, overall concept, landscape strategy, and reception. Smaller projects, or those where there was limited information, did not receive this ordered analysis. The case study method prompted us to ask questions about the project's political context and public reception, queries that may have been overlooked had we limited ourselves to strict project analyses. The case study method also helped us to consider Oberlander's built work over time, which is vital to any account of landscapes. Another consideration was the architecture in Oberlander's projects, particularly since it is so often closely intertwined with her landscapes both conceptually and physically. This incorporation of architectural analyses revealed much-needed insights into the collaborative dimensions of her practice. Case study work was enhanced by site visits and by research at the Canadian Centre for Architecture (CCA) in Montreal. The CCA's Cornelia Hahn Oberlander Archive contains her drawings, correspondences, and project files. These materials were critical in synthesizing textual information and her built works.

Research methods also involved interviews with people who have collaborated with Oberlander and with her clients, particularly on residential projects. Some of these clients worked closely with her, often developing a personal relationship over an extended period of time. Also, Oberlander made herself available for extensive interviews. From 2008 to 2013 she graciously provided hours of discussion during taped video sessions, augmented by informal interviews and e-mail exchanges. Oberlander's contributions were invaluable, as they offered insights that would have been otherwise unobtainable through textual and archival methods.

However, historians have questioned the heuristic premise of "the architect interview." Traditionally the oral interview served as documentary evidence in reconstructing the past; but historians have found that this method has proved to be unreliable. According to the architectural historian Robert Proctor, those interviewed too often act as their own biographer and their recollections of events from an earlier period cannot be regarded as the same as "when they engaged in the act of creation" of a project.[15] For Proctor, "the historian critic approaching the architect interview needs to recognize that it is a self-conscious artistic creation in its own right, requiring the same degree of critical analysis" that would be applied to other historical works.[16] I have tried to stay true to this idea. In fact variations between Oberlander's recounting and my interpretation were highlighted when we both presented her work at a colloquium in 2011.[17] I reminded her that I was going to say things about her life and career that she might not have thought of, and that I hoped she would find this interesting.

In my communications with her, Oberlander has always been very open in recounting both her successes and failures and the many stumbling blocks she has encountered. She believes her work is "an evolving experiment. . . . The art of the possible."[18] By revealing the ideas that did not work out, she demonstrates both the need to experiment and take risks, as well as deal with the consequences, positive or negative, that arise from these actions.[19]

Failures and the struggles inherent in realizing landscapes often get lost in histories that primarily rely on polished images of built work. They can characterize landscape architecture as a series of effortlessly conceived artifacts. Unrealized aspects of a project, such as conceptual ideas, are not only the recordings of history but also the testimonies of intentions that contribute to a practice. For Oberlander, conceptual ideas entertained in unbuilt projects often manifested themselves in later works. For example her references to First Nations landscapes at the University of British Columbia's Museum of Anthropology took almost forty years to be fully installed, although the landscape was never made part of the museum's formal educational programming. Yet, this project would lead her to consider how the design of landscapes communicates ideas about cultural or natural systems — ideas that found expression in her designs for the National Gallery landscape, Library Square rooftop, and the VanDusen Botanical Gardens Visitor Centre.

Structure of the Book

The format of this book is chronological within each chapter. "Identity," the first chapter, and "Invention," the last chapter, bracket the main chapters. Thus "Housework," "Human Environment," and "Ecological Environment" define themes and mark transitions in phases of Oberlander's career from 1947 to the present day. Each of these chapters begins with a contextual account of the times that locates the intellectual coordinates of Oberlander's thinking and situates her work. This is followed by more detailed interpretations of Oberlander's projects that elucidate this context. The semi-chronological structure has allowed me to both distill key objectives in her work and lay bare how they have accrued over time.

As a final note to this introduction, *Cornelia Hahn Oberlander: Making the Modern Landscape* completes a story started long ago. In 1997 I was in a Berlin archive studying the first German kindergartens when I encountered the author Beate Hahn. She was one of the earliest twentieth-century writers to describe the use of gardens in nineteenth-century kindergartens. Despite its seemingly innocuous reputation now, during the late 1840s the kindergarten was considered a radical pedagogy and it was subsequently banned throughout Germany. While the ban was eventually lifted, much of the knowledge about the pedagogical role of gardens in the original kindergartens was lost. Unfortunately, the archive had no publications by Beate Hahn after 1936. When I inquired about Hahn, the archivist casually informed me that she must have disappeared. Years later I was interviewing Oberlander about her play environments. It was then that I discovered I was speaking with Beate Hahn's daughter, and I knew that Cornelia Hahn Oberlander would be a woman whom history could not forget.

IDENTITY

1

The following chronicles Cornelia Hahn Oberlander's life from childhood to her graduation from Harvard University in 1947. It gives an account of her motives as well as the circumstances that have shaped her life, and eventually her practice as a landscape architect. Here, Oberlander's own words order the narrative. These brief passages speak to her identity: her experiences in Weimar Germany and her mother's gardening and writing endeavors, her resolve to assimilate and not let the appreciably traumatic events from her past feature disproportionately in her future, and her sheer determination to be a modern landscape architect. These quotations and the ideas they spark also illuminate experiences shared by others regarding gender and the future of the profession. During and immediately after World War II the notion of women working *and* raising a family was questioned; however, Oberlander was determined to do both. Ultimately it was her experiences at the GSD that nurtured her social convictions and fostered her use of abstraction, her participation in cross-disciplinary collaborations, and her belief in the economic thrift of design. Together these principles formed the poetic pragmatism of her modern landscape architecture.

I've made up my mind to adjust myself, discard sentiments and look into the future. — Cornelia Hahn Oberlander, "Reflective Moments," 1941

Born in Mülheim/Ruhr, in 1921, Oberlander is part of what the historian Walter Laqueur has called "Generation Exodus": German Jews born between 1914 and 1928 who fled Nazi persecution during the 1930s. Laqueur reveals that this cohort of refugees hailed from different classes, from the very poor to the wealthy, and diverse religious backgrounds; some were practicing Jews while others were members of assimilated families. However, an underlying pattern that they commonly shared was their ability to thrive in their adopted countries. According to Laqueur, age mobilized their success. These refugees, who included Henry Kissinger and Ruth Westheimer, were teenagers and young adults when they escaped. Thus,

Oberlander, 1925

they were old enough to feel the gravity of their family's situation but young enough to adapt and survive in their new countries. In fact numerous individuals from this generation, such as Oberlander, made significant contributions to their professions and their newfound communities. Moreover, members of Generation Exodus continued to identify with Weimar Germany. Although they felt the raw sense of loss when they fled their homeland, scores still remember happy childhoods when Germany was a culturally rich, democratic society.

The Weimar period marked a time when modern design and new materials heralded the emergence of a postimperial society and a leveling of social inequities. Oberlander's family actively participated in this effervescent period of art and design. Her mother attended dance performances at the Bauhaus in Dessau, her father studied Bauhaus prefabricated houses, and her grandparents lived in a house designed by Erich Mendelsohn.[1] Jutta, Oberlander's best friend, lived in Mendelsohn's Bejach house in Berlin/Steinstücken. Playing there daily she was impressed by the way the structure extended into the landscape with long terraces and perimeter walls that matched the same materials and design of the house, an integration of landscape and architecture that she would seek in her own work. Indeed, Oberlander's experiences of modern architecture during one of its early evocations in twentieth-century Europe gave voice to her belief that an enlightened life was a modern one, and it propelled her gravitation to modern landscape architecture as a young woman.

The Hahn family's escape from Nazi Germany was a long and carefully planned process. In 1932, when the National Socialists succeeded in dominating parliament, Oberlander's parents, Beate and Franz, pledged to each other that they would leave.[2] Since 1926 Oberlander's father, an engineer, had studied scientific management in the United States with the renowned industrial psychologist and engineer Lillian Moller Gilbreth. Beate and Franz agreed that the United States would be their destination. Tragically, on 12 January 1933 Franz Hahn died in an avalanche while skiing in Switzerland. Although his death may have slowed the family's departure, Beate Hahn was still determined to leave. Now a widow with young children, she kept in close contact with family members abroad and with Franz's colleagues working in England and the United States. Gilbreth, who had been widowed with eleven children in 1924, was a particularly loyal friend. As Nazi oppression and terror campaigns mounted, Gilbreth visited the Hahns in Germany each year to show her support for Beate and the children.[3]

While Beate Hahn planned her family's exodus she attempted to keep things as normal as possible at home in the leafy suburbs of Berlin.[4] The Hahn family continued to ski, despite Franz's accident, as well as skate, swim, and garden together. While seeing a painting of a landscape initially inspired Oberlander's quest to become a landscape architect, tending her own garden was also a motivator. It was during this time period that Oberlander began to garden extensively, learning precepts and skills about working with natural systems that she would build upon as a landscape architect later in life. Using companion plants, amending soil organically, attracting birds and insects that mitigated pests, and working with plants hardy to a location laid the groundwork for the ecological basis of her practice. It was also during this time that Oberlander developed otosclerosis, abnormal bone growth near the middle ear (repaired in 1967). While the condition gradually impaired her hearing, it sharpened her visual acuity. As vision supplanted sound, she developed a predilection for the world as comprehended by the eye, another aspect that would inform her later work.

As a professional horticulturalist, Beate Hahn authored several books about gardening with children and how this activity supported their development and education.[5] For example her 1935 book *Hurra, wir säen und ernten!* (Hooray, we sow and harvest!) linked the seasons of the year with activities and songs that children could perform in the garden. Hahn also studied the work of Friedrich Froebel, founder of the original German kindergarten, and she was one of the earliest twentieth-century writers to acknowledge the use of gardens in his schools. Certainly Hahn's interest in Froebel's gardens is telling. Froebel sought refuge from an increasingly strict Prussian government by creating a

Oberlander was recycling at a young age. She created her costume by reusing the straw baskets from large Chianti wine bottles, Switzerland, 1934.

garden culture, the kindergarten, which was based on the maxim: "Come let us live with our children." For Froebel, the kindergarten provided an idealized world distinct from real-world Prussian oppression — a concept that would have surely appealed to Hahn at the time.[6]

Oberlander assisted her mother with the drawings for her books. Her rendering of a diagram entitled "Natur und Kind" (Nature and Child) for Hahn's 1936 *Der Kindergarten ein Garten der Kinder — Ein Gartenbuch für Eltern, Kindergärtnerinnen und alle, die Kinder lieb haben* (The kindergarten a children's garden — A garden book for parents, kindergarten teachers, and everybody who loves children) is an exquisite example of Oberlander's early exposure to the power of the plan as a conceptual device to communicate ideas. "Natur und Kind" is a plan view of a woodland landscape with paths expressing the passage of time. Along the path, stopping points represent events and people as diverse as Bishop John Amos Comenius, the sixteenth-century Moravian author of *The Whole Art of Teaching;*[7] the nineteenth-century children's garden advocate Erasmus Schwab; and the development of twentieth-century school gardens in Germany. These individuals and events contributed to the development of

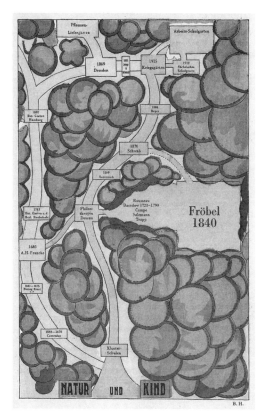

Plan view rendered by Oberlander for her mother's book *Der Kindergarten ein Garten der Kinder—Ein Gartenbuch für Eltern, Kindergärtnerinnen und alle, die Kinder lieb haben*, 1936.

children's gardening and other philanthropic programs in Europe. Froebel, depicted as the largest stopping point on the main path, is a clearing in the woodland landscape.

The metaphor of time as a pathway would continue for Beate Hahn. Years later, Oberlander asked her mother how she was able to cope with the rising violence against Jews during these years. Hahn replied, "I envisioned a path, a long straight path with posts on either side. At the end was our new home. I just kept following that path, never straying from it."[8] On 23 November 1938, two weeks after Kristallnacht (Night of Broken Glass), the Hahns joined the nearly 40,000 refugees fleeing Germany that year. Their escape was not without incidence. Fleeing by train they approached the German border and an officer boarded. He bellowed at Beate and her two daughters to get off the train immediately. Fortunately, Oberlander's uncle, Kurt Hahn, had sent his friend Sir Alexander Lawrence to accompany the Hahns. Lawrence asked the officer why they should get off. Appealing to the officer's fascist adherence to rules of conduct, Lawrence also added that when attending a conference in Germany he was very impressed by the nation's lawfulness. While the pair conversed the train started to move. The officer had to jump out of a window and the train continued on its way.[9]

The Hahns eventually reached the United States in early 1939, and Oberlander spent her first weekend at Lillian Gilbreth's house in Montclair, New Jersey. Gilbreth took a special interest in Oberlander. Sensing her desire to fit in she decided to treat Oberlander like all the other members of the Gilbreth family and assigned her a household task — washing dishes.[10] The Hahns initially moved to New

Oberlander in Berlin, 1938.

Rochelle, New York, living in a house almost identical to one in a photograph given to Beate by Franz in 1932. While the house matched the picture, Hahn needed a larger property so that she could garden and they soon moved to a farm in Wolfeboro, New Hampshire. There, Oberlander spent her first year helping her mother manage the farm, donating their harvests to the war effort, and that winter partaking in her favorite pastime, skiing.

In 1940 Gilbreth took Oberlander along to visit her daughter at Smith College in Northampton, Massachusetts. The Olmsted office had designed the campus in 1893, and Gilbreth knew that this women's college offered degrees in landscape architecture. (By 1938 the Cambridge School of Architecture and Landscape Architecture, founded in 1915 by the architect Henry A. Frost to exclusively educate women, had been made part of Smith College.[11]) In 1940 Oberlander was accepted into an interdepartmental major in Architecture and Landscape Architecture. This was a critical step in Oberlander's adjustment to her new life. Smith provided her with academic courses regarding landscape architecture; but the college environment also gave her a place where she could assimilate into American society. In an essay penned in 1941 for English IIIa, Oberlander offers a glimpse of her struggles to adapt, writing, "There are long periods where I don't think of being a foreigner. But then again, a sudden little

During the summer and school breaks from Smith College, Oberlander continued to work on her mother's farm in Wolfeboro, New Hampshire, 1941.

incident might shake me, throw me back and make me meditate again. It happens sometimes when I go to a house of a friend's. I often have to tell of our escape. I am made to feel like a movie and I don't feel real: I suddenly notice that there is a high wall between me and my hosts, which neither of us can cross. I feel as if I am in borrowed shoes which are much too large for me and no one can make them fit."[12]

While the instructor's comments on her paper indicate a greater concern for Oberlander's spelling rather than the story being told, the essay is a poetic testament to her struggles. Her conclusion is equally revealing. At the end of the essay, Oberlander resolved, "I am determined not to give up. I've made up my mind to adjust myself, discard sentiments and look into the future and learn and understand the demands of America."[13] But as she soon discovered, these demands were not always in keeping with her own views, particularly as they regarded her future as a female landscape architect.

If you have a profession, just get to work! — Cornelia Hahn Oberlander's retort to Betty Friedan (then Bettye Goldstein)

At Smith College Oberlander witnessed heated discussions regarding the dual lives of working women versus those who stayed at home to raise their children.

Day and night these discussions buzzed about Chapin House, her residence hall. While American women had gained numerous rights by the 1940s, Oberlander's classmates such as Betty Friedan, who would later write *The Feminine Mystique* and cofound the National Organization for Women, debated the rights of women to both work and be mothers. Oberlander's dorm room was directly across from Friedan's, and they were constantly at odds. American-born Friedan, then editor-in-chief of the school newspaper, *SCAN*, sought to awaken Smith students to the realities of war, fascism, and being a woman.[14] Oberlander, who had personally escaped fascism, wanted to fit into life at Smith and become a landscape architect. Late one evening Friedan and her friends created a racket while they debated the fate of Smith graduates. Tired by the late-night commotion that was keeping the rest of the students up, Oberlander pounded on Friedan's door and yelled, "If you have a profession, just get to work."[15]

Friedan and her cohort were discontent with the idea of motherhood replacing a professional career or active political life. In contrast, for Oberlander working outside the home and making a difference in the cultural, economic, and political fabric of society, while also having a family, were a given. So she finished her education, married, had children, and continued to practice. Following her mother's course, Oberlander confided in a *National Post* newspaper article in 1999, "I never looked right or left . . . that's the only way that I could succeed in this male-dominated world."[16] Oberlander has also noted that both women and men in her family had a long history of contributing to society, describing herself as a member of "the third generation of women brought up to serve."[17] Not only was her mother a well-known author of children's gardening books, her mother's sister was the archaeologist Elizabeth Jastrow, and her grandmother Anna Seligmann Jastrow was one of the first female teachers in Germany in the 1880s. Anna and her husband, Ignaz Jastrow, were also active in revitalizing impoverished neighborhoods in Berlin during the first decade of the twentieth century. Thus, the tradition of service to society ran deep in her family.[18]

Lillian Gilbreth, who was remarkably successful in the male-dominated field of engineering, influenced Oberlander as well. Gilbreth claimed she was not a feminist, but she may have believed in what Karen M. Offen has called "relational feminism,"[19] which differs from the feminism espoused by Friedan. Many American feminists, such as Friedan, fought for equal rights and personal independence, seeking to transcend gender. Relational feminists, in contrast, sought equal rights as women. Within relational feminism the female gender was traditionally defined by women's ability to bear and nurture children. Although Gilbreth never claimed to be either an equal rights or a relational feminist, she broadened the relational perspective by making porous her life as a woman in the world of marketing and scientific management. For Gilbreth being a woman gave her insights into her work — from the packaging of sanitary napkins, to linking nurse fatigue with productivity, to applying factory efficiency to the logic of the kitchen — and she profited from this understanding as an industrial engineer.[20]

When Cornelia Hahn married Peter Oberlander in 1953 she kept Hahn as part of her married name, but like Gilbreth, she has always maintained that she is not a feminist. Being a woman is also reflected in the territory she has claimed in projects — that of defender of natural elements, particularly plants. From her determination in the 1950s to save the trees on the Mill Creek Housing project in Philadelphia to her reprimand of the contractor who removed trees at Robson Square more than half a century later, she has always positioned herself as the member of the design team who would fight to save both existing and new vegetation. As her work became increasingly complex, involving dense, spatially complicated urban conditions, she consistently assured her collaborators that despite these conditions, she would find a way to sustain healthy plant growth. As the architect Arthur Erickson once remarked, when it came to handling plant material, "no one could strike the fear of God into a contractor like Cornelia."[21] So while Oberlander enjoys telling you that she has cooked 143,000 meals since marrying Peter, she also has, by my estimate, saved just as many trees.[22]

Another facet of Oberlander's gender regards the scale of her practice. She has always kept a small, atelier-style office at home, hiring only two or three employees at a time, principal among them Elisabeth Whitelaw, who worked with Oberlander from 1987 to 2012. By the late 1970s, with her children grown, Oberlander could have expanded her atelier to a large corporate-style office. While there are men who have kept their offices small, James Rose for example, many of her male counterparts formed partnerships, such as the formation of Sasaki, Walker and Associates (SWA) in 1957, Wallace McHarg Roberts & Todd (WMRT) in 1963, and Eckbo, Dean, Austin and Williams (EDAW) in 1964.

Oberlander chose to keep her office at home and found that staying small enabled her to maintain direct involvement in all phases of work. The architect Jim Wright, who worked in Arthur Erickson's office and first met Oberlander in 1974 through the Robson Square project, believes this was a smart move. By keeping her office small she could work directly on all aspects of the project, managing the landscape consequences of architectural decisions and vice versa in minute detail — undoubtedly appealing to architects seeking consultation from the principal landscape architect.[23] Indeed, a modest-size office has allowed her to carve out a special niche in the profession — as a fastidious collaborator with a constellation of famous, and sometimes temperamental, architects.

Despite Oberlander's internal drive and the manner of her practice, she has had to constantly fight for recognition. When she entered the field of landscape architecture in 1947, men dominated the profession. After World War II women faced huge pressures to marry, reproduce, stay at home, and not embark on a professional career. Moreover, the field's eventual transformation from École des Beaux-Arts leanings to a modern conception of the profession presented extra hurdles. Nineteenth-century female landscape designers primarily worked on residential gardens, which were viewed as the natural extension of women's domestic sphere. By the early twentieth century, however, women like Beatrix Jones Farrand, Ellen Biddle Shipman, Martha Brookes Hutcheson, and Marjorie L. Sewell Cautley expanded this work to include shared housing, playgrounds, and campuses.[24]

While the work of these female practitioners certainly supported social motivations embedded in the early years of the profession, the formal qualities of their projects drew from materials and design typologies established in the pastoral, École des Beaux-Arts, and country estate eras. Cautley's landscape for the planned community of Radburn, for example, employed traditional design motifs, with a Central Park–like stone arch pedestrian underpass, low trimmed hedges surrounding each colonial-inspired housing unit, and pastoral open spaces with a Stick Style gazebo.[25] Landscape designs that recycled historical styles could be conceived without the inventive spark of genius, an attribute perceived as lacking in women. Thus the designs created by these early female practitioners did not impede upon the social construction of the modern landscape architect, which linked originality with male genius.

Certainly the realization of new modern forms of habitation and transportation after the war was dependent on the revival of a Kantian genius, a super-endowed individual who was original rather than imitative, who broke rules rather than followed them — and was male. This sentiment is witnessed in the

Museum of Modern Art's 1964 publication *Modern Gardens and the Landscape* by Elizabeth Bauer (Mock) Kassler. It showcases forty-two landscape architects, architects, and artists practicing modern design in Europe, North America, South America, Scandinavia, India, and Japan, but not one woman designer is mentioned. Moreover, excerpts from the book cited in the museum's press release stress the linkage between male genius and modern design, with Kassler proclaiming that "the artist makes his own truth. Like his brothers back through history to the mythical Garden, he will recreate the landscape according to his own subjective image of reality. As he takes hold of earth, plants, and water, the materials unique to his art, let him only beware lest he destroy through his act of possession the genius of that which he has sought to possess."[26]

Modern landscape architecture did have a style, a distinct appearance and intension; however, many of its proponents distanced themselves from the notion of style.[27] Modern landscape architects' cannon of truth lay not in matching historical motifs to use, but in generating new forms from use. According to the architectural historian Mary McLeod, too many connections to the feminine were central to the problems of style. For McLeod, style was linked with the "superficial and the effeminate," so this may be why many landscape architects denied its existence in their work.[28]

Likewise the architectural historian Anthony Alofsin notes that École des Beaux-Arts modes of representation were also aligned with the feminine, and thus, were rejected by faculty and students inspired by Walter Gropius. While sketching was still the chief approach to visualizing form and space, "the skills of drawing that rested on centuries of tradition were equated with effeminacy, and reliance on the vocabulary of the past was seen as an aping of classical forms and an implicit lack of concern with the demands and rational requirements of construction."[29] In landscape architecture, modern forms of representation, the planting plan for example, were to reflect technical knowledge of the project rather than artistic skills expressed in watercolor renderings.

Despite these incongruities between modern design and perceptions of women, it was the promise of practicing modern landscape architecture that solidified Oberlander's commitment to the profession. As she recalls, "Here I was this crazy girl who wanted to design modern landscapes."[30] Her passion for modern design was undoubtedly compelled by her life in Weimar Germany. Yet, her desire to become a modern landscape architect was also part of her adaptation to North America. Working as a woman in her chosen field was part of her adjustment to her new country, which itself was in the midst of transformation. These changes required new ways of living and working, and for Oberlander her participation in this new life — as a wife, mother, and landscape architect — is what made her modern.

Asked to lecture on the subject of "women and leisure" in 1975, Oberlander opened her talk with a quote from G. B. Shaw's "A Perpetual Holiday Is a Good Working Definition of Hell." She then declared, "I am not a women's libber but I believe in Women working and participating in shaping our society. In this, I believe lies the challenge of our times. Whether we participate as a full-time, part time, or volunteer worker, in order to do this we must be educated and have aspirations and confidence in ourselves that we can plan our lives and work hard, and assume responsibilities willingly and gladly. We are made of the same stuff; we have brains, we can decide and act and we need work just as we need food — and most of us need work in order to eat especially to-day. Work gives us a feeling of purposefulness and usefulness and we derive much satisfaction from this."[31]

In many ways Oberlander's unfaltering support for modern design was in step with changes taking place in North American society. The new project types demanded by society needed new forms and materials. Upon entering Harvard University's Graduate School of Design, however, she found that those teaching in the landscape architecture program did not necessarily understand the need for these changes.

I didn't come here to do washes! — Cornelia Hahn Oberlander's
reply to Professor Bremer W. Pond

After the attack on Pearl Harbor, the Smith College Board of Trustees voted to close its Cambridge School of Architecture and Landscape Architecture and to transfer the remaining students to Harvard's Graduate School of Design.[32] Until that point the Graduate School of Design had denied women full-time enrollment, but with the country's sudden immersion into war, the school had lost two-thirds of its student body. On 19 January 1942 the governing boards authorized the Faculty of the Graduate School of Design to admit women.[33] This news was momentous enough to warrant coverage in the Boston Herald with an article exclaiming "TO ADMIT WOMEN" in May 1942 and the July 1942 issue of Landscape Architecture magazine. Henry Frost, a professor of architecture at Harvard and an instructor at the Cambridge School of Architecture and Landscape Architecture, announced the closing of the Cambridge School and the first transfer of female students to the Graduate School of Design between 29 June and 19 September 1942.[34]

On 23 March 1943, Oberlander received a letter from Frost, who was her former teacher at Smith, accepting her into the Graduate School of Design and outlining her course work. "The school at present," he noted, "is in the process of course changes in relation to the post-war period."[35] A month later she received a new curriculum that superseded the 23 April 1940 catalog descriptions of course work.[36] Other changes were taking place in the program as well. Faculty members and students were leaving in droves to join the war effort, and for the first time since its inception, a woman, Elizabeth Bird Barnes, graduated with a Bachelor of Landscape Architecture degree.[37]

Given the type of practice Oberlander envisioned for herself, the move to the GSD could not have been more advantageous. She entered the school with the intent to study modern landscape architecture and her enrollment in the program in 1943 coincided with a time when the GSD played an unprecedented role in defining modernism in education and practice in both landscape architecture and architecture. Other architecture programs experimenting with modern curricula, such as the Institute of Design in Chicago (formerly the New Bauhaus), did not offer landscape architecture. In contrast, the GSD's dean and founder, Joseph Hudnut, had brought the programs of landscape architecture, architecture, and planning together in one school to form a unified modern curriculum in 1935.[38] The school's modern fate was further sealed by Hudnut's hiring of Walter Gropius, founder of the original German Bauhaus. While Hudnut and Gropius fought over the exact nature of this new educational endeavor, these two developments were instrumental in creating a modern landscape architecture curriculum at the GSD.

Oberlander had read articles by Dan Kiley, James Rose, and Garrett Eckbo in *Pencil Points* (now *Progressive Architecture*) and she was confident that these young landscape architects embodied the future. They knew the world was rapidly changing and that the profession had to change its clients, projects, methods of design, and aesthetics to meet these transformations. She also read, and still has her copy of, Christopher Tunnard's *Gardens in the Modern Landscape* (1938, 1948), the first manifesto in the English language proclaiming a modern design ethos for landscape architecture. Prior to Oberlander's arrival, Tunnard

Oberlander after graduating from Harvard and looking very American, Cambridge, Massachusetts, 1947.

had taught site planning and landscape architecture at the GSD, and he introduced students to large-scale, complex problems. The architectural historian Jill Pearlman notes, "In one example, his students planned a 1,200-family residential complex for a proposed industrial town in eastern Massachusetts. To do so they carried out extensive research (much as they did for Gropius's and Wagner's design problems) on economic issues, land use and manufacturing processes."[39]

Tunnard had left Harvard by 1943, but in the intervening years before accepting a permanent position at Yale University he occasionally lectured there.[40] He also displayed his projects (primarily from England) as part of the 1947 and 1950 exhibits hosted by the landscape architecture department.[41] Thus, despite his official departure by the time of Oberlander's arrival, Tunnard's ideas made an indelible impression on her, as well as the school at large. Unfortunately not all landscape architecture faculty and students embraced these ideas. Oberlander recalls that apart from Lawrence Halprin, who sat across from her during her first semester, most of her classmates "didn't get Tunnard."[42] Likewise, she found some of the current landscape architecture faculty to be disinterested in modern design. As a result Oberlander was constantly challenging what she considered to be their "old-fashioned ideas."[43]

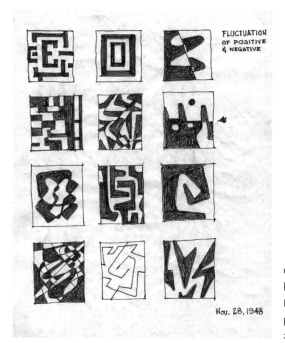

FLUCTUATION
OF POSITIVE
& NEGATIVE

Nov. 28, 1948

George Tyrrell LeBoutillier's lecture notes on the Basic Design course showing positive and negative space, 28 November 1948.

Luckily her introductory studio course — commonly referred to as the Basic Design studio — on Mondays, Wednesdays, and Fridays, from 2:00 to 5:30 p.m., proved to be exactly what she was looking for.[44] While the studio took place in Robinson Hall, a Beaux-Arts edifice designed by McKim, Mead, and White in 1904, the course marked a distinctly modern turn in landscape architectural pedagogy. Basic Design was to be modeled after the Bauhaus Vorkurs, or Preliminary Course, which stressed individual creativity and a diversity of materials marshaled into the universal language of form.[45] It was required for both incoming landscape architecture and architecture students so as to give them a common language of visual communication. For Gropius, who viewed it as his seminal contribution to the new curriculum, Basic Design gave a student "a foundation of solidarity for his spontaneous expression in art; it will free him from the sad isolation which he is suffering from at present since we lost the common key for understanding the visual arts. . . . At least toady we are able to feed the creative instinct of a designer with the knowledge of visual facts, such as the phenomena of optical illusion, of the relations of solids and voids in space, of light and shade, of colour and of scale; facts instead of arbitrary, subjective interpretations or formulas long since stale."[46]

Oberlander, like Eckbo, Kiley, and Rose before her, deeply appreciated the fresh perspective Gropius brought to the GSD. She recalled that on the first day of classes, Gropius gathered all of the new students together and asked them to "find something" by the end of the day. Olivier Messier, an exchange student from France, found the best "something." He returned with mistletoe, dipped it in India ink, and created an abstract pattern on white paper. According to Oberlander this exercise was about "learning to see": perceiving how ordinary elements found in everyday life could be transformed into art.[47]

Marcel Breuer, a graduate of and later teacher at the Bauhaus, joined the Harvard faculty in 1938 and had a tremendous influence on studio culture thereafter. His lectures reveal not only more detail regarding the Basic Design method but they also link this pedagogy to fostering self-guided exploration. In a 1948 lecture at Yale University, Breuer describes the investigative nature of the course: "Today a drawing of a bird, or a figure (nearly academic) — tomorrow a study in materials and textures, collected on the waste dump (nearly Dadaistic); after tomorrow a composition in colors organized in 3 simple shapes on a sheet of paper (nearly abstract). This method is to expose the student to varied opportunities, to let him choose and select his media, to develop inventiveness, and his probably not too obvious creative instincts."[48]

Oberlander's instructor for Basic Design, George Tyrrell LeBoutillier, did not exude the spontaneity Breuer captures here. Nonetheless, he inspired Oberlander in ways that recalled some of the concepts that guided early kindergarten activities, precepts that Beate Hahn had embraced. In fact, Johannes Itten, who devised the original exercises for the Preliminary Course at the Bauhaus, was a former kindergarten teacher.[49] Froebel's kindergarten pedagogy stressed self-directed exploration through the manipulation of physical materials, and the discovery of visual patterns and forms that he thought were universal to both the animate and inanimate world. The author Norman Brosterman has argued that Froebel's kindergarten pedagogy tacitly advanced abstraction in the work of modern artists and designers who were exposed to this pedagogy as children.[50] Likewise, Basic Design's emphasis on physical and visual experiments where students learn to see and interpret by exploring the effects of color, light, texture, and composition may have also influenced the aesthetic practices of students. Certainly, as a daughter of a mother well-versed in kindergarten pedagogy, Oberlander had already acquired the idea of distilling the common properties of observable phenomena, and this ability to abstract remained vital in her years of practice as a landscape architect.

Unfortunately Oberlander's studio with Bremer W. Pond proved to be more frustrating than enlightening. Pond, who had taught at Harvard University since 1914, was particularly resistant to the new curriculum. As a consequence, Oberlander was constantly at battle with Pond and every time they argued she would throw a piece of plasticine on the ceiling over her desk. By year's end its surface resembled a field of stalactites. The effect was not appreciated by Robinson Hall's longtime custodian, who informed Oberlander that he was not looking forward to cleaning the ceiling.[51]

Pond and Oberlander's arguments centered on the subject of modern needs versus the traditional modes of landscape design and representation that Pond cherished. Pond had a fondness for topiary, historical landscapes, and private residential gardens rendered in watercolor washes. When he asked Oberlander to grade a residential property to include a formal entrance for the owners' house and a separate drive for servants, she argued, "We don't have service drives because we don't have servants anymore. Everyone enters through the same drive."[52] When he asked her to render the project in watercolors, she replied, "I didn't come here to do washes!"[53]

We'll be hearing from you some day, Miss Hahn. — Scoop Furnell
when firing Oberlander from SOM, 1944

While Pond was unsuccessful in hindering her quest to study modern design, it was Oberlander's mother who presented her with the most formidable test to her resolve. Hahn saw in Oberlander, unlike her other children, a hardy specimen who thrived when served up a challenge and whose ambition she continually kept in check. In the spring of 1944 Hahn met with Professor Frost without Oberlander's knowledge. She was concerned that her daughter's drafting skills were insufficient. Together they decided that Oberlander would take the 1944/45 school year off so that she could fine-tune her drafting skills while working in an architectural office.[54]

A bit miffed, but undeterred, Oberlander sent out numerous letters requesting employment. She eventually found work at Skidmore Owings and Merrill (SOM) in New York. There she drafted working drawings with ink on linen, since materials such as vellum would not come into common practice until the

1950s. Linen was a difficult drafting surface because the ink could easily bleed. While she excelled at lettering, line drawings without ink spots remained elusive. Three months later she was fired. Her manager, Scoop Furnell, had mixed feelings about her dismissal, as he admired her energy and determination. Upon giving her notice he added, "Regardless, I think we'll be hearing from you some day, Miss Hahn."[55] And he did. The 13 September 1954 issue of *Life* magazine featured Oberlander's 18th and Bigler Street Playground in Philadelphia.[56] She mailed Furnell a copy and he wrote back a letter of congratulations.

Oberlander was unemployed that winter, but in the spring Albert Mayer and Julian Whittlesey, also in New York, hired her. The architecture and planning firm was working on public housing projects that gave Oberlander firsthand experience with the technical drawings required by public projects. Mentored by Emiel Newbrun and James Johnson, she perfected her drafting with ink on linen, while becoming familiar with drafting conventions and the lexicon of drawn lines needed to convey information in construction drawings. Oberlander also learned how to work with men. As she later admitted, she was the only female and the other employees kidded her a lot. One day a project manager asked her to go to the drafting store to pick up some vanishing points. At the store she searched in vain for them. Giving up, she asked the owner if he carried vanishing points. He gave her an odd look but double-checked his inventory books — no vanishing points. Returning to the office she announced that the store did not have any vanishing points and she was promptly met with a round of laughter. Newbrun took her aside and said, "We were just kidding."[57]

Oberlander's return to graduate studies in 1945 was a rare move for the time. While educational opportunities for women in landscape architecture and architecture programs had been increasing across the United States, the female students at the Graduate School of Design did not always finish. During the 1940s a woman who enrolled in the GSD faced a more than 50 percent dropout rate among female students. The dropout rate among males was 23 percent, even though these were the war years when men were drafted or joined the war effort voluntarily.[58]

Although Oberlander had to work as a nanny during her first semester, things were looking up. The war was over, she had become a U.S. citizen, and during a picnic at Walden Pond she met her future husband, a new urban planning student originally from Vienna. Like her, Peter Oberlander had fled Nazi persecution.[59] While they shared a comparable history, it was their similar ideas about the

H. Peter Oberlander, Montreal, 1945.

future that bound them. They both sought a life that was less about the past and more about the present and the future, and in this present tense they would meet the demands of society. Without doubt, this mutual vision was forged by a determination whose gravity and clarity would eventually unite them for life.

Oberlander's reenrollment in the GSD was also marked by the return of a younger generation of landscape architecture professors, such as Norman T. Newton, Walter L. Chambers, and Lester Collins. Unlike the old guard, they were keen to transform the program. Newton in particular had been incorporating Basic Design principles into his landscape architecture studios.[60] In his 1951 publication *An Approach to Design,* Newton offered a glimpse of the transforming curriculum at the school. He noted that the revised curriculum stressed a new attitude towards design, which included cross-disciplinary courses and studios. For Newton, "Above all, let us not seek in this procedure any clear-cut lines of cleavage that separate the professions . . . into mutually exclusive 'zones of jurisdiction.'"[61]

Oberlander thrived in the collaborative atmosphere of large-scale projects assigned to students during this time. For her group work in South Boston she became well acquainted with not only the landscape architectural dimensions of the project but also the planning and architectural implications.[62] This prepared her well for working in New York and Philadelphia after graduation. With the inception of National Defense Housing projects in the 1940s, collaboration between architects, engineers, and landscape architects on these complex urban projects was made mandatory.[63]

Oberlander's willingness to work with architects and planners, as well as artists, scientists, and sociologists, was crucial in the realization of the multifaceted projects later undertaken in Vancouver and other cities. Her early collaborations also instilled in her the idea that she could make valid suggestions on architecture, especially when it intersected with the landscape. Describing her process in a 1956 article in *Community Planning Review,* Oberlander notes,

"After such a job is completed, it is hard to tell precisely which parts of it were contributed by the architect, the engineer, the landscape architect, the department officials and the residents of the neighborhood."[64] This interest in the complete project, including the architecture, continued throughout her career. Oberlander's longtime colleague Arthur Erickson reported, "I can't over emphasize the contributions Cornelia has made to my buildings. She approaches every assignment almost like a thesis project."[65]

A pragmatist at heart, Oberlander greatly appreciated the research and technical skills she acquired during these final semesters at Harvard. According to Oberlander, Walter Chambers taught students to "sculpt the earth," an idea that has shaped her belief that grading is the landscape architect's most powerful tool. Since design was a currency that should be affordable to everyone, students were also asked to prepare financial analyses and cost estimates for their projects.[66] This technical and research-intensive approach to design has also remained with Oberlander and contributed to the exceptional economy of her work. The thrift of her thinking is evident in one of her early publications for *House and Home* magazine (1956). Using a title that draws upon the basic operations of calculation—"Good Land Use + Good Architecture = Long Earning Life"—she demonstrated that landscape design need not come at great expense. Moreover, she revealed that by preserving the trees, fitting the road and structures to the slope, and trenching the wiring, the landscape design actually added value to the land. Referring to the Cherokee Village project, Oberlander points out, "The original appraisal of land was $5,000 per acre. After construction it increased to $12,000 per acre."[67]

In June 1947 Oberlander was one of two students (the other was Stanley Burnett Underhill) to graduate with a Bachelor of Landscape Architecture degree (two master's students also graduated). Peter had already graduated with a Master of City Planning degree and was awarded a Wheelwright Traveling Fellowship for 1946/47.[68] There was also an amicable denouement to her academic experience with Bremer Pond. While her years with Pond had been stormy, his letter of recommendation reveals a change of heart. Written in 1947, he describes her as "an excellent draughtsman and a rapid, conscientious worker . . . she is a person of imagination, efficient and capable."[69]

HOUSEWORK

2 An analysis of the 1951 *Landscape Architecture* exhibit catalog opens this chapter. The project types and modes of representation featured in the catalog are a testament to the growing conviction that the profession must design for all segments of society—a belief realized by the fact that numerous socially germane projects were made available after the war. Historically, landscape architecture has always included some measure of social responsibility, but in the postwar years this thinking was tied to a new aesthetic that would help give form to the social efficacy of landscapes. Borrowed largely from architecture, I describe how abstraction, function, and honesty played a role in fulfilling this social agenda. While there were discussions about space during this time, the idea of experiential space in landscape architecture would evolve more fully later.

Oberlander unequivocally embraced these ideas as they formed the moral center of her practice. Thus in the following I examine her early collaborations on the design of public housing projects, and how she sought to hone her site design and technical skills to realize the social aims of her chosen profession. During this stage of her career, Oberlander worked as a planner in New York and Philadelphia, spearheading community design methods that involved the voices of the disenfranchised. In 1951 she joined Dan Kiley as an associate and became immersed in the radical rebuilding programs for public housing in Philadelphia. Kiley and Oberlander's plans for Schuylkill Falls Public Housing and Mill Creek Public Housing were ambitious in scope and laden with promise, but many of their ideas never materialized. Nonetheless, the experience prompted Oberlander to think of ways in which notions of both individuality and equality could be delivered in the design of a shared landscape.

Citizen Landscape Architect: Public Landscapes

Oberlander's early career, from 1947 to 1967, centered on community planning and close collaborations with architects for the design of public housing and private residences. During this time period she also designed her first landscape for children. While these projects are not as well-known as many later works, they played a formative role in realizing her practice as an agent for social change. Her classmates and teachers in Harvard's landscape architecture department did not always share this vision, but by midcentury it was clear that a modern conception of both the education and practice of landscape architects was unfolding. The 1951 *Landscape Architecture* exhibit catalog gives an informative account of the trajectory of midcentury practice and its commitment to modern landscape architecture.[1]

The work of Oberlander as well as that of Beatrice L. Zion appears in the exhibit catalog, accompanying forty-five male landscape architects that included Thomas Dolliver Church, Garrett Eckbo, Lawrence Halprin, Daniel U. Kiley, Ian L. McHarg, John Ormsbee Simonds, Hideo Sasaki, Christopher Tunnard, and Robert L. Zion — figures who would define landscape architecture in the second half of the twentieth century. Surprisingly even Bremer Pond seems to have warmed to the idea of a modern landscape architecture, and even to the presence of women in the school as well. In the foreword he notes, "This publication is not a cross section of what all the students have accomplished during this first half century; it is a selection taken from contemporary work done by men and women from the Department. This volume also contains a few essays about Landscape Architecture. I am proud of what is presented here."[2]

Immediately striking is the way projects are represented in the catalog. Gone are the colored-wash perspective views bejeweled with historic motifs. In their place is the graphic dialect of *Architectural Graphic Standards,* which was revised and published that year.[3] Black-and-white plan diagrams with Leroy lettering characterize drawings in the *Landscape Architecture* catalog. Consider Oberlander's drawings, her plans for two residential landscapes are for modest homes. Landscape features such as deciduous trees are presented as simple circles with a dot at the center to stand for trees. Planted areas and other surfaces are

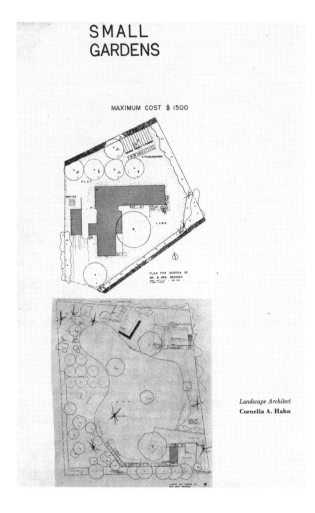

SMALL
GARDENS

MAXIMUM COST $ 1500

Landscape Architect
Cornelia A. Hahn

Oberlander's plan views in the *Landscape Architecture* exhibit catalog, 1951. Oberlander was the only solo female whose work was presented in the published catalog of the 1950 exhibit celebrating the first fifty years of the Department of Landscape Architecture at Harvard's Graduate School of Design.

represented with symbols, such as hatching and stippling. Many areas of the plans are labeled with Leroy lettering denoting lawn, kitchen garden, service, and play. Numbers refer to plant types and materials that correspond to a key.

Certainly the absence of pretense that comes with unrendered line drawings and the labeling of use areas uphold the image of function. Moreover, the dominance of plans in the catalog reinforces a view that lent itself effortlessly to the construction process. If *Landscape Architecture* records the profession's indoctrination with the representational conventions of a modern practice, it also gives testimony to the evolution of landscape architecture with not only a new visual vocabulary but also a social purpose. Previously, the City Beautiful movement was linked to reform ideas that positioned design to serve a common good. Yet, changes during and after World War II reaffirmed the profession's social obligations and created unprecedented opportunities to realize these commitments.

The social project in landscape architecture was conceived in several ways. First, the nature of projects available to landscape architects (housing, schools, highways, and recreational spaces) was geared towards a range of socio-economic classes and to the general public. The projects fulfilled the exigencies of a society just emerging from the war, beset with deteriorating urban cores and in need of affordable housing. This was also a society that was determined to prove to communist regimes that the market systems of the West could provide a new and superior social infrastructure. In fact a year after World War II, the American Society of Landscape Architects was receiving direct requests for services from "city planning, parks and highway commissions, housing agencies, and department and agencies of the federal government."[4] Projects profiled in the *Landscape Architecture* exhibit catalog include subdivisions, housing projects, modest private residences, schools, college campuses, highways, and parkways. They represent prototypical building programs through which landscape architects hoped to realize modern principles of social responsibility, functionality, abstraction, technical ingenuity, and economic thrift.

Affordable housing and recreational facilities, in particular, were central to realizing a more egalitarian society. Landscape architects had worked on social housing projects as part of New Deal programs. Garrett Eckbo, for example, had been hired by the Farm Security Administration to design housing camps for migrant workers, and during the war he had worked on defense housing. Dan Kiley produced twenty-one shared housing projects between 1941 and 1952.[5] Even Thomas Church, known for his private residences, designed public housing landscapes in the San Francisco Bay area. These socially oriented projects prefigured a new concept of the landscape architect's clientele for postwar practice. Writing in *Ontario Housing*, Oberlander describes this new clientele, a segment of society that landscape architects must address. Noting that roughly 20 percent of the population in Vancouver requires better housing and recreational areas, she reminds readers that this client "will not belong to affluent society" or be a member of a country club or have access to distant regional parks, so "landscape architects bear the responsibility to create an environment meeting this population strata."[6]

Indeed, midcentury landscape architecture was defined by its social projects, but also by changes in the design vocabulary and rationales for its use. Historians have suggested that landscape architects looked to modern artists and architects to develop their own version of modern design. While landscape architects may not have always fully grasped the intentions of these architects, references to architects such as Le Corbusier and Mies van der Rohe abound — first in the writings of Tunnard in *Gardens in the Modern Landscape* (1938, 1948) and in its successor, Eckbo's *Landscape for Living* (1950). These texts did not reject history with the voracity of many architectural manifestos, but they did echo many claims voiced by modern architects. One well-documented claim was the idea that space — an area shaped by mass, form, and line — was the logical substitution for style.[7] Likewise, abstraction, honesty, and function were also ideas interpreted from modern architects, and they were central to a profession with social purpose. As with many translations, the landscape architects' version of the way modern tenets benefited society often altered and in some instances expanded the architectural reference. Specifically their translations of abstraction, function, and honesty are relevant in the distinguishing of the landscape architectural endeavor from the architectural.

The use of abstraction rather than the imitation of historical patterns was promoted as a means to align landscape architecture practice with that of modern architects. In a 1945 issue of *Landscape Architecture* magazine, Lockwood Deforest decries that "the architects are getting ahead of us! If you don't believe me, look at any of the magazines that publish pictures of houses and gardens. They are full of abstract composition rather than traditional decoration."[8] During a 1955 lecture in Toronto, Oberlander suggests that adopting the language advanced by modern architects would provide more job opportunities, noting that "the contemporary architect is often reluctant to associate himself with a landscape architect, for he can rarely find one who can speak his language aesthetically."[9] Yet, abstraction had a social rationale as well. In *Landscape for Living* Eckbo argued that one of the main currents in modern art and architecture was to distill a vocabulary that could be understood by all people rather than to seek self-referential forms. He notes that a current among modern artists and architects recognizes "the existence of people in relation to the creative process in the form of the controversy 'is art for art's sake — or for people?' This has been expressed in various ways — the new techniques of representation developed by the cubists, the rejection of subject matter by abstractionists and non-objective painters, the search for new subject matter by dadaists, futurists, surrealists, etc. The housing and planning activities of Le Corbusier, Gropius, and Neutra — express art for people rather than for its own sake."[10]

Thus it was thought that employing abstract shapes and unadorned lines in landscape design would tap its potential as social currency. Unlike École des Beaux-Arts projects, which emulated the past and for which historic interpretation was vital to their appreciation, abstraction produced simple forms that did not require labored interpretations. This deemed abstract design more egalitarian. Eckbo was unwavering about this point: "If our concept for design is held on a higher plane than our concept of people we introduce a contradiction in our work . . . how about the majority who experience our park designs? Do they require a course of training before they enjoy them?"[11]

Importantly, landscape architects did not limit themselves to basic shapes; rather, abstraction served as a starting point to integrate these shapes with features of the site, such as contours, structures, and property lines. According to M. E. Bottomley, writing in *Landscape Architecture* magazine in 1947, "The new idea would be to take the shape of the area which is available. Why be restricted to squares and rectangles when a variety of equally pleasing shapes may be derived if we follow the suggestions of the plot?"[12] This design vocabulary was also thought to accommodate uses more directly than historically determined features. For example, if a client requested a pool in which to swim laps, the form of the pool would be determined by site features and the direction and length of the lap — rather than matching the pool shape to the historical style of the house. Thus, abstraction was also tied to function.

According to the architectural historian Adrian Forty, from the eighteenth century onward "function" referred to a number of ideas that differed from the modern usage of the term.[13] Andrew Jackson Downing, for example, wrote on the importance of expressing the purpose of architecture through design. In 1844 he disapproved of domestic dwellings in North America that borrowed from ancient temple architecture. For Downing, "Houses should express historic domestic styles, otherwise they are buildings appearing to be what they are not."[14] More than a hundred years later, function resurfaced as the rationale against style and a driver in the logic of the plan. Writing in *An Approach to Design*, Norman T. Newton outlined the comprehensive role that function played in landscape architecture. According to Newton functions involve two categories: Natural and Assigned. Natural functions are biological and mathematical and exist without conscious human intervention.[15] The category of Natural functions commonly fell under the rubric of "science" in writing on landscape architecture, and this is poignantly described by Lester Collins in his essay "Of Landscape Architecture": "The landscape architect works primarily with the site. Although he uses structural elements such as wood and glass, he also has at his command a series of forces — elements which are not inanimate — water, sunlight, wind plants. These are subject to scientific analysis. They can be used to fulfill functions. They are involved in building shape volumes, in establishing indoor-outdoor relationships, in disclosing spatial experiences. They are part of the art which is achieved after form has followed function."[16]

Newton's second category, Assigned functions, involves an "area of conscious intent, that we assert our stature as designers."[17] Newton defined Assigned functions as use functions and affective functions. Plant material in particular played a use-functional role. According to Ian Thompson, for modern landscape architecture "planting could no longer be ornamental, but had to have a functional justification such as dividing space or providing shelter."[18] Use functions, in particular, would occupy discourse and practice in modern landscape architecture as specific activities, their spatial allocation and their proximity to each other in plan shaped the design process from bubble drawings to functional diagrams.[19]

Affective functions comprise lines and forms in a design that communicates to people. For Newton, there should be an *interplay* between functional design and our appreciation of it. A circle designating a place to gather, for example, would become a hallmark in Oberlander's work, from her public housing projects and playgrounds to residential projects and even her own yard, where, she notes, "the first thing we built was the sandbox — circular, with a big rim for mother to sit on."[20] Her landscape design for Residence Y (the owners wish to remain anonymous), which she began in 1963, is a superb example of Natural and Assigned functions. The owners requested a place for breakfast that would receive ample morning sun in spring and early summer (when they used their garden the most). Oberlander conducted a sun/shade analysis of the site and determined the exact spot that received the most sun during the morning hours in those seasons (Natural, math function). She planted sun-loving vegetation (Natural, biological function), and planned a deck big enough to accommodate the family's outdoor furniture (Assigned, use function), and designed it as a circle to denote where to gather for breakfast (Assigned, affective function).

Demonstrating Norman T. Newton's definition of function in Oberlander's landscape design for Residence Y, Vancouver, circa 1964. Architects: Thompson, Berwick, Pratt, and Partners.

Function was also linked to honesty, which can be traced to the nineteenth century in the writings of John Ruskin. In *The Seven Lamps of Architecture* (1849), he stressed function's importance regarding structure. Ruskin chastised architects' fraudulent "introduction of members which should have, or profess to have, a duty, and have none."[21] Nor did he approve of camouflaging material, decrying that "to cover brick with cement, and to divide this cement with joints that it may look like stone, is to tell a falsehood."[22] Ruskin's critiques formed the basis of some of William Robinson's assessments of parks twenty years later. During his visit to the Parc des Buttes Chaumont in Paris, for example, Robinson admonishes the use of artificial rock, complaining that "instead of true rockwork" we find "plastering over heaps of stones. . . . A hole is left and there is this mass from which may spring a small pine or an ivy, but the whole thing is incapable of being divested of its bald character."[23]

The pursuit of honesty continued among modern architects and landscape architects as it signaled distrust with illusion, particularly historical.[24] For Oberlander, honesty meant keeping truthful to the times. An advocate of Tunnard's early ideas, she noted that his advice to study production landscapes, such as truck farms and oil refineries, was honest because these were facilities on which modern life depended.[25] Materials, in particular, played an important role in honest expression. Tunnard states that "there is no artificiality where there is no attempt to disguise materials. Most concrete paving aims at being a substitute for stone; the deception is even encouraged in laying, when crazy or random courses give a path or terrace of this material an ill-conceived air of inappropriateness in any surroundings."[26] For example, he describes the pavers at St. Ann's Hill House in Surrey, England, as those "which do not pretend to be other than they are; the texture and shape of each slab is as precise and formal as a machine — there is no attempt to make them appear natural."[27] Linking appreciation with function, Tunnard continued by noting that we should also appreciate the components of concrete that serve a purpose. The sparkle imparted by the concrete's surface in the sunlight, for example, is appropriate to admire because this shimmering is the product of carborundum — a material added during the floating stages of the construction process to prevent slipperiness.

So it was within this context of an emerging modern landscape architecture that Oberlander entered the profession. As post–World War II articles and letters in *Landscape Architecture* magazine attest, the transformation was slow. Nonetheless, this was a profession that was increasingly asked to design landscapes addressing all segments of society. In response its practitioners employed a design vocabulary drawn from basic forms rather than historical motifs, producing landscapes that sought to accommodate both Natural and Assigned functions, and supporting the honest use and appreciation of materials reflective of the times.

NEW YORK AND PHILADELPHIA

When Oberlander graduated in 1947 the opportunities for landscape architects were still scarce as the economy was recovering from World War II. While trying to secure work, sending out forty letters to landscape architecture offices across the country including Hawaii, she designed residential gardens on her own.[28] Eckbo replied with enthusiasm in 1947, but he was not hiring.[29] Dan Kiley also responded to her letter of inquiry, writing, "You impressed me very much," and hinting that she might work for him in the future.[30] Finally she was given an opportunity to work with James Rose. Oberlander, along with Elizabeth Herd, was hired to help build a modular garden for Rose's show garden in Great Neck, Long Island. Constructed as part of his modular series for *Ladies'*

Home Journal, the garden consisted of three birch trees, a hedge, 2 feet × 2 feet concrete pavers, a bench, trellis, and bulbs. Oberlander appreciated the experience but show gardens did not capture her vision of modern landscape architecture.[31] She was eager to work on the practical problems of the city—housing, transportation, and the provision of open spaces—and work directly with the people she was serving.[32]

During the war years, many architects and landscape architects engaged in planning since opportunities to build landscape projects were limited. In fact Louis I. Kahn confessed to Oberlander that his postwar work in Philadelphia was the realization of all of his wartime planning efforts.[33] The architectural historian Andrew M. Shanken notes that planning provided a robust concept to strategize life after the war. "As a metaphor for the future, planning embraced seemingly unrelated fields, linking the most intimate aspects of family life with community and nation."[34] With the war over, Oberlander thought planning would provide her with an opportunity to directly engage with the power structures that were directing postwar development. In 1949 the Regional Plan Association (RPA) of New York hired her. The goal of the RPA "was to improve the quality of life and economic competitiveness" for thirty-one counties located in New York, New Jersey, and Connecticut.[35] Oberlander helped develop plans for small communities in the metropolitan area and she performed research on commuting times from home to work. She also helped compile progress reports for the Planning Board of the Township of Mendham, New Jersey.[36] Positions at the RPA were temporary, lasting only one or two years. Nonetheless, the position gave her valuable analytical skills.

An ingredient missing from Oberlander's RPA experience was working directly with communities and incorporating their views into the design process. For Oberlander this was an extension of the collaborative process and a true mark of a socially oriented practice. These ideals eventually led her to Philadelphia—the epicenter of experimentation with urbanism. At the RPA, Oberlander met James Marshall Miller, an architect working with practicing planners and students at Columbia University's School of Architecture. He brought her into contact with the Citizens' Council on City Planning (CCCP) in Philadelphia, one of first organizations in the United States specifically established to facilitate citizens' participation in the urban planning process.[37] Philadelphia had undergone a revolution in city politics and was quickly becoming a model of urban development for the nation. During the war years the city had embarked upon extensive planning initiatives that determined postwar projects. By the early 1950s there was a revamped architecture program that embraced modern design at the University of Pennsylvania, and these plans began to materialize under the supervision of Edmund Bacon, who, from 1949 to 1970, served as the executive director of the City Planning Commission.[38]

The Citizens' Council, spearheaded by Bacon in the early 1940s, was formed to act as an intermediary between the Planning Commission and community groups.[39] In 1950 Oberlander left the RPA and was hired as a community planner with the Citizens' Council. The job was an ideal post since major renewal plans for parts of Philadelphia would have a direct impact on people living there. Her move coincided with Peter's relocation to Vancouver when he was appointed to create the School of Community and Regional Planning at the University of British Columbia. Although separated by thousands of miles, they continued to keep in touch and encouraged each other in their chosen fields.

At the CCCP, Oberlander held community meetings, conducted interviews, and sought to integrate people's opinion into the planning, design, and building process. She initiated a number of community gardens and Fix Up events that involved painting houses and helping families tend their yards. She also led tours of the finished projects. On Sunday, 19 February 1950, for example, Oberlander facilitated a Germantown Gardens Exploration Trip, a tour that took people up to the roof to view their neighborhood from above and down to walk among the community gardens created by residents in Operation Fix Up.[40] While we tend to attribute 1960s counterculture to participatory design, Oberlander had already developed questionnaires and was conducting workshops with community members in the early 1950s.[41] She also represented a new breed of women working in the public realm. For example, women's organizations such the Massachusetts Emergency and Hygiene Association were instrumental in working with disenfranchised communities and establishing playgrounds for them at the turn of the twentieth century.[42] Oberlander possessed the design and technical skills that enabled her to directly link people's needs with the creation of physical designs for parks, community gardens, and other urban landscapes, adding to this trajectory of women serving communities.

Her work as a community planner at the CCCP also exposed her to some of the most powerful planners and architects working in Philadelphia. However, it was her dexterity in employing a modern design vocabulary in a small park for the John Hay Neighborhood Association (now Gold Star Park) that caught the

Oberlander (with hat) worked directly with community members to construct and tend gardens as part of her work with the CCCP in Philadelphia, circa 1950.

attention of the architect Oskar Stonorov. Trained in Europe and a member of the council's Public Improvements Committee, Stonorov had partnered with Louis Kahn during the 1940s. He was deeply committed to the social goals of art and design, and he was eager to bring European concepts of public housing to the city.[43] Stonorov was impressed with Oberlander's modern design vocabulary and the way she applied it to landscape design.[44] He asked to meet with her after work. Upon entering his office, Stonorov immediately produced a drawing of Solidarity House, the international headquarters for the United Auto Workers in Detroit, Michigan. He requested that she prepare a landscape plan that evening, which he would pick up in the morning to take to Detroit. Never one to shy away from a challenge, Oberlander preserved the site's mature trees and stone walkways, and created an abstract design with Andorra juniper and grass. It was implemented in 1951. Although she did not know it at the time, the existing site had been owned by Edsel Ford, and the landscape designed by Jens Jensen.[45]

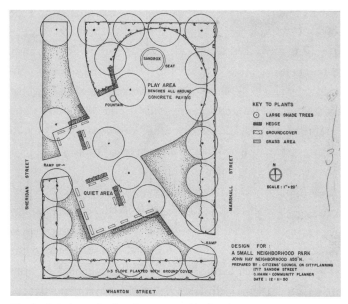

Oberlander's design for the John Hay Neighborhood Association
(now Gold Star Park) for the CCCP, Philadelphia, 11 December 1950.

Solidarity House with Oskar Stonorov's addition, Detroit, 1956. Oberlander preserved the mature
trees planted by Jens Jensen. The old Ford mansion can be seen on the right-hand side of the
photo, 15 January 1958.

Schuylkill Falls Public Housing

A few months later Stonorov asked Oberlander to collaborate on a recently commissioned public housing project, Schuylkill Falls. While she was concerned about leaving the CCCP, Stonorov was persistent and confessed that there were only a few landscape architects in Philadelphia who understood modern design, a sentiment Arthur Erickson would express years later in Vancouver. Oberlander was persuaded, and began a twenty-year professional relationship with Stonorov and close friendship with his family.[46]

Public housing is often a neglected chapter in landscape architecture history, particularly during the 1950s and 1960s when the architectural typology changed from low-density, two- and three-story brick structures to concrete high-rises with double-loaded corridors and minimal access points to the landscape. The tower form, which defined much of the public housing from the 1950s onward, departed dramatically from the garden apartments that afforded direct access to the landscape from each unit. This typology demanded new conceptions of the urban residential landscape because increased density created residual open spaces removed from the street gridiron that could be assigned to accommodate a range of communal uses.[47]

In Philadelphia, the Schuylkill project was a new model of this high-rise public housing for the city. According to the architectural historian Eric Mumford, towers were relatively new types of public housing in Philadelphia.[48] Stonorov sought to base Schuylkill on the prewar housing developments he was familiar with in Europe. He thought that this earlier work was affordable, yet the design was of a high quality.[49] Stonorov asked Oberlander to study these housing developments in preparation for working on the project. She was to accomplish this learned study by chaperoning the European leg of Stonorov's exhibit on Frank Lloyd Wright, *Sixty Years of Living Architecture.* The exhibit opened at the Palazzo Strozzi in Florence in June 1951, and Oberlander, along with two Swiss architects, accompanied the models and drawings by truck from Florence to Zurich, Paris, Munich, and Rotterdam before returning to North America.[50] While the intent was to study public housing, the trip was sidetracked by a truck accident, and as Oberlander later admitted, too many ski trips.

When she returned to Philadelphia from her European tour, Oberlander was given another assignment. Stonorov asked that she spend the rest of the summer working with Dan Kiley, who had joined the Schuylkill design team. At the time Kiley was receiving commissions throughout the United States and needed extra help in the office. Oberlander had hoped to work with him since graduation and immediately accepted. Learning to write specifications for a major urban project was the main objective of this apprenticeship experience. During the 1950s the written documents accompanying construction drawings, known as specifications, were just being formalized as part of the profession.[51] They describe the scope of work, materials, methods of installation, and quality of work under contract, and they became increasing important in public projects as one basis for the construction bidding process.

At Kiley's highly unconventional residential office nestled in the rural enclave of Charlotte, Vermont, Oberlander met Richard Haag, who was joining Kiley as an apprentice for a second summer.[52] Together, Haag and Oberlander compiled a single set of comprehendible specifications for Kiley's office. This was completed amidst the execution of extensive grading plans and a large three-dimensional model for James Rouse's Mondawmin Shopping Center in Baltimore. While Kiley did not give them the mentoring they had hoped for, both Oberlander and Haag were enthralled by his command of design and his ability to bring a range of functional requirements and site issues into a simple and elegant diagram.[53] Kiley also instilled in Oberlander the importance of treating ecological systems with great care. During one of her morning walks through the woods with Kiley, he said, "Cornelia, tread lightly on the land."[54] This was advice that she would take to Philadelphia and beyond.

Returning to Philadelphia that fall, Oberlander began work on Schuylkill Falls housing in Stonorov's office. The project entailed six phases, with one phase containing two sixteen-story towers and outdoor recreational facilities. The remaining phases comprised five to eight low-rise housing structures in each phase. The terrain was extremely challenging, with a seventy-four-foot drop from the north to south sides of the site. Oberlander worked closely with Kiley, who went through numerous rolls of tracing paper before settling on the right solution. She recalls that he would always say, "That's my final drawing — but it never was."[55] While working on Schuylkill, Oberlander developed a formula that determined the number of trees and the amount of open space per acre dedicated to each unit.[56] She also devised a tree typology of large shade trees, street trees, and ornamental trees for each of the six phases. A planting plan for Phase A from 14 November 1952, which included eight grided rows of garden apartment blocks, shows how Oberlander attempted to break up the monotony

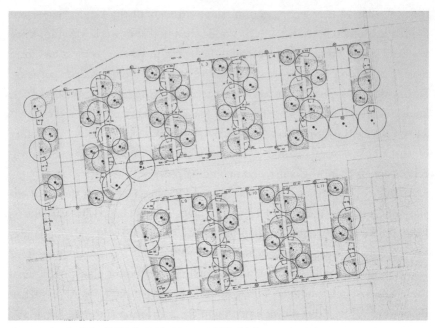

Planting plan for Schuylkill Falls Public Housing, Philadelphia, 14 November 1952. Landscape Architects: Dan Kiley and Cornelia Hahn (associate). Architect: Oskar Stonorov.

of the grid with angular planting areas outside of each unit. When their drawings for Schuylkill were finished, Kiley was so impressed with Oberlander's work ethic that he gave her Warren Manning's can of pounce, powder used to prepare a drawing surface to receive ink, an object she has kept ever since.

Working with Kiley introduced Oberlander to Louis Kahn, who was working on Phase One of Mill Creek Public Housing. Kiley was regularly consulting with both Kahn and Stonorov at the time, and soon Oberlander joined him at Kahn's as well. This arrangement of working directly in an architect's office was a pattern that she has repeated throughout her career. Together, Kiley and Oberlander worked from 9:00 a.m. to 3:00 p.m. at Stonorov's office and from 4:00 p.m. to midnight at Kahn's. Kiley also gave her advice on working with architects. Oberlander once informed Stonorov that they were late for Kahn's office. Kiley took her aside and told her never to mention that they were consulting with both architects at the same time.[57]

Mill Creek Public Housing

In 1948 the Mill Creek area, approximately 290 acres, became one of nine certified redevelopment areas in West Philadelphia designated by the City Planning Commission for renewal. Phase One of the project was prompted by a 1950 cave-in at 47th and Fairmount Streets and Kahn was hired to design the four-acre site to accommodate 218 units, with a net gain of 76 additional units compared to the existing site.[58] The neighborhood's frequent cave-ins can be traced back to the nineteenth century when Mill Creek supported numerous mills, giving the area its name. In the 1880s this alluvial system was funneled into an underground brick and masonry sewer and an entire community materialized above. As Anne Whiston Spirn has revealed, by the early twentieth century the system was failing due to the increased weight of the structures above coupled with an overload of waste from half of West Philadelphia and the suburbs upstream.[59] The failing sewer resulted in numerous cave-ins that swallowed up entire buildings and cars. People were regularly evacuated from the area and houses were routinely condemned and demolished. Despite this calamitous history, the design of Phase One commenced with great optimism as Kahn's office (Kahn, McAllister, Braik, & Day) sought to create a new viable model for the city's public housing program.

DESIGN PROCESS As Kiley's associate, Oberlander worked alongside Kenneth Day, Louis E. McAllister, and Anne G. Tyng, and there she found the collaborative atmosphere she had sought since graduating from the GSD. Tyng also stressed this integrative character of practice at the time, noting that in the "1950s there was a great synthesis — we didn't think of traffic plans of the city as not being related to architecture. And we worked at various scales — large areas of the city, individual houses. . . . There was not the differentiation in architectural engagement at the time; there was a broad and exciting atmosphere."[60]

Initially the design team manipulated rough models that allowed them to study the relationship of massing to open space.[61] Later, Oberlander worked with the engineers and architects on grading, parking, pathway layout, and outdoor sitting areas. Given the sensational promotion of Kahn and Stonorov's planning schemes for Philadelphia during World War II, Kahn's postwar rendition for Mill Creek received unprecedented attention from the press and architectural magazines. Drawings as well as construction photographs of Phase One were published internationally.[62] Oberlander and Kiley developed several variations of Mill Creek's planting plan as the building layouts evolved. Initial iterations of the housing scheme were quite different from what was built. A working model of an early scheme displayed ten high- and low-rent apartment buildings of fifteen stories, square in plan view and surrounded by shared open spaces.[63]

While many urban renewal schemes perceived the demolished site as a tabula rasa, Oberlander argued to preserve some of the foundation walls of the removed housing, and to incorporate these remnants into the landscape design. This effort was later commended in *Architectural Forum,* where the author notes that the landscape is "based on a bright idea: leave some of the old weathered masonry walls standing when you clear old buildings from the land. Design them into the new scheme as economical retaining walls, play courts, and 'ground sculpture.'"[64] Oberlander also specified to save the existing fruit trees and three paulownia trees.

LANDSCAPE STRATEGY An important landscape strategy connected the site to the existing urban fabric with a network of green spaces and tree-lined streets. Working with traffic plans and a wide range of information regarding off-site conditions, a system of pedestrian areas, called a "promenade architecturale," was developed to connect the site to the city.[65] In 1953 Kahn described the project as brimming with green spaces, noting that "over the entire area, trees are planted for shade and rest."[66] A landscape plan by Kiley and Oberlander, dated 15 January 1953, depicts this idea with trees planted around the parking areas for the towers, with an allée from Fairmount Avenue leading into the large grassy common.

Another strategy was to treat each household equitably. This is best illustrated in the garden-style apartments where Kiley and Oberlander provided each unit with the same type and number of landscape elements. Thus, every tenant had a courtyard with a small grass lawn, shrubs, a large canopy tree to the north, a smaller ornamental tree to the south, and an area for growing vegetables or other plants. Since the building units were staggered, the trees created a diagonal line across the block, uniting the individual courtyards into one landscape pattern. Specifications compiled by Oberlander reveal the extent of this planting — calling for 75 trees, such as red maples, locust, and Washington hawthorn; 1,691 shrubs; and more than 4,000 vines. The variety of plants used was small compared to the number required, another hallmark of modern landscape architecture. For

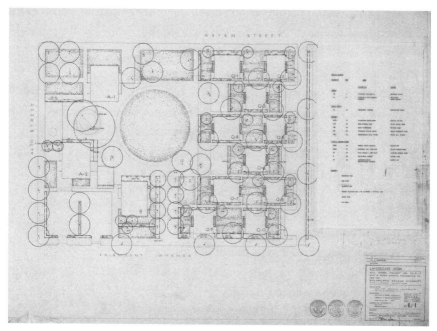

Landscape Work for the Mill Creek Public Housing, Philadelphia, 15 January 1953. Landscape Architects: Dan Kiley and Cornelia Hahn. Architects: Louis I. Kahn, Kenneth Day, and Louis E. McAllister.

example, while 4,981 vines were planned, there were only five types of vines selected. This reduced palette not only brought equality to the individual courtyards but also unified them visually as a whole with broad strokes of color and texture.

RECEPTION Phase One of Mill Creek was constructed between 1953 and 1954. The plight of high-rise public housing structures of this era has been well documented — most poignantly by Jane Jacobs in *The Life and Death of Great American Cities* (1961). Eric Mumford posits that public housing policies of the 1950s did not allow for experimentation or extensive landscape design.[67] While Mill Creek is one of the more polemical examples of her work, Kiley and Oberlander's plans for Mill Creek were not fully implemented and the green network planned to connect this new development to its surroundings was never realized either. Photographs of the site shortly after construction depict only patches of grass and a few trees. The important role of specifications was also undermined. Although Oberlander had specified preserving three mature paulownia trees (with a $1,000 penalty fine if they were damaged), the contractor nonetheless removed them without penalty — destroying the only mature vegetation from the site's past.[68]

The fact that their planting plan was not implemented was a sign of the severe budget constraints that many of these projects faced, but it was certainly not the sole cause of Mill Creek's failure. The forces that doomed many public housing projects associated with urban renewal are complex. The nineteenth-century housing type permitted businesses, such as beauty parlors, at ground level, which provided a means of economic support and served the local community. This older housing type also provided space for gardens, which could potentially provide food. The tower typology curtailed these self-sustaining activities and concentrated people with little means of support in an architecture that greatly contrasted to its surroundings.

Less than fifty years after their construction, both Schuylkill Falls and Mill Creek housing were imploded. Spirn, who for decades has studied and worked with people living in the Mill Creek area, found that between 1950 and 1970 the overall population in the area declined and that the public housing projects built there "contributed to the racial segregation of a neighborhood."[69] She also describes how Mill Creek is a testament to our inability to include natural systems into the planning of cities, an omission that has had disastrous effects at Mill Creek given the area's continuous cave-ins. Spirn's critique is evident in the City Planning Commission's rationale to redevelop the Mill Creek area in the first place. Despite decades of cave-ins, the certification letter to redesign the area did not mention the buried alluvial plain or even the sewer.[70] This omission is also evident in the 1954 report by Kahn, which depicts the "Mill Creek Sewer Right of Way" as a block-long serpentine swath, seemingly unconnected to the rest of the urban systems they were analyzing.[71] Interestingly, it would be this very issue — the presence of functioning natural systems in the urban environment — that would eventually become central to Oberlander's work.

Cherokee Village

Despite some setbacks, Oberlander also had successes during her years in Philadelphia. With Stonorov & Haws, and Robert Venturi as draftsman, she worked on the site plan for Cherokee Village housing in the early 1950s. The site was a stark contrast to the Schuylkill Falls and Mill Creek sites. Located in the tony Chestnut Hill area of Philadelphia, it was part of the fifty-one-acre Stonehurst estate formerly owned by Sallie and Charles Wolcott Henry. The Henrys, a prominent Philadelphia family, owned a sprawling French chateau designed by McKim, Mead, and White and between 1904 and 1914 they had hired the Olmsted Brothers to design their landscape. When Sallie Henry died in 1938, the family, under the direction of Donald Dodge, decided to demolish the chateau, and after World War II they enlisted Oskar Stonorov to develop 10.5 acres of the property as a residential development.[72] By the 1950s the Omlsted brothers' trees had matured and covered much of the undulating property, features of the site that Stonorov and Dodge sought to preserve.

Oberlander worked directly in the architects' office and collaborated with both Stonorov and Venturi to lay out 104 garden apartment units in fifteen buildings on the heavily wooded and sloping site. Dodge's desire to keep the trees immediately resonated with Oberlander, who had lost her battle to preserve trees at Mill Creek. While there seemed to be little sentiment regarding the chateau, Dodge sought to retain as many of the existing trees as possible.

A tree inventory was conducted at the beginning of the project with the location, size, condition, and species (mainly lindens, oaks, maples, and other hardwoods) plotted to ensure that building footprints and infrastructure did not adversely affect the trees.[73] Based on the Olmsted Brothers' plans of the Stonehurst site dating from 1904, the side drive was lined with twenty-four elm trees and the main drive with sixty-eight maples.

Predating the overlay method espoused by McHarg, roads and building masses were overlaid with the tree survey to guarantee their preservation. Drystone retaining walls were also designed to maintain elevations around the trees' drip lines, thus preserving their root systems. Stonorov and Oberlander were able to preserve ninety mature trees, which at the time were more than fifty years old.[74]

The project also enabled Oberlander to hone other site planning skills. With Stonorov, she designed a new roadway system that traced the old drives and followed contour lines. Together they lobbied the city to narrow the roadways' width to preserve the adjacent trees. The curving streets and calculated location of buildings were conceived together to negate views of long building façades and shorten sight lines, thus giving an intimate, human scale to the landscape spaces. The rural character of the site was also maintained by burying the electrical lines. Since many of the structures were split-level, Oberlander graded the land around the changing access points.

According to the art historian Malcolm Clendenin, Stonorov's architecture blended traditional and modern materials and construction. "The architects responded to the architectural and historical context in a way they did not in other Philadelphia projects — using (shallowly) pitched roofs, and traditional Philadelphia brick along with concrete and plate glass. At the same time Stonorov was still attempting to answer the same underlying challenge as those earlier developments: housing that is affordable, yet high-quality in its design."[75] Perhaps Cherokee Village was a solution. The project's mixture of rental houses and owned homes and the sensitivity of the site plan contributed immensely to its success. Oberlander visited the project half a century after its completion in 1959. She found the trees they had fought to preserve were still largely extant. As of this writing the project is still standing, and serves as a model of landscape and structure fitting the hilly wooded context.

18th and Bigler Street Playground

Oberlander's first solo public project was the 18th and Bigler Street Playground (now Barry Playground). In the early 1950s the City Planning Commission designated the defunct sports fields at this location as a capital improvement site as part of a program to convert playfields and abandoned lots into new playgrounds that featured more varied play opportunities. Given her working knowledge of the community and her background at the CCCP, Oberlander was hired as landscape architect. The 18th and Bigler Street Playground was the first project to be realized under this program; thus, it was to be a model for Philadelphia's thirty-one new playgrounds and a testament to the city's progressive planning for youth.[76]

Located on a 3.5-acre city block of defunct sports fields in South Philadelphia, the park primarily catered to older children playing organized sports, and to fighting, about which the local community expressed concerns. Oberlander also discovered that the site was located at the threshold of several competing groups (African Americans, Italians, Irish, and Poles), and they used the field to negotiate their differences. As the lead designer, Oberlander immediately embarked on the type of research she had performed in her planning roles: collecting information on age groups and population composition along with traffic studies from the city and school locations from the Board of Education. She then conducted public meetings to exchange information and update the community on her progress. One of her goals was to create play spaces for

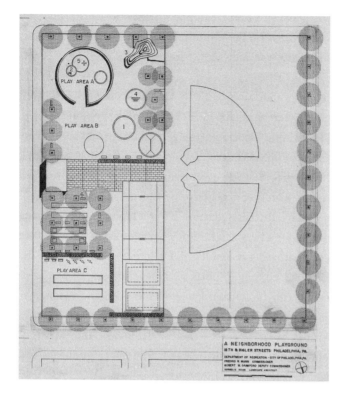

A NEIGHBORHOOD PLAYGROUND
18TH & BIGLER STREETS PHILADELPHIA, PA.

DEPARTMENT OF RECREATION - CITY OF PHILADELPHIA, PA.
FREDRIC R. MANN COMMISSIONER
ROBERT W. CRAWFORD DEPUTY COMMISSIONER
CORNELIA HAHN LANDSCAPE ARCHITECT

Plan (in preparation
for reverse printing)
of the 18th and Bigler
Street Playground
(now Barry Playground),
Philadelphia, circa 1954.
Landscape Architect:
Cornelia Hahn.

different age ranges and shared spaces where children from different backgrounds could play cooperatively.[77] She was also keen to design a new line of equipment, working with sculptors and playground manufacturers.

Bounded by 18th, 19th, Bigler, and Johnston Streets, Oberlander used the geometry of the city block—a defining element of historic Philadelphia's development—to divide the playground into discrete rectilinear spaces that addressed different groups using the playground. Given that it was to be a model for other communities, Oberlander's geometric organization could be easily adapted to other sites in the city. The southeast quarter of the site was dedicated to younger children, with a series of circles cut from the ground plane or defined by low curbing, which doubled as child-size seat walls. These circular spaces provided opportunities for sand manipulation, sliding, water play, swinging, and climbing. The northeast quarter of the site accommodated spaces for adults and older children, with plenty of sitting areas and more formalized opportunities for play. A small bosquet of nine trees shaded games tables as well as a bocce area and horseshoe pit. This section also contained spaces for basketball, shuffleboard, badminton, and a small service building. The entire west half of the site was dedicated to ball sports, with baseball fields outlined in plan.

Oberlander installed play sculptures by Egon Moeller-Nielsen, whose work she had discovered with Peter in a park in Stockholm. The sculptures were reminiscent of the plasticity and associative imagery of Isamu Noguchi's playscapes. For example, a reinforced-concrete sculpture resembling a seashell morphology provided an inner stairway and an outer surface that served as a slide. Oberlander devised a sculpture herself; she designed the biomorphic concrete *Goat Mountain,* which reinterpreted steps in topographic relief. Reaching eight feet in height with varying riser heights and curving treads, the structure allowed for climbing and gathering in small groups. In her descriptions of the playground Oberlander referred to both of these unusual structures as equipment, making a concerted effort to encourage people to think more imaginatively about what a play apparatus could be.

It took Oberlander three years to realize this model playground, which finally opened in September 1954 to a large group of children, city officials, and the press. At the inaugural ceremony, Commissioner of Recreation Frederic R. Mann announced that this "is a carefully planned recreation facility with different and outstanding attractions, many which have never been used in any part of the nation."[78] These were not empty words. The playground was featured in *Life* magazine in 1954, *Progressive Architecture* in 1955, and *Community Planning Review* in 1956. The author of the *Progressive Architecture* article observes that "passing the stereotyped, cindery city 'playground' with its grid rows of iron-and-wood exercise equipment behind spiked fences is heralded in Philadelphia by the adoption of a new kind of landscape, informal areas for family recreation as the standard for the redevelopment of dozens of the municipal playgrounds."[79] The playground was also featured in European books about innovative playgrounds in the United States. Alfred Ledermann and Alfred Trachsel selected it as among the best of the playgrounds from the United States, and they applauded the way areas for different age groups were spatialized over the site.[80]

The 18th and Bigler Street Playground is extant, and Oberlander's main organization scheme still exists, with baseball fields on the western half, a smaller children's area in the southeast quarter, and the play courts in the northeast. The street trees she planted along Johnston Street survive, as do a group of trees

Goat Mountain at the 18th Street and Bigler Street Playground (now Barry Playground), 1954. Landscape Architect: Cornelia Hahn.

in the younger children's play area. Tennis courts have replaced the badminton area, and the small children's circular zone now contains ganged playground equipment. A swimming pool has replaced Oberlander's *Goat Mountain,* the wading pool, and Moeller-Nielsen's sculptures.[81]

Oberlander admits that the playground did not reduce tensions among its users. Children continued to fight. However it did instill a new conception of what an urban playground could be and how landscape architects were uniquely positioned to create these spaces for a wide range of age groups. The 18th and Bigler Street Playground also demonstrated how an enlightened city government was a contributing factor to innovation. This was stressed in her first address to the Canadian Society of Landscape Architects and Town Planners. She notes that under past regimes "a playground constituted a piece of ground with an eight-foot-high cyclone fence, usually large enough for ball games with a few isolated swings and slides, if the little ones wanted to come too. The grass was always worn, and in a most unimaginative shelter sat a guard." She then described how the realization of the 18th and Bigler Street Playground was directly tied to the new progressive government in Philadelphia.[82]

Her understanding of the vital connection between the city politic and public projects served her well when she moved to Vancouver, a small resource-based city that was rapidly transforming into a modern one. She married Peter Oberlander in 1953 and during the first few years of their marriage she traveled back and forth between Canada and the United States, starting projects in Vancouver and completing ones in New York and Philadelphia. In 1954 the Oberlanders moved back to the United States so Peter could complete his Ph.D. in Urban and Regional Planning at Harvard. They agreed to live in New York, as he could commute to Cambridge and she could oversee projects in the Northeast. However, they eventually returned to Vancouver and settled there permanently. This decision warranted considerable thought on Oberlander's part. She knew she would miss her friends and colleagues who shared her vision of a modern landscape architecture. An exchange of letters between Oberlander and Ian McHarg in April 1958 regarding the Rockefeller Research Project in Landscape Architecture reveals how this feeling was mutual. McHarg writes that despite her snippy retort to his request for her latest research, "I am delighted to have a letter from you under any pretext. Therefore dear Cornelia, will you gather together representative work and representative thought and let me have it for the research project? I am sorry you have left Philadelphia. You are sorely missed."[83]

VANCOUVER

Vancouver provided numerous opportunities for Oberlander's emerging practice. Certainly, the city's location near the ocean, and its watery sun and mild climate, greatly expanded her palette of plant materials. Compared to cities she had known in the United States, Vancouver was also relatively young. Incorporated in 1886, it was the last stop on the Canadian Pacific Railroad and the managerial hub for forest extraction and shipping. By the early twentieth century, Vancouver featured a major port connecting North American markets to the Pacific Rim, and, with the Panama Canal completed in 1914, to Europe. Fortunately, Vancouver's twentieth-century expansion followed the recommendations of Harland Bartholomew and Associates' planning report of 1929, and subsequent reports in the 1940s. Their comprehensive plan for a city of one million proposed a series of parks along the waterfront and smaller neighborhood parks throughout, ideas from which Vancouver residents still benefit.

Oberlander called Vancouver a "terminal city," the final stop of a transcontinental railroad, settled, "as the saying goes, by 'people who reach for the future or flee from the past.'"[84] To be sure, Oberlander reached for the future, and she has surmised that her move to Vancouver was very fortuitous: "Vancouver was a tiny town, with no theater, no great art gallery, and only two high-rises. . . . I was able to conquer new ground. In the east I would have never been able to do that."[85]

There are other reasons that made the timing of her move fortuitous. When she arrived in the 1950s her skills as a landscape architect were in great demand — Vancouver was transforming itself into a major city needing housing, civic buildings, transportation systems, and open spaces.[86] Vancouver possessed a busy waterfront harbor and port, a vibrant entertainment district, commercial areas for shopping, and two large parks, Stanley and Hastings. Unfortunately, there was a scarcity of affordable housing. According to the historian Rhodri Windsor-Liscombe, "Between 1940 and 1970, Vancouver was remade," requiring forty-five thousand new housing units after World War II.[87] There had been some small experiments with modern housing starting in the 1940s, but otherwise the housing stock (aside from the exclusive Shaughnessy estates designed by Frederick Todd) was a range of hastily erected worker housing, Arts and Crafts bungalows, and Edwardian-styled dwellings.

Never hesitating to participate in the power constituencies that shape a city, both Oberlanders were to quick to participate in this change. She joined the Community Arts Council, Vancouver Housing Association, Urban Design Panel, Community Planning Association, and numerous children and youth organizations. As a female landscape architect she participated in worlds of both genders — the full range of professional associations dominated by men and the numerous women's volunteer organizations keen to make a difference in the life of the city. From removing billboards to conducting media-covered walks in historic districts, these volunteer groups played a pivotal role in transforming as well as preserving Vancouver's urban landscape.[88]

The young couple soon became part of a small cadre of like-minded design professionals, primarily schooled in the East, who brought their modern ideals to the needs of the city. For example, Abraham Rogatnick, who was a recent graduate of Harvard's architecture department, visited Vancouver in 1955 and never left. Rogatnick eventually taught in the University of British Columbia's School of Architecture, but he also contributed immensely to the city's emerging art scene, opening with Alvin Balkind the city's first commercial gallery for contemporary art: The New Design Gallery. Oberlander also met other female professionals like Catherine Mary Wisnicki, an influential architect with the firm Sharp, Thompson, Berwick & Pratt and a faculty member in the School of Architecture.[89]

Peter's connections to the architecture faculty also introduced Oberlander to some of the leading modern architects arriving in Vancouver, including architecture department head Fred Lasserre, and the architect Arthur Erickson. The Oberlanders maintained their East Coast connections as well. Walter Gropius, with whom they both corresponded after graduation, received an honorary degree from the University of British Columbia in 1968. There was also a flurry of exchanges between architects working in other West Coast cities. Richard Neutra, for example, spoke several times in Vancouver. As Windsor-Liscombe points out, the "American Pacific coast exerted a powerful influence on the design community in Vancouver, not only because it was closer and more accessible than even Winnipeg, but also because its culture and climate were more closely related to the conditions in post-war Vancouver."[90]

One reason why the Oberlanders and other newly arrived designers were so successful in effecting change was due to Vancouver's lack of a traditional ruling elite who controlled its cultural institutions. While the East Coast establishment required navigating the entrenched social structures governing everything from fashion to park design, this was not the case in Vancouver. The city was initially a resource town, primarily run by tightfisted Scottish lumber barons who vied to make money from the land — but had little interest in managing it. During the 1950s and 1960s Oberlander found that sometimes a simple suggestion might materialize and become convention. A prime example of this can be seen on Vancouver's numerous beaches. Today they are known for the huge logs that line their sandy edges — an idea that Oberlander achieved with a simple phone call. In 1963 she noticed huge plumes of smoke rising from Jericho Beach. Upon closer inspection she found that park workers were burning logs washed ashore after breaking away from a log boom. While this was common practice, she thought it was a terrible waste and called the Vancouver Park Board superintendent Bill Livingston. Oberlander proposed that the logs be saved and spread out on the beaches for people to sit on. Livingston thought this made sense and followed her advice. Now, for more than half a century, people have enjoyed relaxing on these logs.[91]

Vancouver also created unparalleled opportunities for Oberlander because she had little competition at the time. While the Canadian Society of Landscape

Architects had been established in 1934, most of its members lived in Montreal and Toronto. The first landscape architect to work in the Vancouver area was the British-born Thomas Mawson. In 1912 he made an ambitious, high-profile proposal for Vancouver's Stanley Park and Coal Harbor. Envisioning the relationship between Stanley Park and the city as an urban ensemble that would recall the "grand manner" of Paris — replete with axial boulevards, formal gardens, and recreational areas — his scheme was promptly ignored and he set his sights on Calgary.[92] In 1951, Desmond Muirhead & Associates formed the only Vancouver-based firm to specialize in landscape architecture. Clive Justice studied landscape architecture at the University of California, Berkeley, and joined the firm in 1953. He was followed by the artist Harry J. Webb in 1955.[93]

As one of the few landscape architects practicing in Vancouver, Oberlander promoted the contributions the profession could make. Writing in *Canadian Architect* in 1956, she condemns the paucity of professionally designed homes and gardens in Canada: "During the last year, more than 100,000 single family dwellings have been built. How many of these were planned in [an] architect's offices or had the advantage of advice from a landscape architect? A walk along our suburban streets easily convinces us that the majority of small single family homes have been neglected in their development of the out-of-doors."[94] She also informed North American audiences about modern garden developments abroad. That year she reviewed in *Landscape Architecture* magazine the 1955 *Neue Gärten* (New gardens) by the Swiss garden designer Ernst Baumann. Ironically, her book review faced Bremer Pond's review of Cecil Stewart's 1954 *Topiary: An Historical Diversion.*

Scant opportunities for professional training were another factor contributing to the shortage of landscape architects in Canada. As early as 1956 Oberlander recommended that Canada develop landscape architecture programs in its universities, arguing, "Today modern architecture has won its battles all over the world. But with very few buildings can the work of a landscape architect be seen . . . modern architecture needs the landscape architect and we must train students to fill this gap."[95] At the University of British Columbia she embarked on an extensive campaign to create a landscape architecture program. On 14 July 1960, she wrote a formal proposal to Fred Lasserre, then head of the architecture school, and the architecture professor Wolfgang Gerson. She proposed a program integrated with architecture and planning so that the academic setting would model the desired professional one.[96]

Oberlander also promoted landscape architecture to women's groups. In her 1975 lecture to a largely female audience at the University of British Columbia, Oberlander advised that if you want to be a landscape architect in Vancouver: "Leave women — enroll in Guelph, Toronto, Manitoba or Montreal or U of W or Washington State, which is a little nearer and take a full degree." Alternatively, she added that women could take credit and noncredit courses in horticulture and gardening so that they could engage in "'peripheral activities' such as illustrating articles and textbooks."[97] Five years later a landscape architecture program at the University of British Columbia finally opened, but in the Faculty of Agricultural Sciences with John Neill as its first director. Finally twenty-five years later, the landscape architecture program joined with the architecture and environmental design programs to form the School of Architecture and Landscape Architecture.

During these early years in Vancouver, Oberlander stood out from her peers. Not only was she female, but she also had strong convictions regarding the future of the profession. Modern design was not simply an image she saw in the glossy pages of magazines, but something she had experienced directly during her childhood in Germany. According to the landscape architect Ron Williams, for the handful of landscape architects practicing in Vancouver at the time, modern design was not the all-encompassing drive that it had been for Oberlander. Most practitioners felt equally comfortable designing projects based on modern principles or traditional modes of design depending on the situation.[98] Thus, Oberlander sought out other design professionals who shared her commitment to modern design, and this brought her into contact with other architects, artists, and planners.

In their coauthored article "The Spirit of Architecture in the Canadian Northwest" for *Progressive Architecture*, Peter and Cornelia observe "a meaningful synthesis of the arts in architecture" in Vancouver.[99] Oberlander not only identified with the modern artists and architects she was encountering in Vancouver; she also felt strongly about maintaining the social commitment of modernism that she had envisioned in the 1940s. This sentiment was evident in her lecture in 1955 to the Canadian Society of Landscape Architects and Town Planners. Oberlander reminded landscape architects that they were no longer working for only the very rich, but for a *new* client base. She stresses that "the landscape architect must acquire a thorough understanding of this new client, namely the community."[100]

Canada's version of modernism was more accepting of the social dimensions of European modernism.[101] By 1966, for example, a national health care plan had been established, and in Vancouver experiments in modern housing for all classes were largely an urban phenomenon, with market-rate high-rise housing in the West End and subsidized high-rise housing in the Strathcona area.[102] New housing was needed not only to accommodate the rising population but also to replace the deteriorating nineteenth-century housing stock and infrastructure. As such, affordable housing was one of Vancouver's key areas of concern, especially for retired forest, train, and port workers, as well as young immigrant families and an oppressed aboriginal populace who lived in many of these older neighborhoods. When Vancouver planners began discussions on the creation of subsidized housing, Oberlander, with her experience in Philadelphia, was the undisputable choice as landscape architect.

The location for this new public housing was based on extensive surveys conducted by the Canada Mortgage and Housing Corporation (CMHC) and Vancouver city planning departments in the 1950s.[103] Planners assessed the age of the dwellings, their quality, and existing land use. The older portions of the city were identified as sections in need of renewal, and "blight" became the operative word to describe these areas. The mayor sent residents in every fourth house a letter in English and Cantonese requesting an interview. These interviews revealed that seniors comprised 14 percent of the population, and that 20 percent of the respondents required social assistance. Interviewers also found that while many residents liked their neighborhood, many did not have hot water or heating, and dampness was a constant problem. The study is portrayed in the CMHC film *To Build a Better City* (1964), and while the film today may strike one as fatally paternalistic, the deleterious conditions — documented through interviews, photographs, and film — poignantly convey the grim environment in which people lived. Between 1961 and 1967 clearing began on twenty-eight acres destined for public housing and industry in the Strathcona area in northeast Vancouver.[104] Redevelopment plans identified two new public housing projects, McLean Park and Skeena Terrace.

McLean Park and Skeena Terrace Housing
Phase One of the McLean Park Rental Housing Project occupied four city blocks in Strathcona, a working-class neighborhood largely born out of its association with the railroads. By the 1960s the expanding trucking industry drastically

reduced railway use and the jobs it afforded. Strathcona also bordered China-town, home to a close-knit community living in the neighborhood since the nineteenth century, a group that would dramatically shape future plans for the area. Phase One began on the block containing McLean Park Playground, re-located a few blocks east. The city's redevelopment efforts began with the park because it was the only block that was not occupied by housing. As the three remaining blocks containing housing were cleared, residents were relocated east to Skeena Terrace, the largest low-income housing project in Vancouver.

McLean Park Housing was comprised of a nine-story apartment building with one-bedroom apartments and studios, and a series of three- and four-story maisonettes.[105] Erwin C. Cleve was the chief architect working with Under-wood McKinley Cameron.[106] As landscape architect, Oberlander was respon-sible for site planning, grading and drainage, the planting plan, and the design of recreational spaces for young and old. She also specified the retention of old chestnut trees, a legacy of the site's former life as a park. Unfortunately, during the design phase Oberlander contracted mumps and was unable to design col-laboratively with the architects and engineers as was planned. In fact she was required to sterilize all of her drawings before submitting them to the CMHC.

The drawings Oberlander produced in 1962 for the McLean site included a number of variations on open space design. E. Georgia Street, which divided the site, was redesigned as a sidewalk to ease pedestrian movement from north to south. To the north the masionettes were paired to create two linear open spaces with semiprivate yards linked by a sidewalk. The west side of the site contained the majority of parking, and an apartment tower with a surrounding open space at its base. Like Cherokee Village, eleven three-story structures were staggered along the site's edge to take up the slope and disrupt a potentially block-long length of building surface.

McLean shared some similarities, as well as differences, with Mill Creek. At the main courtyard a circle of grass, eighty-four feet in diameter, provided the communal area and counterpoised the scale of the nine-story tower. Ober-lander also designed play sculptures that were reminiscent of the 18th and Bigler Street Playground, a chess area for older people, ample seating, and a freestanding curved wall at the base of the tower. A planting plan by Ober-lander, dated 15 October 1962, depicts a tree palette similar to her Philadel-phia work, with large deciduous trees at the project's street edges and smaller trees in the interior courtyards and along the linear spaces. The 1962 plan also identifies small entrance gardens and sites for individual gardening in front of the three- and four-story maisonettes. Individual entrances and small green areas with high fencing between the units, but low fencing on the street side, were intended to allow residents to make their own personal marks on the landscape with gardens or outdoor sitting areas. In contrast to her Philadelphia projects, the site design does not turn its back on the adjacent neighborhood. The lower floors of the maisonnettes flank the site's edges with doorways that open to semiprivate spaces echoing the individual yards of the older housing across the street. Significantly, the mature chestnut trees were preserved and root fed during construction.[107]

Skeena Terrace, located on the eastern edge of the city, was designed during the same time period. Underwood, McKinley, Cameron, Wilson & Smith, Architects designed one eight-story apartment tower and twenty-seven three-story maisonettes. The twelve-acre site for Skeena Terrace presented Oberlander with a formidable challenge. Similar to Schuylkill, there was approximately a one-hundred-foot change in elevation from north to south. Added to this, prior to Oberlander's joining the project, the engineers had cut a roadway through the site connecting Cassiar with 5th Avenue, thereby dividing the site in two. Using a series of retaining walls that created shelf-like building pads, the outdoor terraces for the maisonettes were created to provide garden areas for tenants, as well as views over the city. Resembling her other housing projects, large deciduous trees were planted on the project's street edges and smaller trees were located at the residential spaces. She also designed play sculptures for small children and several recreational and social spaces.

Both projects were only the start of a larger redevelopment scheme. However, the Chinese community consistently spoke out against the renewal process, and when plans involved building a highway through the neighborhood, the process was halted.[108] Interestingly, Peter Oberlander played a key role in stopping this construction. Although the planning commission had supported renewal housing and the highway, Peter personally disagreed. In protest, he announced his resignation as chairman of the commission "to a standing ovation of 800 residents."[109] As a result no highway was constructed, and much of the public housing in Vancouver was reduced dramatically in scope. Small developments, like McLean Park, were left intact as part of neighborhoods that still contained a cohesive social structure as well as amenities. According to Windsor-Liscombe, "The proximity of shopping and community facilities and

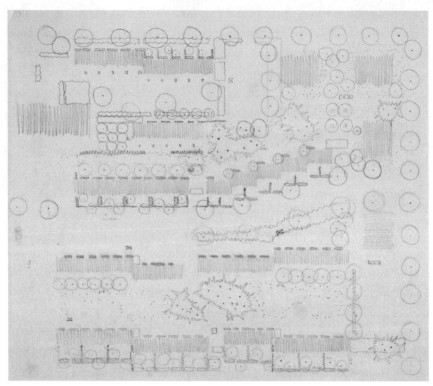

Skeena Terrace schematic tree planting plan, circa 1963. Landscape Architect: Cornelia Hahn Oberlander. Architects: Erwin C. Cleve with Underwood, McKinley, Cameron.

the developments' relatively small scale, protected them from the disastrous concentration of social problems that afflicted Toronto's Regent Park South, to a lesser degree Montreal's Jeanne Mance housing complex."[110] The architect Martin Lewis notes that the "institutional and social services support from CMHC" also contributed to the sustainability of the projects when compared to their U.S. counterparts.[111]

In the tenant location plans for McLean Park Housing and Skeena Terrace, age was considered to be the main factor determining residents' assignment to high-rise versus garden-style accommodations. In her interview with Oberlander for *The Province* newspaper, the journalist Nikki Moir notes that both McLean Park and Skeena Terrace "follow the pattern of urban living; high-rise apartments for the older or senior citizens; garden types housing for younger marrieds and designed play areas for the children. Theory is that olders should be able to mingle with the children when they wish."[112] Given that many former

public housing towers in cities like San Francisco have been renovated for seniors, this pattern of locating seniors in high-rise structures and families in
garden housing may have contributed to the livability of McLean Park Housing
and Skeena Terrace.

While both projects have suffered from crime and vandalism they have not
been as extreme as at Mill Creek or Schuylkill in Philadelphia. The building
envelopes and energy systems for McLean Park and Skeena Terrace were renovated in 2009. However, the landscape has largely remained intact and many
of the spaces at McLean Park that Oberlander allotted for gardening are still
maintained as semiprivate spaces, some teaming with vegetables and flowers.
During a visit in 2010, it was noted that about half of these spaces contained
vegetable and/or flower gardens. While the benches and play area in the courtyard have been modified, the curving wall and play sculpture installed in 1963
are extant. Additional areas for gardening by tower residents have also been
provided in the courtyard.

At Skeena Terrace, there are fewer individualized spaces with gardens — but
there is an extensive community garden next to the new childcare center. The
garden is quite expressive, containing plants and artworks produced by the
residents. It is informative to compare these projects to Oberlander's public
housing landscapes in Philadelphia. While the Canadian projects share similar architectural typologies to their U.S. counterparts, Oberlander's landscape
plans for McLean Park and Skeena Terrace were installed. It would be naïve
to suggest that the landscape alone was the reason the Vancouver projects are
still in use. Nonetheless, today the stately trees contribute greatly to the atmosphere of the Vancouver projects, providing dappled light and color. Likewise
they counterbalance the scale of the towers and knit the project into the surrounding neighborhood, a quality that many public housing projects of the
time lacked.

McLean Park and Skeena Terrace brought Oberlander into contact with
Vancouver's leading modern architects. The office of Semmens & Simpson in
particular, was part of the Vancouver School, a group of architects who had
been experimenting with modern architecture since the 1940s.[113] The projects
also reinforced her belief that thoughtfully considered design need not be expensive and should be available to all. By the 1980s, however, another serious
social issue emerged: homelessness. In the following decades Vancouver grew
to have some of the most expensive housing in North America. As the disparity

↗ McLean Park Housing individual gardens, 2010.

» McLean Park Housing entrance, 1968. Landscape Architect: Cornelia Hahn Oberlander. Architects: Erwin C. Cleve and Underwood McKinley Cameron.

between wealth and poverty grew, numerous people already plagued with mental illness and drug-related problems began living on the streets of Vancouver's Downtown Eastside.

Portland Hotel

In 1995 Arthur Erickson with Nick Milkovich Architects began work on the Portland Hotel project, a permanent accommodation for eighty-six adults with mental illnesses, addictions, and other problems.[114] As Milkovich recalls, they

both immediately thought of involving Oberlander because she had social commitment.[115] Located on a city-owned site in the Downtown Eastside, the new Portland Hotel was around the corner from the demolished Portland Hotel. It was the vision of Liz Evans and Mark Townsend, members of the Portland Hotel Society. Arriving in Vancouver from Britain they were discouraged by the city's treatment of homeless people. Subsidized housing was only available to those who had recovered from addiction, so many people with compound issues of drug dependency, HIV/AIDS, and prostitution were forced to live on the streets or in seedy hotels. Evans and Townsend were also critical of the single-room-occupancy facilities being revived in North America at the time. They found them institutional and not respectful of the residents as human beings. According to Elisabeth Whitelaw "they sought to change the institutionalized feel of these places and to allow people who had not recovered from their addictions to be residents."[116]

For the project, Oberlander designed both a main entrance courtyard and the parking garage rooftop landscape. Every effort was made to create spaces that were, in Liz Evans's words, more "home-like."[117] For example, Oberlander selected outdoor furniture, mainly benches and picnic tables, which were made of wood instead of more durable metal. Displays of annual flowers, a common feature of institutional settings, were avoided. Instead Oberlander selected plants associated with Vancouver's domestic gardens: small trees, woodland ferns, and perennials. Erickson brought the idea of home inside the building with Dutch doors that allowed tenants to partially open their units to the corridor — affording some privacy with an opportunity to socialize. To mediate the scale of the buildings surrounding the sunken courtyard, Oberlander planted trees and grew vines on the courtyard walls. Milkovich designed a water feature at the end of the courtyard to muffle noise.

The rooftop landscape called the "backyard garden" is reminiscent of a classic Vancouver residential space, a landscape typology that many of the residents knew about but may have never experienced. A thick arborvitae evergreen hedge defined the yard. Two lawn areas and picnic tables also suggested a domestic space, rather than an urban plaza. The backyard was originally intended for gardening but the shadows cast by a tower built to the west in the intervening years prohibited this. In response Oberlander planted apple trees, strawberries, and blueberry shrubs for the residents to pick. Today, a poignant moment in the scheme is the stairway that connects this rooftop landscape to the lower courtyard. The measure of the stairway is wider and more gracious than the building code requires and provides an unexpected moment of grandeur. As of this writing, the rooftop backyard serves as a gathering spot for barbeques and music and is a space for residents to exercise their pets, as well as enjoy programmed events. Unfortunately, the contemplative courtyard has served an unplanned use — a commemorative site for those residents who have died of their afflictions.

Along a similar vein, in 2002 with Diana Gerrard of gh3, Oberlander designed a one-acre park for Wellesley Central Place in Toronto. A long-term care and outpatient facility for people with Alzheimer's disease and those with HIV/AIDS, Wellesley Central Place also sought to evoke a home-like environment. However, the landscape reflected a public more than a private space. For this urban site, Oberlander helped lay out a grid of forty-two London plane trees in a base plane of crushed granite. Given Toronto's dramatic changes in weather, the trees created varied atmospheres from winter versus summer. Against this geometry of plant life, a variety of large rocks for seating were scattered throughout. Many of the rocks have polished top surfaces that reveal textures and a rich variety of colors hidden in their rough state.

Oberlander also revisited public housing in the twenty-first century. While the 1980s had witnessed a general retreat from government-funded projects, such as social housing, by the end of the twentieth century there was a renewed willingness to experiment with different typologies and new combinations of rental, subsidized, and owned homes. Oberlander returned to the United States to collaborate on New Holly Park.

New Holly Park Phase III
In early 2000 Oberlander was hired by Daniel Solomon ETC Architects as landscape architect for New Holly Park Phase III, located in South Beacon Hill outside Seattle, Washington. Originally called Holly Park, the housing site was designed between 1940 and 1942 for defense workers and their families. Butler Sturtevant, who had recently formed a partnership with Edwin Grohs, was the original landscape architect. The architects John Paul Jones, Frederick T. Ahlson, and Paul Thiry designed 896 primarily two-story units.[118] After World War II, veterans and their families lived in Holly Park but during the Korean War it again housed defense workers. In 1954 the project was converted to public housing under the jurisdiction of the Seattle Housing Authority.

Like much defense-worker housing, Holly Park was hastily erected and built of cheap materials. Sturtevant had prepared the landscape plans but it is doubtful the planting scheme was ever installed, as pictures of the site before renovation show dilapidated structures set in large expanses of dead grass. By the 1980s Holly Park was identified by the Seattle Housing Authority as one of the most distressed areas of the city, and by 1995 the authority received redevelopment money to revitalize the entire project. A year later residents were temporarily relocated as the entire area was transformed.

The redesigned New Holly Park was a combination of 1,200 dwellings and a mixture of market-rate and subsidized homes. Phase III contained 219 rentals and 121 owned properties. The character of the new dwellings and layout reflected a nineteenth-century urban fabric with densely spaced street-facing façades and back alleys. A 30 January 2002 plan depicts a dense mixture of apartments, duplexes, and single-family homes laid out around a market park for the entire community. Gardens became a major theme in Oberlander's design response as she planned not only the central market park but also numerous pocket parks and a greenhouse. The final phase was opened and occupied in 2005. Five years later, the project remains a testament to Oberlander's social engagement and commitment. Half a century ago she sought to bring gardening opportunities to people through her work at the CCCP and with less success in the public housing landscapes she designed with Dan Kiley. At New Holly Park Phase III her landscape plan was installed and the community gardens are thriving.

Oberlander's relocation to Vancouver enabled her to continue the social aims of her work, starting a trajectory that would last into the twenty-first century. In addition to landscapes for shared housing at McLean Park and Skeena Terrace, the Portland Hotel, and New Holly Park Phase III, she also designed gardens for numerous single-family residences. If her public housing work represented landscape architecture's commitment to the social dimensions of modernism, her private residences stressed the psychological.

Landscape played a key role in the conception and production of postwar single-family homes as well as in Oberlander's private residential projects. While this dichotomy of housing — public housing in the city and private housing in the suburbs — would eventually have its own social and ecological consequences, the demands of the private client enabled her to explore in detail the fitting of site and structure, how different compositions move the eye, the role

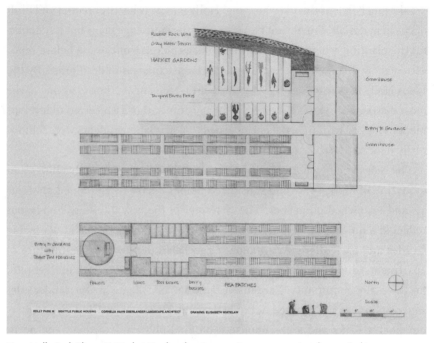

New Holly Park Phase III Market Garden drawings, 30 January 2002. Landscape Architect: Cornelia Hahn Oberlander. Drawn by Elisabeth Whitelaw.

of empathy in design, and the use of historical references. Moreover, while the psychological impacts of the landscape, such as providing privacy, would be considered in her design work for shared housing projects, it was the private realm of home and garden where the psychological import of landscape was given its greatest attention.

Desire Lines: Private Landscapes

Oberlander's move to Vancouver brought a wave of private residential work to her office as well. Vancouver did not witness a housing boom at the scale of the American Sun Belt states; however, by the 1950s thousands of veterans who had fought in the Pacific during World War II were demobilized in Vancouver — and they stayed.[119] Similar to California, many of these veterans married and sought inexpensive housing. Furthermore, many had no longings to replicate the tired historical designs of a class from which they were largely excluded, so as a whole they were relatively accepting of modern design. At the same time previously restricted war-related materials and modes of fabrication became fungible resources for civilian use. Indeed, many young Vancouver architects eager to explore these converted postwar commodities and systems incorporated them into their emerging practices.[120] As a consequence there was a shared willingness to break with tradition for both those needing housing and the new generation of architects seeking to define a modern design vocabulary.[121] As a champion for modern landscape architecture, Oberlander had numerous opportunities to design residential gardens.

Her professional prospects, however, were not borne entirely out of location. The postwar rise of lifestyle magazines, with their colored photographs and widespread distribution, created unprecedented opportunities for architects and landscape architects to publicize their work. As the architectural historian Beatriz Colomina notes, this generation "understood that to be an architect in the 1950s was completely different than what it had for the previous generation. Images had become the raw material of their craft."[122] Moreover, images of projects were not only crucial to this publicity but also for the designers themselves. As a young professional pair, modern in their taste and lifestyle, the Oberlanders received much attention from the local press. Describing them as the ideal couple in *The Province* newspaper, Moir writes, "Father Peter is an architect and member of the UBC School of Architecture. Mother is a trained landscape architect."[123] The article was accompanied by a half-page photograph of Oberlander drafting at her desk with an image of her Philadelphia playground photomontaged in the background. When they designed their own home, the highly publicized Tick-Tack-Toe House, it was hailed as a model design that embraced British Columbia's most valuable commodity: lumber.[124]

In Vancouver the architectural photographer Selwyn Pullan, a classmate of Julius Shulman and a student of Ansel Adams at Los Angeles's Center for Creative Photography, returned to Vancouver after the war. He played a pivotal role in capturing images of the midcentury homes built at the time and promoted the careers of Vancouver's modern architects and artists. Like Shulman, Pullan had a flair for presenting these homes as veritable stage sets awaiting owners, who would inhabit them effortlessly, and of course, without clutter. Oberlander recalls that "Selwyn had the eye," and he photographed not only her private residential gardens but also her playgrounds.[125]

Demonstrating the valuable contribution that gardens made to the conception of modern homes, Oberlander's residential projects were featured in lifestyle magazines, such as *Western Homes and Living,* as well as in professional magazines, such as *Canadian Architect.* Certainly, a professionally designed garden could offset the standardization found amongst many single-family homes built en masse. Dianne Harris observed that *House Beautiful's* coverage of gardens by Thomas Church, Lawrence Halprin, and James Rose from 1945 to 1965 illustrated how a custom-designed landscape could distinguish one's home from the monotonous backdrop of suburban housing.[126] Moreover, the contributions of landscape architects to middle-class housing became as vital as the architects. While many middle-class homeowners relied on off-the-shelf and prefabricated structures, they were still accountable for locating and adapting these structures to the site.[127] Homeowners needed to know how to read surveys of their property, interpret zoning restrictions, and often deal with unforeseen site complications when locating their houses, tasks commonly performed by landscape architects.

For Oberlander the private residential project, compared to public housing, allowed for more control. Residential sites were generally smaller and the building time frame shorter, so she was able to exert greater influence in the design process from concept to construction and maintenance. The finer-grain detail of design engagement required by private residences also gave her more opportunities for experimentation. She not only explored the use of new materials, forms, and technical details but also historical references (at times suggested by the clients themselves). Importantly, she developed a close rapport with many clients; some of these relationships have lasted more than fifty years.

KEY FEATURES OF PRIVATE GARDENS

Working on Cherokee Village, Oberlander had demonstrated her ability to handle difficult sites and to fit the land to the structure, but it was her 1954 encounter with the Wong site on S. Cambie Street in Vancouver that presented her with the most formidable challenge. At the time every other lot on the street had been developed, only the Wongs' site lay vacant. The main impediment to construction was a huge rock outcrop created by an upwelling of magma from nearby Little Mountain (now Queen Elizabeth Park) thousands of years ago.[128] Since this geologic fragment intruded into the sidewalk by three feet, the city required that any development of the site necessitated blasting the rock. However, the Wongs were originally from China, where the adoration of rocks is a long-standing tradition. According to their son Milton Wong, "people didn't

The Wong residence with rock, Vancouver, 1959. Landscape Architect: Cornelia Hahn Oberlander. Architect: Duncan McNab.

like the rock outcrop, but their family loved it" and they asked Oberlander to save it as they planned their new house with the architect Harry Lee from Duncan McNab's office.[129] Oberlander argued to the city that saving the rock and situating the house behind it would reduce traffic noise from the street and also create a visual barrier. Keeping the rock would also avoid added costs for the Wongs and loud disruptions to the adjacent neighbors. She prevailed; the rock was saved and she began the design work for the Wongs' new garden, which is largely extant today.

Oberlander also explored fitting the structure to the site for the houses she designed with Peter. Both their own Tick-Tack-Toe House and Ravine House presented diverse site constraints and in turn distinct design responses. Their first home, Tick-Tack-Toe, was located in South Vancouver where the water table was notoriously high. Their solution raised the main living area to the second floor. They called it Tick-Tack-Toe because the house was square in plan and made up of nine distinct square-shaped spaces. The center square contained the utility core for the house, which extended down to the ground where it provided access to the upper floor.[130] Oberlander noted that the raised structure also created a dry space for the children to play in when it rained, and the elevated position provided a "good view across the evergreen tree-tops to the Gulf of Georgia beyond."[131]

Tick-Tack-Toe House night view, Vancouver, circa 1965. Landscape Architect: Cornelia Hahn Oberlander. Architect: Peter Oberlander.

Their second home, Ravine House, was located in the sparsely developed University Endowment Lands (UEL) of the University of British Columbia on a site characterized by a steep gorge and ample vegetation. Given the dramatic slope and the sensitive ecology of the ravine, the UEL in 1968 held a competition for a residential development. The aim was to design a house for the site that would have the least impact on the existing ravine. The winner would receive the site as the prize. Working with Barry Downs Architects, the Oberlanders conceived of a long structure that lay parallel with the site's contour lines to minimize grading. To avoid the need for a building pad, concrete pillars supported the structure, enabling it to float above the gorge. The Oberlanders also proposed that the erection of the house generate zero soil import and export. They won the competition and the house was completed on 29 July 1970.[132] Since then the ravine's plant material has grown substantially, creating a thick green mantle around the house that is immediately visible from the interior's expansive glass walls.

Another distinct feature of private residential work was its intimate nature. Designing for a family's private life meant getting to know its members and understanding their interpersonal relationships, in short their psychology. In fact many midcentury modern landscape architects embarked on a psychological, if not confessional, design process. Thomas Church in particular encouraged homeowners to reveal their wants and desires. In the opening pages of his 1955 classic, *Gardens Are for People,* he cautions the homeowner, "No one can design intelligently for you unless he knows what you need, what you want, and what you are like. If you won't tell, he will have to guess."[133] Years later Oberlander remarked that due to the personal demands of residential work she often had to function as an analyst. This corresponds with Sylvia Lavin's claim that due to the growing field of psychoanalysis and an overtly psychologized culture after the war, architects often considered themselves analysts and their clients the patients.[134] Eckbo also stressed these roles, underscoring the benefits of creating reciprocity between the designer analyst and client patient. In *The Landscape We See* he recommends that designers and their clients partner in the design process, which "makes the therapist and his client teammates," and achieves something greater than if they worked in isolation.[135]

In order to understand the psychological impacts of the site and her design on her clients' daily lives, Oberlander read Richard Neutra's *Mysteries and Realities of the Site* (1951), and later Ernst Hans Josef Gombrich's *Art and Illusion: A Study in the Psychology of Pictorial Representation* (1960). Referring to *Mysteries and Realities of the Site* as a starting point for her 1956 *Canadian Architect* article on residential landscapes, Oberlander suggests, "The mood of a lot, even the smallest one, say 100 feet by 50 feet, must be studied and analyzed. Its potential must be understood and the land allowed to influence the design solution."[136] In this article, she also offered a psychological sketch of the average homeowner's relationship with their garden. Reminding the reader that no two families and no two sites are the same, she described three different solutions for three different clients and sites. There was the active family looking to use the yard for leisure activities, but "not too much gardening."[137] The second owners were enthusiastic gardeners, tending to vegetables and flowers. The third owners enjoyed their yard as an outdoor living room with a minimum of maintenance.

Not only were landscape architects analysts in their working relationships with clients, but long after the contract was finished, the design itself was to have a psychological impact. According to Lavin, key to the architect as analyst was the psychological theory of empathy. "Empathy allowed the analyst to identify with the client, but remain distant and objective."[138] Tunnard foreshadowed this dynamic in *Gardens in the Modern Landscape,* where he contended that an empathic approach (along with functional and artistic) was key to designing modern landscapes. In theory, empathy allowed users to apprehend animation in static forms (seeing a line as movement), or project human qualities (hearing the stream as a babbling brook), or ascribe moods to color (a cheerful yellow).[139] For the architectural historian Mark Jarzombek, empathy in architecture became "the prime philosophical project of modernity."[140] Likewise, in landscape architecture it supplied a powerful currency. Empathy linked modern design with popular culture, and gave the landscape a purpose by validating a psychological need for it.

The attribution of emotion to lines and forms was not entirely new to landscape architecture. Picturesque theories of the eighteenth and early nineteenth centuries associated human emotion with the formal qualities of landscapes. However, by the twentieth century, the effects of composition on human perception had the full-blown weight of psychology and a society ready to accept them. The idea of creating a feeling of movement and unity communicated through design became paramount to society immediately after the war. Movement was particularly salient as it also provided an argument against symmetry, which was equated with elite gardens and stasis. In short, asymmetry caused the eye to move; thus, it became a recurring design feature in the work of Oberlander and other modern landscape architects.

Tunnard's writings on empathy, form, and movement forecast this view, and he even extended the discussion to the selection of plant material. In *Gardens in the Modern Landscape* he observes that plants can contribute to "the shape of atmosphere of certain familiar settings."[141] For example, the weeping European spruce "is a curiosity of variable form. Its main stem, draped with short pendulous branches, usually develops more sensuous bends, which give the tree an apparently unstable character. In landscape planting this convulsive habit of growth introduces an arresting quality of movement."[142] Eckbo would continue the emphasis on the line, composition, and the movement of the eye. In *Landscape for Living* he notes that "a garden laid out in straight lines and right angles, but without bilateral symmetry, can be interesting, stable, and restful without being dull or monotonous. Likewise a garden planned in large simple circles, again without bilateral symmetry, would have a sense of plastic motion."[143]

The architectural historian Harry Francis Mallgrave maintains that the visual practice of empathy was abstraction.[144] Abstraction allowed designers to distill the emphatic dimensions of their work by isolating the formal attributes of design, such as line, color, and shape. Whereas the use of abstraction in shared and public housing projects provided a vocabulary that could be understood by everyone, abstraction in private gardens went beyond ideas of conscious interpretation and effected the psychological. For example, abstraction facilitated a singular design vocabulary that could enhance the feeling of unity between house and garden. This was a vocabulary that could express a line as a building edge, a garden wall, a hedge, or a separation between planting areas. For Oberlander this was paramount; she argues that "the relationship of the house to the land is most important. House and garden must *flow* into one another as if they were one."[145]

While this flow is often thought of as horizontal, many of Oberlander's schemes exploited vertical relationships to the building as well. This can be seen at the Friedman residence, one of Oberlander's first commissions in Vancouver. For the Friedmans' split-level house designed by Fred Lasserre, Oberlander used the lines from the structure, the property line, and contours to integrate the site with the house. Given the steep slope of the land the entrance is located at the ground floor, where a line created by a bank of heather leads the eye away from the house to join the invisible lines of the site's contours. On the second floor the upper patio area is defined by a fence, which parallels the property line to the south, and a scrim wall pulled directly from the building edge to the east. While providing privacy the enclosure integrates the site conditions and the building as a unified composition.

Architectural unity can also be seen at Oberlander's design for Residence Y, from 1963, where lines and surfaces are treated as a series of horizontal strata extending from the house out to the landscape. At the roof plane a wood framing system continues past the structure's edges to create a deep awning. The measure of the awning matches the ground plane surface with a divider that separates the pebble area from the planting area. A sunken living room with a glass corner allows the owner to sit and observe a view of the garden at seated eye-level. This careful attention to the level of the viewer is also found in the sitting area that looks out to the back garden. Here the owner enjoys reclining on her lounge chair and viewing the plantings. However, she did not want to see the walkway between the house and this planting area. So a small berm hides the walk, but yields a seamless view of the plants.

A common psychological need for most homeowners was privacy. Colomina observes, "Not only did the open plan eliminate individual private spaces inside the house, but the picture window and the glass wall exposed everything to the ruthless public gaze."[146] Landscape designs for the single-family suburban residence often stressed the important role of vegetation and grading in providing

Garden design for the Friedman residence, Vancouver, 3 March 1953. Landscape Architect: Cornelia Hahn Oberlander. Architect: Fred Lasserre.

⌄The planting lines flow from the structure for the Friedman residence, Vancouver, 1956. Landscape Architect: Cornelia Hahn Oberlander. Architect: Fred Lasserre.

⌄⌄ The garden is graded to unify land and structure for the Friedman residence, Vancouver, 1956. Landscape Architect: Cornelia Hahn Oberlander. Architect: Fred Lasserre.

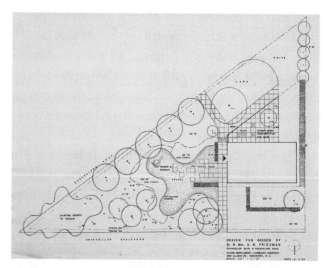

Unification of structure and land at Residence Y, Vancouver, circa 1964. Landscape Architect: Cornelia Hahn Oberlander. Architects: Thompson, Berwick, Pratt, and Partners.

a barrier against the glare of nosy neighbors and passersby. Harris's analysis of *House Beautiful* from 1945 to 1965 shares this view. The magazine's editors declare in large typeface, "Good Living is NOT public living" and ask readers, "Do the neighbors know your business?"[147]

For new suburban residences that lacked the screening provided by mature trees, privacy was particularly important. Oberlander's correspondence with a homeowner in 1964 disclosed that their biggest priority was blocking the views into their corner lot. She addressed the problem with a fence and mounds. She also demonstrated the important psychological contribution of privacy in her garden design in the late 1970s for Dr. and Mrs. Norman Keevil Sr. Their site was steep, dropping sixty feet east to west. The first floor of the house featured floor-to-ceiling windows that looked down on the property. Oberlander carefully designed large mounds to screen visual intrusions into this glass façade as well as views out. The height of the mounds was designed to match the height of the top of the mullions on the first-floor windows — a veritable act of camouflage.[148]

Another perceived emotional need of homeowners at this time was organization. The psychologically healthy home and garden were organized units, and

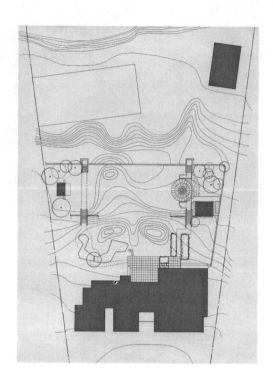

Grading plan of the Keevil residence, Vancouver, circa 1977. Landscape Architect: Cornelia Hahn Oberlander.

they could function as one because they were organized. In *Landscape for Living* Eckbo ranks organization as a primary goal for landscape architecture, stating, "The fundamental thesis of this book is that landscape design is a problem in the unified organization of specific units of outdoor space."[149] Oberlander echoed this sentiment in her 1954 lecture entitled "Planning and Living in Your Garden" given at the Vancouver Art Gallery. She advises, "Just as each room in your house serves a specific function, each of the areas in your garden must do the same. You want to rest, you want to relax, you want to play — all of these desires can be taken care of in the smallest lot if you arrange the house well on the lot. This is part of the functional approach to design."[150] Not only were spaces organized to support the leisure and domestic tasks of homeowners; the planting itself should also be orderly. "Plant material, in order to be meaningful, must be organized," Oberlander explains. "It must be used with restraint and discrimination. It is not wise, for instance, to use too many varieties of plants in a small area. It is much better and more effective to use one plant type in one area. Just as the architect organizes spaces in the interior of the house, so ought the spaces in the outdoors be organized."[151]

Keevil residence with windows camouflaged, Vancouver, circa 1977.
Landscape Architect: Cornelia Hahn Oberlander.

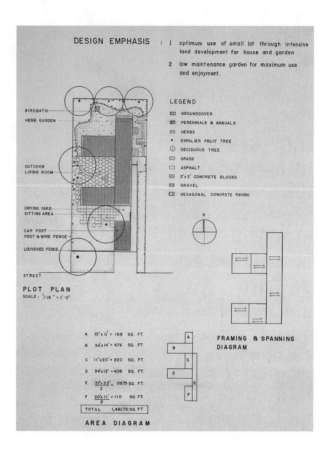

DESIGN EMPHASIS : 1 optimum use of small lot through intensive land development for house and garden

2 low maintenance garden for maximum use and enjoyment.

LEGEND

GROUNDCOVER
PERENNIALS & ANNUALS
HERBS
ESPALIER FRUIT TREE
DECIDUOUS TREE
GRASS
ASPHALT
2'x 2' CONCRETE BLOCKS
GRAVEL
HEXAGONAL CONCRETE PAVING

BIRDBATH
HERB GARDEN

OUTDOOR LIVING ROOM

DRYING YARD
SITTING AREA

CAR PORT
POST & WIRE FENCE
LOUVERED FENCE

N

STREET

PLOT PLAN
SCALE : 1/16" = 1'-0"

A	15'x 11' = 168 SQ. FT.
B	34'x14' = 476 SQ. FT.
C	11'x20'= 220 SQ. FT.
D	34'x12' =408 SQ. FT.
E	57'x3.5' = 99.75 SQ. FT.
F	20'x 11' = 110 SQ. FT.
TOTAL	1,481.75 SQ. FT

AREA DIAGRAM

FRAMING & SPANNING DIAGRAM

Home Design Competition, 1954. Landscape Architect: Cornelia Hahn Oberlander. Architect: Norman Rice.

Oberlander's drawings of residential gardens of the midcentury stressed the importance of organized space. Likewise, labels ascribing assigned use functions to different parts of the plan served in part to validate the proposed organization. In Oberlander's 1956 *Canadian Architect* article, labels on a plan view drawing for a house designed in 1954 with the architect Norman Rice indicated zones of use in relationship to orientation and the house's spatial disposition. An herb garden faces the east edge, the outdoor living space extends directly from the interior living room, the sitting area faces the street, and the drying yard is tucked in behind the carport.

Lastly, another feature of midcentury private gardens was the owner's ability to control the landscape, and this served both psychological and pragmatic needs. In discussing how abstract art versus organic art forms reflected degrees of human control, the art historian David Morgan notes that organic life and the changes it brought expressed "a finite human existence."[152] It would be difficult to exclude all organic life in a garden. Yet, paved and gravel areas often replaced lawn areas in many midcentury modern residential gardens. Certainly these surfaces did not express the type of organic change characteristic of many plants. Moreover, many of these gardens featured low maintenance plants, such as junipers, that did not change dramatically with the seasons.

On the pragmatic side, flat, inert areas provided surfaces for outdoor furniture, barbeque grills, and storage. These surfaces were also viewed as low maintenance. Harris states, "Essentially, the garden was to be designed for stasis. If it didn't change its owner needn't spend the time on it."[153] Echoing a combination of the psychological and the practical, Church advises homeowners that "large areas should be under permanent control . . . this garden is calm, restful, and serene, inviting contemplation. Why? Because maintenance is minimal."[154]

The Oberlanders' Tick-Tack-Toe House featured a sixteen-foot-wide paved perimeter around its central core for these reasons. Likewise, she used a wide expanse of gravel at the Friedman residence, noting that in the lower garden they encountered hardpan, making extensive earthmoving impractical. Oberlander was honest about the maintenance involved in this solution for the Friedmans' garden, writing, "A large free-form area of raked gravel replaces the conventional lawn at the front of the house. This is flanked by wide banks of mountain laurel, andromeda, euonymus and heather, which will eventually provide a self-sustaining year-round display. (At the moment, of course, it requires a considerable amount of weeding.)"[155]

Eventually, Oberlander would discard the idea of controlling organic processes as her landscape designs for private residences would make visible these very changes. This idea is most poignantly conveyed at the Wright residence, a project where landscape change was fully expressed.

Wright Residence

DESIGN PROCESS In 1979 Arthur Erickson asked Oberlander to join him in the design of the Wright residence, a nine-acre property in The Highlands, a residential community located north of Seattle and designed by the Olmsted Brothers in 1911. For decades Virginia and Bagley Wright had amassed an extensive collection of modern art. Their main residence was in Seattle, so The Highlands setting was to be "at once a gallery for their important collection of contemporary art, a work of art in itself and eminently livable."[156] Oberlander had crossed paths with Virginia Wright before. She and Peter had attended the

1952 solo exhibit of Jackson Pollock at the Janis Gallery in New York, where Wright had been an assistant. Erickson and Oberlander shared Wright's conception of art as something that one lives with, and the project presented a unique opportunity for both to integrate art, landscape, and architecture.

The site was one of the largest lots in The Highlands properties; it was heavily wooded, with a 10–15 percent gradient that sloped to a steep ravine, affording views to Puget Sound. Erickson recalls, "As always, the landscape was done before the house. The whole piece of property was a forest, and basically the house follows the idea of a clearing in the forest."[157] Virginia Wright's father, Prentice Bloedel, was one of the original partners of the lumber giant MacMillan Bloedel, so the forest played an important role both literally and figuratively in the design response. The Wrights encouraged the designers to take their cues from the landscape surrounding Virginia's family home on Bainbridge Island, now known as the Bloedel Reserve. The family estate contained a French chateau, originally the Agate Point Farm; a Japanese inspired guesthouse; Thomas Church and Richard Haag's majestic reflection pool and formal yew hedge; and one hundred and fifty acres of managed forest and gardens.[158]

LANDSCAPE STRATEGY The Highlands site's thick, unmanaged forest growth presented a challenge of considerable proportions. Although considerably larger in size, the Wright landscape is often compared to the hedge-enclosed pool at the Bloedel Reserve. Nevertheless, the landscape design for the Wrights unabashedly referred to its own site conditions. Reminiscent of the block cutting associated with the timber industry, the design team cut a rectangular clearing roughly 600 feet by 100 feet, beginning at the site's cliff edge and extending deep into the forest. To locate the cut, a tree survey was conducted to determine a line of the largest (over 100 feet) and healthiest trees that would mark and define the cut.[159] As Erickson remarks, "Instead of a hedge of yew, a wall of fir and cedar was exposed, reaching 150 feet up. . . . The clients gained a huge forest room."[160] Oberlander and Erickson also forced the perspective by narrowing the south end of the forest room to 80 feet wide so that from the house the space appeared longer.

Locating the house was born both in plan and section — demonstrating the use of abstraction to link architecture and site. Siting was determined by drawing a centerline through the forest room in plan and a centerline through the cross slope in section. The house was located at the crosshairs.[161] To counter the strong vertical lines of the forest, Erickson created a one-story structure with a series of H-shaped portals.[162] The house further connected to the landscape by acting as a north–south view corridor. From the main entrance the view extends through the structure to the landscape in either direction. To the north lies Puget Sound, to the south is the somber forest. Reflecting pools on either side of the house reinforce this view.

The entire property has served as a setting for art. Yet as the landscape architect Jory Johnson and the photographer Felice Frankel have observed, no pedestals for display interrupt the flow of space and separate the art from the landscape.[163] Oberlander and Erickson created a subtle palette of materials to serve as a backdrop emphasizing the art. A warm neutral hue of concrete permeates the patios and house; for the most part the plantings mimic what Oberlander saw at the site prior to construction, reminding us to "plant what you see."[164] However, this reserve would be abandoned on the south side of the house where the main view extends past the reflecting pool into the forest room. Within the depths of this three-dimensional frame Oberlander seeded a meadow of grasses and Shasta daisies to create a mutable display of color and reflection, providing a dramatic image of landscape change.

RECEPTION The project was completed in 1984 and with time the Wrights acquired an even more extensive collection of contemporary art. Both house and landscape have served to display this collection. Meg Webster's *Conical Depression* occupied one patio, while Oberlander's forested walking areas featured work such as Tony Smith's *Wandering Rocks* and Mark di Suvero's *Bunyan's Chess*. The daisy meadow remained clear of any art, without a doubt because it was a work of art in and of itself. In 2008, the Wrights pledged their collection to the Seattle Art Museum and the museum's Olympic Sculpture Park, and over time all sculptures were removed.

Given Oberlander's approach to planting what she saw growing on the site without maintenance, the plantings have required little watering over the years. This was a wise move, as many Highlands residents were castigated by the local newspaper for irrigating their gardens during the water shortages of 2004. The Wrights were spared this public scorn. Another redeeming aspect of the landscape is the long winding driveway. Distinct from the asphalt driveways of other Highlands residences, the Wrights' drive is gravel. Today the drive is covered with brilliant green moss that has been carved by the passage of tires to reveal its gravel surface below.

Wright residence forest room without and with daisies, The Highlands, Shoreline, Washington. Landscape Architect: Cornelia Hahn Oberlander. Architect: Arthur Erickson.

In 2010 the views to Puget Sound were completely blocked by vegetation but the striking view of the meadow remained. Although it was not widely published, Oberlander also designed a kitchen garden in a small courtyard on the west side of the building, adjacent to the family breakfast area. Enclosed by a high concrete wall with a slit aperture, the garden is bordered with a small boxwood hedge, espalier pear trees, and herbs. According to the caretaker of the house, the breakfast room and kitchen garden area were among the Wrights' favorite places. Even though a kitchen garden might seem like an odd addition to a modern house, Oberlander would increasingly use historical landscapes as a generator of form.

USE OF HISTORIC REFERENCES

Oberlander's inclusion of historical precedents in the design process began with her residential work. Many modern landscape architects did not completely reject history. Tunnard, who eventually dedicated his career to preservation issues, made this evident. In *Gardens in the Modern Landscape* he began

Kitchen garden, Wright
residence, The Highlands,
Shoreline, Washington, 23 July
2010. Landscape Architect:
Cornelia Hahn Oberlander.
Architect: Arthur Erickson.

with a history of landscapes and gardens — with modern design as the logical outcome of this historical narrative — and he validated many of his theoretical points with examples of historic Japanese gardens. Even when Tunnard was surrounded by the scions of modern architecture at the Museum of Modern Art's 1948 symposium "What Is Happening to Modern Architecture?" he acknowledges the valuable experiences to be gained by studying historical architecture, stating, "We have to look, I think, at the buildings which, as Thomas Jefferson said, have received that approbation of all good modern critics, and I think we have to look at the building of the past that we have been instructed not to look at."[165] Eckbo echoed Tunnard's strategy in *Landscape for Living.* He began with a brief historical account, in an attempt to understand the organization and conceptual underpinnings of historical gardens, rather than trying to imitate their styles.[166]

Historical ideas also featured in 1950s housing by Oskar Stonorov and Frank Haws for Cherokee Village, which blended traditional forms with new materials and spatial relationships. The architecture critic Sarah Williams Goldhagen has observed Louis Kahn's use of historic precedent during this time period as well.[167] Oberlander may have also been influenced by Dan Kiley, who was one of the first modern landscape architects to revive the muse of history in his work. For example, the influence of Le Nôtre has been well documented in Kiley's postwar projects.[168] The difference between Oberlander's and Kiley's use of the past and later postmodern treatments of history lies in their intent to express history through typological configurations, the replication of dimensions, or in the case of Oberlander, even the reworking of historical elements into a design. In general their intent was not to use precedent as a way of making the landscape appear historical, but rather to use precedent for generative purposes in the design process.

Use of historical precedent was also suggested by the clients themselves. Returning to the Wong residence, once the rock was saved, the Wongs requested a house and garden that reflected traditional Chinese values, which centered on family and food, but also resonated with the verve of modern art and design.[169] They suggested that Lee and Oberlander look to the pattern of the *hutong*—the alleys and courtyard residences that were the hallmark of time-honored neighborhoods in China. In response, Oberlander designed a main walkway paralleling the side yard property line to connect S. Cambie Street to the rear alley. Off of this passage, a veritable *hutong*, or U-shaped courtyard, with a traditional south-facing orientation served as the main outdoor space. Floor-to-ceiling glass windows enhanced the visual connection between inside and outside. The dining area, the most important room for the Wongs, opened onto this courtyard, where Oberlander designed a play space and installed a bubbling fountain that could be heard from the inside. Milton Wong, the second-youngest of the Wong's nine children, and his wife, Fei, lived in the house for decades. They replaced the grass play area with a small pool, but the remainder of the landscape has been kept largely intact. Visiting the courtyard today one is immediately struck by its tranquility. The courtyard captures the light and heat of the sun and blocks the wind, a quality of the traditional *hutong*. Thus, the historical references are subtle and spatial rather than symbolic and literal.

Oberlander's return to Residence Y is an example of her integration of historical elements into a modern composition. In 1966 the owners had returned from an extensive tour of Japan, where they had acquired nine stepping-stones and an ancient stone lantern from Kyoto. When Oberlander arrived on-site the

Traditional Japanese elements integrated into the Residence Y garden, Vancouver, circa 1968. Landscape Architect: Cornelia Hahn Oberlander. Architects: Thompson, Berwick, Pratt, and Partners.

stones and the disassembled lantern were neatly stacked in the driveway, each piece individually wrapped in washi paper and tied with a bow. Recalling the lectures on Japanese gardens given by Lester Collins at the GSD, Oberlander considered the integration of these elements into this garden. In a traditional Japanese garden, lanterns often stood at the water's edge so their light would be mirrored in the liquid surface; the light also guided those strolling through the garden at night. This garden was without water, so she used the stones and lantern as a guiding device, connecting the house with the beginning of the woodland walk, which had been designed in 1963 and was the owners' favorite part of the garden. Working in-situ, Oberlander placed the largest stepping-stone at the doorstep and situated each of the remaining stones approximately twenty-seven inches on-center. She located the stone lantern at the terminus of the stepping-stone path, signaling the beginning of the woodland walk. Very little was changed to the garden itself. Oberlander did not install a Japanese stroll garden or import other Japanese references. Rather, this ensemble of steps and lantern linked a modern landscape with an ancient garden-making tradition, through the ritual of movement.

Work on the garden of Dr. Paul and Josephine Hwang, which Oberlander started in 1980 with Erickson, provided another opportunity for Oberlander to

Garden edges of the Hwang residence, Vancouver, circa 1985. Landscape Architect: Cornelia Hahn Oberlander. Architect: Arthur Erickson.

distill aspects of a garden tradition and translate them into modern form. The classical houses and gardens of Suzhou, China, greatly impressed the Hwangs, and they asked Erickson and Oberlander to consider these historical works in their conception of the house and garden. Oberlander enclosed their yard with a high fence and mounds to ensure privacy and to reduce sound from the adjacent busy road — within these walls the property was entirely transformed.

Working closely with the Hwangs, Oberlander and Erickson situated the two-story house at the far end of the site to maximize the size of the main garden and its southern exposure. Like the gardens of Suzhou, water dominated the ground plane. However, whereas the gardens of Suzhou have craggy edges of weathered rock, this water basin floats under one side of the building's crisp lines and on the other side meets the soft boundary of planting.

Erickson's linear open plan for the Hwang house contained a series of spaces oriented towards the water garden. The ground-floor family room, kitchen, and dining room were based on a fourteen-foot module expressed on the exterior with decks cantilevered over the water from each of the three rooms. Stucco walls with openings that recall the gateways in Chinese gardens defined the decks. However, instead of a circular aperture or decorative shape — like the

View of the garden from the Hwang residence, Vancouver, circa 1985. Landscape Architect: Cornelia Hahn Oberlander. Architect: Arthur Erickson.

famous plum blossom door of the Lion Grove Garden in Suzhou — these openings were lozenge-shaped.

The sunken living room, with its large windows facing the garden, allows for a unique view of Oberlander's plantings. At close range one can see the water-loving plants such as lilies and horsetails in the pond, but the earthbound plants were also carefully selected and situated to enhance the view. Between the water's edge and the mounds with vegetation, Oberlander employed the traditional practice of layering foreground, midground, and background with varied plant textures. Plants with fine textures were selected for the background, shrubs with slightly larger leaves such as azaleas occupied the midground, and larger-leafed plants such as ferns filled the foreground. With the size of leaves decreasing with the plant's distance from the house, a living picture and an illusion of depth unfolds. Together they make this standard-size lot look larger than it measures.

These three examples reveal Oberlander's use of historical precedents drawn from Asian gardens. As we know from the writing of Christopher Tunnard and other modernists, Asian gardens, particularly Japanese gardens, have never been banished from modern landscape architecture's memory. Tunnard even declared "the fundamentals of Japanese landscape art as a significant modern example."[170] Accordingly, it was relatively straightforward to blend design principles from Asian gardens with a modern house and garden.

In 1994, however, Oberlander was commissioned to design the landscape for a historic house in Toronto, Residence X, which distinctly recalled a Western tradition rather than Asian. Conceived by John Lyle in 1924, the house was steeped in architectural and personal significance. Lyle was a member of the Society of Beaux-Arts Architects and he employed an architectural language that blended historic European forms with regional motifs. Residence X is a fine example of his work, melding French and Italian architectural forms with Canadian-inspired ornamentation. The dining room ceiling, for example, features a crown molding carved with images of plants and animals associated with the Canadian harvest. For the original owner, a wealthy Toronto banker, the house provided an elegant setting to host a series of important guests visiting the city. In fact, as a young girl the current owner of the house watched a relative dance with the Duke of Windsor at a ball held here in his honor.

Keeping this tradition alive, the new garden was to provide a venue for the opening of the Barnes Exhibit at the Art Gallery of Ontario (AGO) in Toronto. The owners, philanthropists, were instrumental in bringing this world-renowned collection of impressionist art to the city. They sought to hold an opening reception at their home that would measure in direct proportion to the significance of this cultural event. Given the historic nature of the house, Oberlander may have seemed like an unlikely choice, and at that point in her career she was working only on residences designed by Arthur Erickson. However the owners were persistent and finally convinced her to take the commission. Simply put, they wanted the best landscape architect in Canada. She was hired in January 1994 and the garden was finished nine months later.

Oberlander's first scheme, an angular composition, which they called the Frank Stella Garden, was rejected because they envisioned something more curvilinear. In response the second scheme involved meandering forms that extended from the rectilinear lines of the house. Like many homes in this stately Toronto neighborhood, the principal façade of the house was oriented perpendicular to the street with the conventional front and back of the house facing the side yards. At the rear of the house a large sunken area for congregating extended the limits of the original outdoor terrace. Stone walls, at the perfect height for sitting and eating during the reception, defined the architectural edge of the

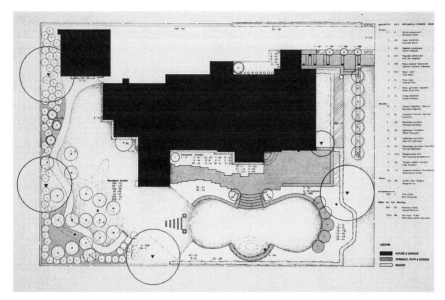

Residence X landscape plan, Toronto, 1994. Landscape Architect: Cornelia Hahn Oberlander. Original Architect: John Lyle.

area. Clipped beech trees paired with juniper and an earth mound defined the southeast edge. Oberlander worked closely with the owners to choose a simple color palette for the garden that would herald spring, eventually settling on only two types of flowers used throughout the design: light apricot-colored tea roses and cream-colored lilies.

The owners were also avid collectors of architectural details salvaged from buildings torn down in New York City and Toronto. They had incorporated these items into a new addition to their house, and they encouraged Oberlander to include some details into their new garden. Oberlander reclaimed two ball-style finials and a series of stone treads for the lawn area. The finials and steps were used to denote the entrance to the upper lawn. A gravel path begins at the end of the upper lawn and leads to a grove of seventeen birch trees. The owners later purchased marble herm figures depicting philosophers. Oberlander located these figures amongst the birches to create a white and green composition linking the eternal wisdom of the ancients with the fleeting changes of the garden.

By 1996 the owners of Residence X had acquired the adjacent property to the north, demolished the house there, and more than doubled the area of their garden. Oberlander was hired to combine the yards as one. To unite the

Recycled ball finials leading to the Philosopher's Grove at Residence X, 30 August 2011.
Landscape Architect: Cornelia Hahn Oberlander. Original architect: John Lyle.

Herm figure at Residence X, 30 August 2011. Landscape Architect: Cornelia Hahn Oberlander.
Original Architect: John Lyle.

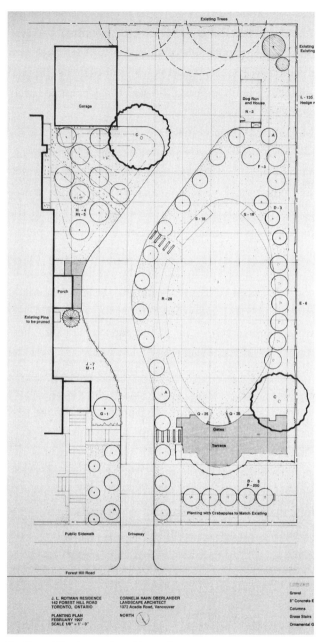

Existing Trees

Existing
Existing

L - 120
Hedge v

Dog Run
and House
N - 3

Garage

C ○

A

F - 3

H - 4
H1 - 5

S - 18

S - 18

D - 3

E - 6

Porch

R - 28

Existing Pine
to be pruned

J - 7
M - 1

A

C ○

G - 1

Q - 25

Q - 25

Gates

Terrace

B - 5
P - 250

Planting with Crabapples to Match Existing

Public Sidewalk

Driveway

Forest Hill Road

J. L. ROTMAN RESIDENCE
142 FOREST HILL ROAD
TORONTO, ONTARIO

CORNELIA HAHN OBERLANDER
LANDSCAPE ARCHITECT
1372 Acadia Road, Vancouver

LEGEND

Gravel

PLANTING PLAN
FEBRUARY 1997
SCALE 1/8" = 1' - 0"

NORTH

8" Concrete E

Columns

Grass Stairs

Ornamental G

Residence X landscape plan addition, Toronto, 1997.
Landscape Architect: Cornelia Hahn Oberlander.
Original Architect: John Lyle.

formerly separate spaces she extended the birch walk around the side of the house. Further, she created an elliptical lawn, defined by columnar beeches, to mimic the curving forms on the south side of the property. A wrought iron gate, salvaged from the demolished house, served as an entrance to the elliptical lawn — a form whose silhouette upon entering the yard today is immediately evident by the now-mature beech trees.

The early years of Oberlander's career witnessed her commitment to the social goals of landscape architecture; private residential designs helped her fine-tune the handling of site and structure, the emphatic contributions of design, and even the integration of historical references. As Oberlander's career progressed through the 1960s her conception of space would expand to include the idea of environment and the shaping of human experience. This development is poignantly echoed in her 2007 design of Milton and Fei Wong's summer residence. The site was located on Quadra Island, one of the puzzle-like pieces of land in the Strait of Georgia between Vancouver Island and the lower mainland of British Columbia. It was thick with old-growth trees as well as fallen logs draped with moss that were strewn across the site — a forest character Oberlander sought to preserve. The Wongs located their new house amongst the trees spared from felling, and Oberlander designed a rooftop landscape as an experiential extension of this forest system. Employing her method of "planting what you see," for the roof she used material she found on the Wongs' site. Equally striking, she designed the roof without railings, giving one the impression of walking on the forest floor rather than on a roof. Upon completion of the project Milton Wong remarked that up on the roof, "I am the figure, my experience is the art."[171] This idea of experience would be the essential ingredient in Oberlander's designs for children's environments and urban landscapes, and is the subject of the next chapter, "Human Environment."

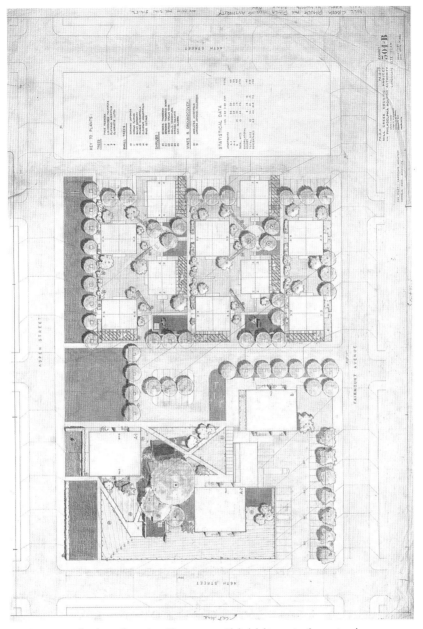

Landscape site plan for Mill Creek Public Housing, Philadelphia, 17 April 1952. Landscape Architects: Dan Kiley and Cornelia Hahn. Architects: Louis I. Kahn, Louis E. McAllister, Douglas Braik, and Kenneth Day. (Louis I. Kahn Collection, the University of Pennsylvania and the Pennsylvania Historical and Museum Commission)

McLean Park Housing grass
circle and play sculptures
(*top and bottom*) and entrance
planting (*middle*), Vancouver,
late 1960s. Landscape
Architect: Cornelia Hahn
Oberlander. Architects:
Ian Maclennan, Erwin Cleve,
and Harold Semmens and
Underwood McKinley
Cameron. (Selwyn Pullan)

Oberlander with her children in their
newly constructed Ravine House, 1970.
(Selwyn Pullan)

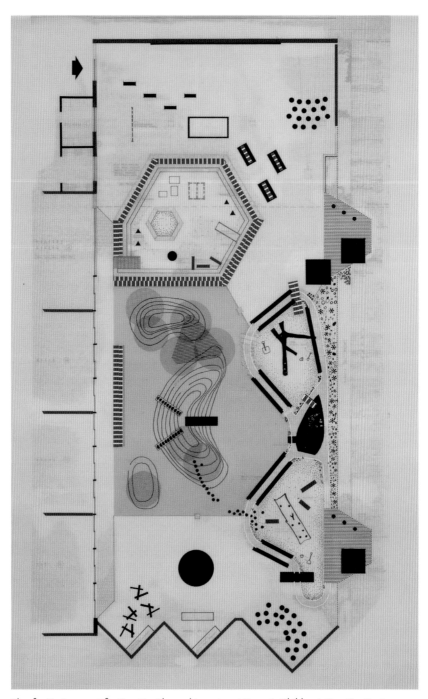

Plan for Environment for Creative Play and Learning at Expo 67 Children's Creative Centre, Montreal, 1967. Landscape Architect: Cornelia Hahn Oberlander. (Collection Centre Canadien d'Architecture/Canadian Centre for Architecture, Montréal)

Top to bottom: Op Art Wall (Artist: Gordon Smith), a rocking Nova Scotia dory, and the sunken position that allowed for optimal viewing of the Environment for Creative Play and Learning at Expo 67 Children's Creative Centre, Montreal 1967. Landscape Architect: Cornelia Hahn Oberlander.

Above: Robson Square and the Provincial Law Courts, alternating plantings on building façade, Vancouver, 2011. Architect: Arthur Erickson. Landscape Architect: Cornelia Hahn Oberlander. (Turner Wigginton)

Opposite top and bottom: Arthur Erickson and Oberlander, Vancouver, 2008, *and* Robson Square and the Provincial Law Courts, replanting, Vancouver, 2011 (Architect: Arthur Erickson; Landscape Architect: Cornelia Hahn Oberlander). (Tom Fox/Turner Wigginton)

Above: Evergreen Building (formerly the Laxton Building), replanting, Vancouver, 2011. Architect: Arthur Erickson. Landscape Architect: Cornelia Hahn Oberlander. (Turner Wigginton)

Opposite top and bottom: A rare view inside the New York Times Building, showing replanting of moss with ferns and grasses, New York, 2010 (Landscape Architects: HM White and Cornelia Hahn Oberlander; Architects: Renzo Piano and Fox & Fowle), *and* the Waterfall Building entrance courtyard, Vancouver, 2011 (Architects: Arthur Erickson with Nick Milkovich; Landscape Architect: Cornelia Hahn Oberlander). (Courtesy of HM White, New York, N.Y./Turner Wigginton)

Above: Wosk Reflecting Pool and the UBC Museum of Anthropology, Vancouver, 2011. Architect: Arthur Erickson. Landscape Architect: Cornelia Hahn Oberlander. (Stuart McCall/North Light)

Opposite: Oberlander's Haida grass mix reestablished at the UBC Museum of Anthropology landscape, Vancouver, 2011. Landscape Architect: Cornelia Hahn Oberlander. (Stuart McCall/North Light)

Green roof, VanDusen Botanical Gardens Visitor Centre, Vancouver, 2011.
Landscape Architects: Sharp and Diamond and Cornelia Hahn Oberlander.
Architects: Busby, Perkins + Will. (Stuart McCall/North Light)

Entrance, VanDusen Botanical Gardens Visitor Centre, Vancouver, 2011.
Landscape Architects: Sharp and Diamond and Cornelia Hahn Oberlander.
Architects: Busby, Perkins + Will. (Stuart McCall/North Light)

Rooftop garden, Library Square, Vancouver, 2010. Architects: Safdie Architects Planners with Downs/Archambault Architects. Landscape Architect: Cornelia Hahn Oberlander. (Author's photograph)

HUMAN ENVIRONMENT

3

The following describes how more spatially complex experiences afforded by the idea of environment increasingly occupied Oberlander's and other landscape architects' thinking in the 1960s and 1970s. While the use of the term "environ" in the English language dates back to the seventeenth century, it proved to be a particularly fertile concept for the design professions starting in the 1960s, when it conjoined ideas of experience with the physical world and the human condition it espoused. As a consequence, the interest in experience, environments, and psychology changed the way landscape architecture history was conceived. Instead of a strictly formalist interpretation of gardens and landscapes from the past, historians' experiences with these spaces figured into their descriptions. This development was abetted by the growing conviction that environments spoke to our subconscious and could therefore unleash creative powers and instincts suppressed by modern society.

Adventure playgrounds and play spaces like Oberlander's Environment for Creative Play and Learning came to symbolize the ability of the environment to tap the creative will of those with the most uncurbed instincts, children. Oberlander expanded the conception of children's landscapes by incorporating these ideas and knowledge gleaned from the growing field of developmental psychology. Her play environment for Expo 67 used basic landscape elements to foster children's imagination, creativity, and exploration. It also provided ample challenges for the children. The project met with tremendous success and she later played a formative role in shaping policies regarding children's environments in Canada at national and local levels. Despite the radical changes to children's play spaces in the intervening years, Oberlander stayed true to her belief that basic landscape materials, forms, and spaces could provide creative opportunities for play, as witnessed in her design for Jim Everett Memorial Park.

Play Spaces as Environments

During the 1960s Oberlander's conception of space as an area shaped by mass, form, and line was expanded to include the idea of environment, a multi-dimensional setting for experience. While the term "environment" in landscape architecture would eventually be associated with the nonhuman, biophysical elements, early conceptions of environment also focused on shaping human experience. Interest in environment followed trends in modern art, as formal-ist concerns with lines, form, and color gradually gave way to concerns with bodily experience. The art historian Juliet Koss has observed that empathy and form were increasingly "embedded within an idea of embodied perception . . . while vision was crucial initially, perception ultimately proved to be a bodily phenomenon."[1]

As emphasis shifted from the way the eye follows a line of movement ex-pressed by a swimming pool's edge to the movement of the body through space, landscape architects looked again to architectural texts as sources for under-standing space and experience in design. In 1969 Eckbo appropriated the archi-tect Erno Goldfinger's diagram of pictorial and volumetric space, and their dif-ferent influences on people's experience. Flat pictorial space was apprehended consciously, while three-dimensional space was apprehended subconsciously. For Eckbo, such a diagram could be connected with the "landscape which exits around us by a kind of psychological topology. That is where design begins."[2]

Expanding Goldfinger's approach, John Ormsbee Simonds, in his influential book *Landscape Architecture: A Manual of Site Planning and Design*, produced an elaborate set of sketches explaining how certain environments might afford different experiences to different people. For Simonds the base plane, overhead plane, and vertical plane acted together to support and express function, but they also influenced people's psychological states: "On an open plain? A timid person feels overwhelmed, lonesome, unprotected; left to their own devices they soon take off in the direction of shelter or kindered spirits. Yet, on the same plain bolder people feel challenged and compelled to action; with freedom and room for movement they are prone to dashing, leaping, and Yahooing."[3]

Equating landscape architectural design with the design of human experience, Simonds advised the reader to design for experience that spanned the gamut of human feelings.

Oberlander developed a deeper knowledge concerning human experience through the design of numerous children's landscapes, where volumetric space and materials became the conduit for play and exploration. For these environments she devised her own spreadsheet-like diagrams for understanding the relationship of human actions as they related to design features. These diagrams enriched the work of Goldfinger, Eckbo, and Simonds by including a regard for child development. Since children's play changes dramatically with age, these diagrams were particularly complex. They not only addressed different types of play activities but also how the actions of a developing child evolved from infanthood to the end of adolescence in relation to design and program features.

Experience itself — its duration, quality, and dimensions — was a rich subject of exploration in the design fields, as well as in history and philosophy. The phenomenology of Edmund Husserl, Martin Heidegger, Jean-Paul Sartre, Gaston Bachelard, and Maurice Merleau-Ponty included bodily engagement with the world as a salient method of philosophical inquiry. While phenomenology had established itself in North American philosophical discourse during the 1940s, it made its impact in landscape architecture in the 1970s.

Environment and experience found surprising allies with architectural historians as well. The architectural historian Sigfried Giedion's *Space, Time and Architecture* (1941) laid the groundwork for understanding history through human experience, furthered by the architectural historian Bruno Zevi's *Architecture as Space: How to Look at Architecture* (first published in Italian in 1948, translated in 1957, and revised in 1974). As an alternative to memorizing historic facts and styles, architectural historians could access history through experience.[4] Not surprisingly, their approach to history proved extremely appealing to students.

This dynamic was not lost on Norman T. Newton. In 1971 he published his classic landscape architecture history text, *Design on the Land,* which brought the experiential attributes of space to the study of historical landscapes. Stressing in his foreword that historical landscapes are not simply neutral spaces but are in fact experiential, he asserts, "Space must be appreciated as a material with which to work — as a vibrant, pliable fullness, not emptiness. To speak of space as a void is to dismiss one of its chief potentials."[5] Fittingly *Design on the*

Land chronicled historical landscapes from ancient Egypt onward, which have spatial qualities that still impacted Newton's own contemporary experiences. Four years after Newton's publication, the landscape architects Geoffrey and Susan Jellicoe produced *The Landscape of Man,* a global survey of landscapes from Genesis to the twentieth century. Here the Jellicoes present historical landscapes as "expressions of man's alternating psyche in relationship to his environment,"[6] illustrating the designed landscape as an elaboration of the internal desires of a collective psyche. This was a particularly relevant thesis given the growing uneasiness with modern social systems, which were perceived as limiting individuality.

Indeed, postwar optimism regarding the advantages of modern life in capitalist society had given way to deeper suspicions regarding how modernism — its institutions, economic systems, and conventions — operated to suppress human instincts and desires. Foreshadowed in *Eros and Civilization: A Philosophical Inquiry into Freud* (1955, 1966), by the German philosopher and social critic Herbert Marcuse, "the very forces which rendered society capable of pacifying the struggle for existence served to repress in the individuals the need for such a liberation. . . . The people, efficiently manipulated and organized, are free; ignorance and impotence, introjected heteronomy is the price of their freedom."[7] For Marcuse, Freud mistakenly limited his understanding of the psyche to its biological factors, ignoring culture and the environment as social determinants. Marcuse proposed to expand this limited understanding of the psyche, and to counter repression with a return to instinctual behavior reacting to the environment.

Certainly if people's desires had been banished from consciousness in order to conform to modern life, it had become common practice among landscape architects to move beyond the simple moods and emotions of their clients to their subconscious through design. From the domestic sphere to the public realm, it was suggested that landscapes might satisfy sublimated needs and desires. These ideas were foregrounded by the landscape architect Sylvia Crowe in 1958, but were most notably championed by Sir Geoffrey Jellicoe.[8] Jellicoe thought if artists could draw upon the subconscious in their work, why could not landscape architects? Between 1957 and 1963, Jellicoe sought to "sublimate" his design work by "inserting within it an invisible idea that only the subconscious could comprehend."[9] In 1965 he turned to the work of Carl Jung and Taoism to access the subconscious. In his University of Guelph lectures, widely read by landscape architects in Canada, he encouraged other landscape architects to sublimate their designs. He later cautioned, "Tell no one, if you can, for this is a message from one subconscious to another."[10]

Garrett Eckbo also encouraged landscape architects to get in touch with their own repressed feelings — through creativity. In *The Landscape We See* he surmises, "Most people do not know how they feel because they are too busy feeling as they are supposed to. Unexpected feelings are suppressed by unhealthy people. Creative emotional health knows how it feels."[11] Accordingly, this knowledge not only helped in the art of the design process but it also enabled the designer to channel the untapped desires of the client. Eckbo even suggested that in connecting to the subconscious, landscape could actually unleash their repressed wishes and inborn patterns of behaviors, noting, "The artist-designer must know when to follow his client's desires and when to lead him to experiences he could not have imagined were available."[12]

For Oberlander if there was one image that most vividly captured the idea of the physical environment unleashing human desires and creativity it was the child creating her own environments through play. To be sure, a child engaged in spontaneous exploration emerged as a symbol of unrepressed human origins and of free will yet to be tethered by societal norms. Likewise, by the 1960s children's natural need to play was viewed as increasingly limited — particularly in the city, where opportunities for children to freely manipulate their surroundings were largely eclipsed. In 1967, Oberlander argued, "Playgrounds should encourage absorption in activity and unselfconscious concentration. They ought to provide seclusion from disturbing or diverting influences, afford a release from everyday pressures and give the child at play the possibility of a make-believe world."[13] Oberlander's belief that play environments afforded opportunities for children to use their instincts to guide play and exploration would fit perfectly with the development of adventure playgrounds in a North American context.

CREATIVE ENVIRONMENTS FOR PLAY

Many North American landscape architects looked to Scandinavian and European adventure playgrounds for inspiration. In 1943 the Danish landscape architect Carl Theodor Sørensen designed Emdrup, the first "junk playground" in a cooperative housing area on the outskirts of Copenhagen. As the landscape historian Jan Woudstra notes, "Sørensen had designed standard playgrounds for children" and he was "taken aback by the fact that they remained unused, whilst the adjoining building sites were used for play."[14] Unlike traditional playgrounds with static fixed equipment, Sørensen's play environment contained recycled junk that was used as building material by the children themselves. Wielding hammers, nails, and saws children created their own places. Adults did not direct the children. John Bertelsen, who worked at Emdrup during the first four years of its inception, described the adult role as "that of an instructor trying to foster a child's ability to use the creative elements in play, so that they aid development whilst acting as the psychical safety valve so sorely needed by every child in our preset repressive society."[15] In fact, earthen mounds and extensive planting surrounded Emdrup for not only microclimatic reasons but also for keeping adults at bay.[16]

The English landscape architect Marjory Allen, Lady Allen of Hurtwood, visited Sørensen's playground in 1945. Changing its name from Junk Playground to Adventure Playground, she was responsible for creating play spaces similar to Emdrup throughout Britain and other English-speaking countries. While early European adventure playgrounds were thought to help "heal society and purge itself of the wartime manifestation of violence," later versions stressed that by making spaces on their own, children were challenged to rely on their own free wills.[17] In her widely read book *Planning for Play* (1968), Allen demonstrates that she was quick to adapt the adventure playground to the changing conception of the child as a creative being with inner urges, chastising that "modern civilization interferes with a hard and heavy hand in the spontaneous play of children. Most vast building schemes in many countries are horrid places, planned without love or understanding, creating a kind of psychological pollution . . . most young people, at one time or another, have a deep urge to experiment with earth, fire, water and timber, to work with real tools without fear of undue criticism or censure."[18]

The first adventure playground in North America was a temporary play space in Minneapolis funded by *McCall's* magazine in 1951.[19] Transferred to North America, adventure playgrounds were thought to reduce vandalism.[20] Yet an overwhelming rationale for adventure playgrounds was their ability to tap the child's instinctive drive to create freely. Moreover, as children's biological needs to play became more evident, North American landscape architects began to design local versions of the adventure playground.

Oberlander was part of the first wave of North American landscape architects, including M. Paul Friedberg and Richard Dattner, to design environments of this type. Each designer modified the European model to some degree. For example, Oberlander created what she called an Environment for Creative Play and Learning that contained "loose parts" for use by children.[21] Unlike the adventure playground, however, these loose parts could be handled in a nonsupervised context. Oberlander had first designed adventure playgrounds on Granville Island in Vancouver using the European model. While they were initially very popular, she found that parents were wary of toddlers brandishing hammers and saws; she realized it was impractical to assume that playgrounds would be continually staffed with play leaders knowledgeable in construction. Expo 67 provided an international venue for her to test a new type of play environment.

Expo 67

In November 1962 Montreal was selected to host the 1967 World's Fair, later referred to as the Universal and International Exposition of 1967 or Expo 67. The Expo site appropriated the greatly expanded Saint Helen's Island and the new Notre-Dame Island, formerly a series of mudflats in the St. Lawrence River. Thirty years earlier one of Canada's first landscape architects, Frederick Todd, had identified this site as a potential exhibition grounds. Made from more than six million tons of earth and rock dredged from the river and excavated from Montreal's new subway construction, the islands provided a dramatic setting for ninety national and themed pavilions.[22] The guiding concept for Expo 67 was "Man and His World" and designers aimed to give visitors an ambitious glimpse of the future. The exposition was marked by an unchecked optimism regarding future uses of technology, science, and resources. Indeed the architects in particular were given free rein to reconsider how we might inhabit the future. Ranging from the stacked cubes of Moshe Safdie's Habitat 67 — which sought to provide modular housing for the masses — to the tectonic achievement of Buckminster Fuller's two-hundred-foot-high geodesic dome for the United States Pavilion, Expo 67 provided a unique venue for visionary ideas.

Amid these futurist ambitions for Expo, Oberlander designed an outdoor play environment situated outside the Children's Creative Centre at the south end of Notre-Dame Island. The center was tucked in among the vast network of phantasmagorical structures in the Canadian section that included a monorail system, flowing canals, assorted exhibit spaces, and the towering inverted pyramid Katimavik. The year 1967 marked the one hundredth anniversary of the Canadian Confederation and the host country was determined not only to dazzle but also to educate the world on Canadian values. According to the official description of the Pavilion of Canada section, "an important aspect of Canadian life was the education of tomorrow's citizens."[23] Oberlander's play environment, paired with the Children's Creative Centre, was designated as a prime site to demonstrate these ideals to the visiting public.

The Children's Creative Centre featured "advanced teaching methods which do most to develop the child's creativity."[24] The center contained a model nursery school for children three to five years old, as well as art, music, and drama studios for children six to eleven years old. Polly Hill, director of the Children's Creative Centre, was well versed in the emerging trends regarding self-awareness in children's emotional development and its relationship to creativity. She notes, "The emotional self develops through discovery of who you are, what you feel in a particular moment. What is courage, fear, love, hate? Experiencing these emotions in an environment that encourages personal freedom and choice leads to deeper awareness of one's own emotions and emerging values. The intellectual self grows by stressing intuition and spontaneity."[25]

DESIGN PROCESS More than seventy advisors from all over Canada were selected to develop the Children's Creative Centre. For Hill, they staked "their reputations on the philosophy that through play and total involvement, children are released to create and therefore enjoy themselves, and hopefully grow a bit inside."[26] Oberlander was commissioned to design the outdoor play space for the center in 1964. Her 18th and Bigler Street Playground in Philadelphia had gained international recognition and in Vancouver she had designed play spaces for Skeena Terrace and McLean Park Housing.

Oberlander also combined her participatory methods developed in Philadelphia with her lifelong interest in children's gardening in Vancouver. In 1957 she began working on ways to include children's ideas into the design of school gardens that would serve as extensions to classroom learning. In planning for the University Hill Elementary School's playground she had children draw the plants they would like to see in the garden. The children depicted not just a carrot or a flower but also showed the plants' root systems extending below the ground surface in the soil. Some children even provided conceptual sketches for the play space.

Oberlander's interest in children's environments also reflected changes in her personal life. When she received the Expo commission in 1964, Oberlander was mother to eight-year-old Judy, six-year-old Tim, and three-year-old Wendy, and she gained great insight from observing them play. She recalled to one journalist, "Sitting on the rim of that sandbox, [I] discovered what children really like to do: run, climb, crawl, build, dig, get wet, use their hands and eyes."[27] Oberlander also experimented at home with new equipment forms such as the combination merry-go-round and seesaw.

All three of the Oberlander children participated in the new Child Study Centre at the University of British Columbia.[28] Opening in 1962, the center was progressive for the times, involving interdisciplinary research in child development and early childhood education.[29] Its first director, Alice Borden, believed, like Oberlander, that play and learning were intertwined and that the outdoor environment offered a valuable experience for children. Throughout the 1960s Oberlander worked with Borden and the center's staff to incorporate outdoor play and learning into the curriculum. For example, in 1962 Oberlander directed a Children's Garden Project, which examined food from its agricultural to its industrial life span. It attracted the interest of not only children but also parents and the press. One article noted, "Children are taught about the food they eat by watching plants grow in a garden and by touring whole-sale food distributors and bakeries."[30]

The Expo 67 play space provided a unique situation where Oberlander could align her emerging ideas regarding children's environments with new concepts concerning children's play and creativity. While some advisors initially conceived the outdoor space as a holding area for children waiting to get inside the center, Oberlander quickly convinced them that the outdoor environment itself was a source of creative play. Working with the Children's Creative Centre team and D. W. Graham and Associates of Ottawa, landscape architecture consultants for the Canadian section, Oberlander's plan unfolded.

LANDSCAPE STRATEGY The Children's Creative Centre was located below the grade of the main concourse area in the Canadian section. In comparison to the surrounding architecture it was a modest structure. This approach was intentional—stimulating the children's imagination rather than displaying the architects'. Inside the center, Hill and her team of educators sought to "stimulate and bring out creative potential" in the children by developing programming for ninety-minute classes in music, drama, and visual art.[31] These interior programs were timed, so children were directed to stop and start specific activities.

In contrast Oberlander conceived a much looser experience for the outside play environment, one that was based on children's spontaneous exploration, rather than on the timing that suited adults. Since the Children's Creative Centre sought to encourage self-motivation and creative play, Oberlander's environment did not contain standard equipment, signaling to children specific forms of play. Instead Oberlander utilized the basic elements of landscape — terrain, water, plants, and structures — that were open to use and interpretation. She also knew that when children transform their environment they use their imagination, so the inclusion of loose parts and manipulative materials was also key.

The outdoor play environment was directly adjacent to the center's art, music, drama, and nursery rooms and was also bordered by the canal that meandered across the island. Like the 18th and Bigler Street Playground, the Expo play space served as a model for other communities. Its 125-feet by 60-feet dimension was to approximate the size of a typical urban park lot so that adults could visualize how their own urban sites might be transformed. Oberlander's environment built play features into the land.[32] As in Philadelphia, Oberlander segregated the site according to age group with a small area adjacent to the building for younger children, and the larger remaining areas for older children. However, in contrast to her Philadelphia playground, the flat ground plane was replaced by rolling terrain, looping paths, a wobble walk, and a canal; and giant wooden building pieces and a rocking boat in water replaced static sculptures. A beach-like expanse of sand and driftwood afforded opportunities to balance, and dozens of plants provided play props. Importantly, children were not directed what to do; rather, using their own desires and instincts they responded to the landscape design itself.

Occupying the geographical center of the play environment was a grass play mound with an interior cave, wood slides, and a high platform that could only be reached by an unanchored rope. To the east was a looping water channel that created two islands that could be accessed by bridges — or jumping. To the south Oberlander designed a wobble walk made of short logs embedded in the ground on end for balancing. Large open areas were allocated for building with giant loose parts, lightweight Pan-a-bode interlocking logs. These notched logs were three to four feet long, so children could build their own spaces, and since

Pan-a-bode loose parts at the Environment for Creative Play and Learning at Expo 67 Children's Creative Centre, Montreal, 1967. Landscape Architect: Cornelia Hahn Oberlander.

they were notched they could construct them without hammers and nails. A separate place for the nursery provided ample sand and water play. Underneath the entrance bridge to the north was the interactive music area with four scrims and a thirty-foot-long op-art wall designed in collaboration with the sculptor Gordon Smith.

RECEPTION Between 27 April and 29 October more than 50 million visitors experienced Expo 67's utopian feats of technology, art, and design. The popularity of the playground at the Children's Creative Centre shared this success. A 1968 analysis of children's attendance numbers and accident rates at the Children's Creative Centre found the outdoor play environment "most popular with 30,000 children visiting in six months (150 at one time), ... many came back regularly and there were only four accidents" reported in total.[33] The most frequently used play material was "wood, especially logs, boards and 2 × 4 blocks that made houses big enough to get into, often several stories high.... The single purpose wooden tunnel had the least appeal."[34] Her creative play space was also covered in numerous newspaper articles about the Canadian section, with the *Toronto Daily Star* declaring that "the prized exhibit is the children's playground designed by Cornelia Hahn Oberlander from Vancouver."[35] In fact, it so poignantly expressed the importance of creativity to the future that Marc Beaudet included footage of children creating and building in Oberlander's outdoor play environment for the Canadian Film Board's *The Canadian Pavilion* (1967).

In retrospect Oberlander has speculated that one reason why the outdoor environment was more successful than the indoor component of the center was that the outdoors was free for spontaneous play, while the interior provided specific classes and activities. She recalls, "When it was built I watched a small girl play at the water's edge for an hour, even though it was a bitter cold day."[36] The outdoor play environment also received attention from visitors without children. Its sunken position and the fact that a main entrance bridge to the Canadian section passed over it enabled the play space to be seen by numerous passersby who stopped to look down at the children playing.

Oberlander's play environment at Expo 67 underscored three major ideas critical to children's development: imagination, challenge, and spontaneous exploration. Several features were planned to stimulate children's imagination. Ample amounts of loose parts (sand, water, and movable agate stones) and building materials provided endless opportunities for imagining new worlds. The giant building logs allowed children to build spaces that they could occupy themselves. At the Op-Art Wall three musical partitions made of bells, xylophones, and drums and the fourth with "found sounds invited children to create a range of aural sensations."[37] According to Oberlander, the wall also encouraged visual exploration. "The children were given colourful strings and other items, which they wrapped around the pegs to create an infinite number of shapes, compositions and colour combinations. There were no prescribed designs — nothing the children were 'supposed to' create. They only designed what they imagined."[38]

The climbing and sliding hill provided sufficient challenge for smaller children while the platform above this mound tested older children's strength and courage. As Hill observes, "It is hard for an 11-year-old to climb an unanchored rope ladder to a tree house 10 feet high and descend by a fireman's pole."[39] Likewise, the rocking Nova Scotia dory was extremely challenging as children found it difficult to balance themselves in the boat. The bridges spanned the water channel, but in the period photographs of the playground, children can be seen attempting to leap over the water. The wobble walk, which Oberlander designed specifically for Expo, challenged both children's agility and balance.

Oberlander's design also encouraged spontaneous exploration, a term borrowed from child development, which refers to movement driven by the curiosity and motivations of the child. Spontaneous exploration affords an opportunity for young children to learn to navigate and adapt to the physical environment, skills that would stay with them the rest of their lives.[40] The looping pathway, the varying heights of terrain, and bridges stimulated the children's desire to know where the path was leading or what lay on the other side of the mound. Likewise the forty-foot-long circulating water channel also triggered anticipation and mystery as children followed floating objects as they sailed upstream.

Fifteen years later, upon giving a Smith College Medal to Oberlander, President Jill Ker Conway noted, "The playground for EXPO '67 'so captivated all who saw it that you have since influenced the design of playgrounds everywhere on this continent'"[41] Shortly after Expo 67 Hill wrote a series of articles on planning children's environments, using Oberlander's built work as examples. Indeed many of Oberlander's design features, such as the boat and wobble walk, were adopted in other playgrounds throughout Canada. Moreover, the tremendous success of the Expo 67 play environment positioned Oberlander to bring local and national attention to the importance of children's play, which she did through both her design and advocacy work.

Vancouver Play Environments

A year after Expo, Oberlander designed a Space for Creative Play at the North Shore Neighborhood House in North Vancouver. This not-for-profit charity served some of the city's most vulnerable residents: toddlers and preschool-age children who did not speak English, and/or were experiencing developmental delays. The charity lacked money to create the play space but, with Oberlander's help, they were able to secure funding from the Junior League of Vancouver, the Vancouver Foundation, and the Chris Spencer Foundation.[42]

The two-lot-wide, urban site was assigned specific zones for gardening, sand play, water play, and rest. The goal was to encourage exploration through challenge, for example with the height of the custom-designed structure, and to increase social play with child-size seating. Oberlander designed a story-high platform only accessible by ladder that provided opportunities for children to test their courage and physical strength. To encourage social interaction, the large sand area was stepped to allow for social spaces at its edges. She also preserved many of the mature trees on the site and designed benches around them to provide additional social spaces.

Two lots were merged to create the North Shore Neighborhood House play environment, North Vancouver, 1969. Landscape Architect: Cornelia Hahn Oberlander.

⍟ Treads of stairs dual as child-size seats for socializing at the North Shore Neighborhood House play environment, North Vancouver, 1969. Landscape Architect: Cornelia Hahn Oberlander.

⍟⍟ A wading pool at the North Shore Neighborhood House play environment, North Vancouver, 1969. Landscape Architect: Cornelia Hahn Oberlander.

A tree trunk provides opportunities to test balance at the North Shore Neighborhood House play environment, North Vancouver, 1969. Landscape Architect: Cornelia Hahn Oberlander.

⚥ Oberlander also custom-designed the child-size wheelbarrows at the North Shore Neighborhood House play environment, North Vancouver, 1969. Landscape Architect: Cornelia Hahn Oberlander.

Oberlander's design encouraged intense sensorial experiences. For example, a winding stone-lined pool enabled children to submerge their entire bodies into the water. She also placed an exquisite tree trunk, which could have passed for an abstract sculpture, in the play environment, enabling children to try out their balancing skills at varying heights. Bikeways for tricycles, carts (custom-designed by Oberlander), and other child-size vehicles also enabled children to move through and around the site. By providing these opportunities, children learned from each other and through the language of play. While there was never a formal study of this play environment, North Shore Neighborhood staff noted that the children were beginning to socialize more, facilitating their language development.[43] Oberlander received an Award of Merit from the Canadian Society of Landscape Architects in 1969 for this project.

Between 1969 and 1974 the Vancouver School Board commissioned Oberlander to design playgrounds for eight schools in Vancouver, where she continued her involvement with children's gardening programs. Oberlander was also hired by UBC to design the play areas for the newly constructed Acadia Married Student Housing complex, which operated a kindergarten for twenty children and a combined nursery and cooperative childcare program for thirty four-year-olds.[44] Located on the sparsely developed edge of the UBC campus, the site contained many mature trees. Oberlander paid homage to the trees by retaining the extensive forest edge and making it part of the play area with rope swings suspended between their trunks. Her design also stressed the numerous play opportunities afforded by trees in their many forms — live, gnarly and fallen, or stripped and cut into stumps. She repositioned the trunks of ancient trees as climbing structures and in the largest open area she designed an extreme variation of the wobble walk, with log ends reaching four and five feet high.

In 1970 Peter Oberlander was made the inaugural Secretary to the Ministry of State for Urban Affairs, requiring the Oberlanders to relocate to Ottawa for three years. While she planned to continue her career there, Oberlander quickly learned that as a wife of a public official in Ottawa "one was not expected to work."[45] However, she continued to oversee her projects in Vancouver and "unofficially" traveled to Toronto several times a week to design and realize six play areas at schools and childcare centers throughout Ontario. During this time she expanded the participatory dimensions of her work by including both children and parents in the site analysis and building of play spaces as well as the design process.

At the Rockcliffe Park Elementary School Playground (1972) in Ottawa, for example, Oberlander took test borings of the soil with the parents and children, and described the importance of soil composition to the design solution.[46] Children and parents also implemented the playground at Rockcliffe. The design featured similar elements to those used in the play environment for Expo 67, including a giant sand area, play mound, water faucet, boat, and balancing logs.[47] Later, when advising other landscape architects on the design of creative play environments, she stressed the importance of an enlightened client. In describing her design for the playground at the Almonte Day Care Centre Ontario in 1972, she noted that all the mothers had taken classes in child development at a local college. Thus implementing the creative play environment became an "easy task."[48]

⌃ Children playing on reclaimed tree stumps for the children's play space at Acadia Married Student Housing, University of British Columbia Endowment Lands, circa 1970. Landscape Architect: Cornelia Hahn Oberlander.

« Children climbing on an extreme variation of the wobble walk at Acadia Married Student Housing, University of British Columbia Endowment Lands, circa 1970. Landscape Architect: Cornelia Hahn Oberlander.

In the early 1970s, Oberlander began to take a leading role at both local and national levels in developing policy regarding children's play environments. She also authored *Playgrounds . . . a Plea for Utopia or the Recycled Empty Lot,* which was published in 1972 by the Department of the Secretary of State and a second edition in 1974, by the Department of National Health and Welfare, Canada. Here Oberlander made the case that stationary play equipment was not sufficient. Children must be able to manipulate their play environment.

"Physical activity such as derived from climbing on a jungle gym is not enough if the child is to find self-fulfillment in play; psychological as well as kinetic stimulation are needed for self-development."[49] She also described the materials, which were available to most communities, necessary for realizing an Environment for Creative Play and Learning. Using images, many of her own design, she demonstrated the numerous ways children could manipulate these materials.

From 1973 to 1977 Oberlander served as founding member of the National Task Force on Children's Play, under the jurisdiction of the Canadian Council of Children and Youth. The task force was charged with defining ways that children's play could be supported in communities throughout Canada. Oberlander was instrumental in identifying outdoor play environments as a key area where communities could support children's play and development. The task force's efforts led to the establishment of numerous Children's Play Resource Centres throughout the country. British Columbia led the way, with Oberlander cofounding the Children's Play Resource Centre in 1977. The center, housed at the Action Society for Children in Vancouver (now the Society for Children and Youth), eventually established local guidelines for outdoor play spaces. These guidelines linked children's development with the design of their environment, stressing how simple found materials and natural elements could provide for children's play, manipulation, and exploration.

Since Expo 67 Oberlander has designed more than seventy playgrounds.[50] Her work marks a time when North Americans perceived children as creative beings whose innate desires to play and develop could be supported and heightened by an environment. Unfortunately, by the 1980s the emphasis on children's creativity and free will was eclipsed by concerns with safety, and its corollary — litigation. By the turn of the twenty-first century, most landscape architects felt comfortable ordering only safety-approved equipment that seemingly grew less challenging by the year. Throughout North America, the creative environments designed by landscape architects and community members were replaced by standardized play structures typically anchored on a rubber surface and surrounded by a chain-link fence. Yet, despite these changes, Oberlander continued to use all the materials available to the landscape architect to stimulate play and creativity. This was beautifully evident in her design for the play space at Jim Everett Memorial Park in Vancouver in 2000.

Jim Everett Memorial Park

For years Jim Everett had mentored youth living in UBC's University Endowment Lands (UEL) with a range of sporting activities. He also advocated for a youth recreation program. A year after his death in 1985 the university designated an unassuming triangular site, bordered by University Boulevard, Allison Road, and Dalhousie Road, as Jim Everett Memorial Park. In the intervening years this veritable traffic island supported soccer games and other events, but the flat expanse of grass was often too soggy for use.

In 2000, the university began to increase the density of housing and commercial space in the area surrounding the park. As part of this densification University Village, a six-story mixed-use complex with retail and medical services, and 108 residential units, was constructed across the street. Consequent to this development, university planners identified Jim Everett Memorial Park as an important component in UEL's open space plan. While the nearby Pacific Spirit Regional Park and University Golf Course provided passive recreation, mainly for adults, it was determined that Jim Everett Memorial Park should provide a play area for the young families and children living in the new village complex. The developer of University Village co-funded the park and Oberlander was commissioned as landscape architect.

DESIGN PROCESS In her research on Jim Everett, whom the children called Jamie, Oberlander discovered that the children loved to play at this site under his guidance. The site contained large sixty-year-old trees, which Oberlander preserved; however, much of the site was so poorly drained that it needed to be completely reconceived.[51] She held numerous community workshops with the families living in both the old and new residences surrounding the site. Oberlander learned that none of the apartments had backyards, nor was there a shared space for outdoor play or gardening in the housing complex itself. She knew that as this area became more populated, children would need even more an open space where they could run, play, and roll down hills. Oberlander stressed to participants that this could be a special place, unlike the site-less, prefabricated playgrounds found in other Vancouver parks.

Like many public meetings addressing the fate of a park, competing needs and conflicting points of view ensued. Not all workshop participants could envision a play space without standardized play equipment. One woman complained that a "playground without a swing-set, slides, and teeter-totters was un-Canadian!"[52] Other participants worried about the views of the park from their apartments and houses. In addition to these issues, parents of children on the junior soccer team, which routinely played on the site, voiced their concerns about future access. Furthermore, a number of festival organizers also wanted to maintain use of the land. Oberlander listened carefully and her design team created three-dimensional clay models of design alternatives thereafter. This proved very effective in communicating major design ideas, and the final scheme was approved later that year.

LANDSCAPE STRATEGY To respond to a number of conflicting demands and to order multiple programming needs, Oberlander employed a simple vocabulary of bold forms. Her tripartite scheme entailed a large sunken oval, two smaller circular areas (one convex, one concave), and small gardens on the site's borders. The large sunken oval tackled both the diverse needs of the users and drainage issues. By excavating the poorly draining clay soil, a well-drained soil level was reached, providing a dry area for the junior-size soccer field. Importantly, no soil was removed from the site. The excavated soil was reused to create berms that not only shielded the park from busy traffic on University Boulevard but also created play mounds. These mounds were planted with low-maintenance sheep fescues, birch trees, and seven thousand daffodil bulbs.

Oberlander circumscribed the sunken oval with a retaining wall at a height for parents to sit and watch the game; and it also helped contain stray soccer balls. Low-voltage lighting in the wall illuminated the field without connecting to the grid. Likewise, a proper grass field drained into the wetland, which was circular in form, making it possible to disconnect the park from UEL's storm sewer system. The concave wetland's corresponding convex mound provided a place to climb and roll, and sled during Vancouver's occasional snowfall. In addition to these spaces, Oberlander also created smaller circular gardens at the paved plaza facing the University Village complex. Unusual for a public space, they were planted with vegetation reminiscent of older, domestic gardens. Oberlander refers to these gardens as an "homage to the apartment dweller." The beds were edged with arctic willow and a series of heirloom roses, creating a space where people could sit and relax, and enjoy the changes expressed in plants commonly associated with private gardens. At the east entrance to the

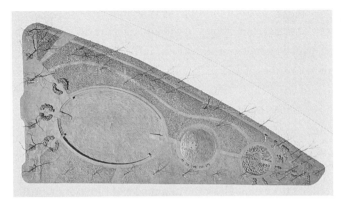

Jim Everett Memorial Park model, Vancouver, 2000. Landscape Architect: Cornelia Hahn Oberlander.

⌄ Although situated on a busy thoroughfare, Jim Everett Memorial Park's mounds and seat walls provide quiet spaces for socializing, Vancouver, 2011. Landscape Architect: Cornelia Hahn Oberlander.

park, Oberlander created another place to pause, a small garden with pines and native plants. The third subspace was a butterfly garden containing coneflowers, rudbeckia, black-eyed Susans, and salvia. Building upon more than thirty years of expertise in creating play environments where the landscape itself provides play opportunities, Oberlander's scheme did not include equipment.

RECEPTION Then-premier Gordon Campbell and members of the Everett family dedicated the park on 16 July 2002. Since then it has become a hub for a range of activities. During the winter, toddlers can be seen climbing the snow-covered mounds and sliding down them on makeshift cardboard sleds. In the summer some children bring their pet hamsters and rabbits for a visit to the park. The sunken grass oval accommodates many other uses in addition to soccer, and the large stepping-stones mounting the nine-foot mound allow even small children to see the world from above. In the fall, the park accommodates the Equinox Festival, which includes music, games, and pony rides. Oberlander later met the parent who thought the park was un-Canadian. Watching her two children run up and down the berms, she admitted to Oberlander that this landscape was, perhaps, not so much a Canadian playground as a human one.[53]

Through her design of play environments Oberlander developed a facile sense of the way people move through and act upon space, and how the landscape itself could serve as a catalyst for creativity. Her designs for children's environments also led her to consider how she might provide environments for adults as well. This is evident in her 1974 article "A Need for Green Streets" in *Canadian Architect.* Here, Oberlander suggested that just as play environments provide refuges for children, landscapes might serve as havens for people living and working in urban environments. She argued that people of all ages lack opportunities to interact with natural elements in the city, and she proposed a network of tree-lined streets and green spaces. Published the same year she joined the Robson Square design team led by Arthur Erickson, her thinking anticipated ideas particularly germane to this major urban landscape.

By the late 1960s and early 1970s, when urban renewal had reached its nadir, the term "environment" provided a common currency among design professionals. In fact, the idea that environment could offer a range of experiences with natural elements and other animate systems guided the design of many urban plazas and other public open spaces. For their execution, these projects required multidisciplinary teams, and by joining the design team for Robson Square in 1974 Oberlander embarked on a significant turning point in her career. Her work on Robson Square with the architect Arthur Erickson expanded her conception of how people moved through space and how landscape features and building systems could be physically and perceptually linked. Interestingly, she did not abandon the idea that composition affects the moving eye; in fact, in many of her descriptions of plantings at Robson Square she discussed both their visual impact and their spatial qualities. This project would lead to numerous other urban projects such as the Evergreen Building and the Canadian Chancery with Arthur Erickson, and the New York Times Building with HM White Site Architects and Renzo Piano Building Workshop.

Cities as Environments

The environment's ability to shape the wordless movement of the body found another application in Oberlander's work—the design of spatially complex urban plazas. The creation of urban plazas during the 1960s and 1970s was largely a reaction to the grim aftermath of urban renewal schemes, which had often left a patchwork of isolated towers set in by large expanses of parking, industrial structures marred by disuse, and fractured neighborhoods. The realities of life in a renewed urban environment were best described by Jane Jacobs in her widely read book *The Death and Life of Great American Cities* (1961). Jacobs revealed how the once noble social goals of organizing a chaotic world were now suspected of only pandering to the very structures that limited human freedom and natural wonder. She warned that modern cities modified our impulses to ones more socially acceptable, noting, "It follows that the exuberant variety inherent in great numbers of people tightly concentrated should be played down, hidden, hammered into semblance."[54] Her insights inspired a generation of landscape architects to reclaim the city for those who lived there.

Catherine Bauer, Lewis Mumford, and William H. Whyte had assumed this critical stance before her. Whyte was initially fascinated by the seemingly duty-bound pressures of the managerial class to conform in the very private world of the suburbs.[55] In time he turned his attention to the city, studying how people actually used outdoor public spaces. In 1970 Whyte led The Street Life Project. Using direct observation and film documentation his team conducted an exhaustive study of human behaviors in the streets and plazas of New York City. His companion film, *The Social Life of Small Urban Spaces* (1980), was shown to generations of landscape architecture students throughout North America. Like an anthropologist studying a strange and unfamiliar society, Whyte's primarily aerial footage of "swingers," "orbiting executives," and others using the urban environment revealed that not unlike other species, humans displayed natural needs and desires. These emerged in conventional habits that the built environment could accommodate, if we only knew they existed.

Jane Jacobs's observations went beyond issues of subjugated human nature, addressing nonhuman nature as well. She thought the urban dweller was given sentimental versions of nature instead of wild patches where nature had not been "improved upon."[56] That connections to nonhuman nature had been repressed appeared in the early writings on modern landscape architecture. In 1940 James Rose, Eckbo, and Kiley claimed that camping and picnicking, summer and winter sports, recreational drama, and arts and crafts fulfilled a "subjective and objective need for contact with nature."[57] They also argued that the exploration and study of vegetation and fauna satisfied emotional needs for the primitive landscape. Likewise, Church echoed this idea by suggesting, "Plants are a link with our primeval past. They offer us shade and shadow, shelter and sustenance and give us color, texture, form, and mass to work with in man-made compositions."[58]

Twenty years later this sentiment provided a basis for environmental theories regarding human instincts and nonhuman nature that combined fields as diverse as landscape architecture, anthropology, and zoology. Certainly, the "urban environment" attracted individuals from a range of disciplines for collaborative practice and research. In the 1960s academic programs based on the notion of "environmental design" developed throughout North America, expanding new areas of interdisciplinary landscape research. Likewise, large multidisciplinary firms began to form throughout North America with the idea that an integrated team of professionals could give them a competitive edge in meeting the demands posed by complex environments.

RECLAIMING THE CITY

Design professionals interested in the urban environment sought to claim playgrounds, vest pocket parks, and urban plazas as places for people in the city to experience natural elements, plants, water, and sculpted terrain. Given their ability to work with living materials, such as plants, landscape architects made a unique contribution to this endeavor. Both Oberlander and Lawrence Halprin developed an expertise in weaving natural systems into the inert surroundings of the city. Halprin claimed that bringing water and plants into an urban environment touched upon our basic natures, for "even in the city, the sound and sight of water stirs the most elemental and basic roots of our human nature."[59] He went on to design major urban plazas and streetscapes in San Francisco, Portland, Minneapolis, Seattle, and Washington D.C. Likewise, in their book *Trees in the Cities* (1977), Oberlander, Ira Bruce Nadel, and Lesley R. Bohm identify the visual and spatial advantages trees offered to the city. "When confronted by hard surfaces, the eye is restless and the body uncomfortable. Trees break up these lines and planes and relate people to their environment; they feel a part of it."[60]

Rehearsed in her designs for children's creative environments, Oberlander developed a great dexterity for understanding people's spatial experiences in the landscape. She transferred this knowledge to the design of Robson Square in Vancouver. Writing about the project in 1981, she notes that "the landscape design integrates the circulation pattern and thereby allows the public to walk down and through the building complex . . . under normal circumstances, in our gridiron cities sidewalks parallel roads and along building complexes; here on Robson Square for the first time pedestrians are encouraged to walk through three downtown city blocks thereby these new buildings were instantly integrated into the fabric of Vancouver's core."[61]

Indeed the concept of environment provided a rationale for integrating animate elements and inanimate features of the city. The idea also furthered the inclusion of nondesigners into the design process. Many landscape architects sought to challenge the autocratic nature of design itself. Since the 1950s Oberlander had developed participatory methods with the CCCP in Philadelphia, and from that time onward she involved children and parents in the design process. She also presented her methods to other professionals and educators, orchestrating workshops such as "Working with Children and Communities in the Planning Process" at the 1976 conference of the Environmental Design Research Association.

A rapidly expanding generation of landscape architects and architects built upon this type of approach, envisioning participatory methods as a more democratic design process — particularly for those who could not afford design fees charged by professionals. Mark Francis, for example, combined the practice of site analysis and mapmaking — once the purview of the landscape architect — with exercises conducted with nonprofessionals.[62] The University of California, Berkeley became a nexus of community design activity with Donald Appleyard and other professionals criticizing environmental injustices, which were often identified as inaccessibility, exclusion, or the unequal distribution of resources or amenities.[63] This movement influenced landscape architectural education in Canada, as Berkeley graduates began teaching in professional programs there — with Ron Williams at the University of Montreal and Moira Quayle at the University of British Columbia.

Much of this activism in the 1960s and 1970s reacted against the uneven socioeconomic geography of metropolitan areas. This geography was characterized by poor and disadvantaged people in the "inner city" and an indifferent middle class in the outer suburbs. As Marcusian suspicions gave way to full-blown attacks on the legitimacy of institutionalized practices of power, many North American cities became sites for antiwar demonstrations, race riots, and other struggles over human rights. In general Canadian cities did not witness the extreme racial and antiwar conflicts observed in the United States. Canada did not participate in the Vietnam War. In fact during the war Canada became home to American war objectors — like Jane Jacobs, who moved to Toronto in 1968 — and a refuge for those avoiding conscription. Even today there are towns in British Columbia that are heavily populated by Americans who relocated there during the Vietnam era.

There was however certainly a political mobilization of Canadian young people in these years. One example was Vancouver's Gastown Riots of 1971, where young hippies were beaten and detained by police for protesting against undercover activity that sought to dismantle their attempts to legalize mari-juana. Vancouver also shared with American cities a major economic trans-formation during the 1960s. Businesses that had been built around the railway stations and ship passenger terminals had all but evaporated; steel, lumber, and other wood product industries had relocated, leaving swaths of abandoned industrial lands in the urban fabric, particularly in the Southeast False Creek area.[64] It was in this context that Robson Square was conceived.

Robson Square

Canada's 1967 centennial had spurred heated debates on the need for a civic complex in Vancouver's downtown core, a complex that tapped the cultural energy generated by Expo 67. Like many cities in North America, Vancouver's urban center hosted few cultural events in the evenings and on weekends. At the same time, the province had outgrown its 1911 courthouse and needed more judicial spaces. Certainly the classically inspired courthouse with its grand ro-tunda, entrance portico supported by ionic columns, and flanking lion sculp-tures did not capture the verve of a city on the threshold of a modern trans-formation. Moreover, the province's recent gift, the courthouse's Centennial Fountain — featuring marble sculptures and a propulsion of water set within a polychromatic basin of broken marble, ceramic, and glass tile — hardly met these expectations either.

With its mission to support the arts and "to act as an advocate for better civic development," the Community Arts Council (CAC) spearheaded discussions regarding a new cultural complex as a means of revitalizing the downtown.[65] Oberlander had joined the council in 1953, and in 1964 she attended the first meeting concerning a pilot project for civic improvement on Robson Street.[66] In 1966 the CAC commissioned Erickson Massey Architects to study the impact of a civic and governmental complex in the downtown core. Erickson presented this study to the council at the Georgian Club on 22 September 1968 and identified three adjoining blocks — 51, 61, and 71 — as a site for the complex.[67] Block 51 was the site of the courthouse (the future Vancouver Art Gallery), while the adjacent blocks, 61 and 71, contained a few isolated structures surrounded by surface parking.

While Erickson Massey was conducting their study for the CAC, the provincial government was planning the creation of a large-scale government office complex of their own making, identifying the same blocks, 61 and 71, of downtown Vancouver as the best location. In 1972 the architect Clair MacDonald designed a fifty-five-story black-glass skyscraper, the Bennett Building (named after Premier W. A. C. Bennett), to house private and government offices. The Bennett Building would have been one of the tallest buildings in Canada at the time. However, a solar study revealed that the shadow cast by the tower rendered unusable the token courtyard spaces planned at its base.[68] Likewise, there were concerns about the gloomy effect black towers would have on the perennially grey Vancouver skyline. The public was also increasingly skeptical of the public-private partnership that was required to construct a skyscraper of that magnitude.

The Bennett tower was dropped in late 1972 after the New Democratic Party (NDP) won the provincial election. The NDP "wanted a clear unequivocal architectural contrast to the free enterprise tower, one that would convince the public that people came first, not economic growth."[69] Erickson, who had established his own architectural practice that year, was hired to develop design alternatives for buildings and a large public open space on the three-block-long site. In the summer of 1973 Erickson presented a master plan that featured a governmental monument "lying on its side."[70] He revealed a comprehensive plan for Blocks 51, 61, and 71 that included a three-block pedestrian and open space spine with 100 percent usable open space on Block 61.[71] This center block also included new provincial offices, public meeting spaces, exhibition galleries, and information facilities. The design of Block 61 encouraged pedestrians to cut across the urban grid using a "series of public roof gardens and terraces which rise gradually from the Robson Street level to about two or three stories at the far end of the site."[72] A new Provincial Law Courts building was planned for Block 71. The old courthouse on Block 51 was to be renovated for cultural activities. For Erickson, the overarching goal of the three-block project was to "intertwine matters of justice and governance within the life of the city."[73]

Throughout 1973 Erickson's office presented schemes to Vancouver City Council. The designs sparked a heated debate captured by local journalists. Some reports complained that the project had "gone from 55 stories to a basement."[74] A recurring concern was a perceived lack of green spaces since many people questioned if rooftop gardens could really serve as open space. Alderman Harry Rankin claimed, "I don't consider rooftops and underground dungeons open space."[75] Later in the year a model of the proposal was displayed in both Vancouver and Victoria. The public was asked to provide its opinions and the city council conveyed requests for revisions to Erickson. Based on this public input, consultation with city planning and traffic engineering officials, and further design studies, a new conceptual plan was prepared during the fall of 1973. Yet by December uncertainties still persisted as to whether Erickson's team could successfully design all the heavily planted areas in the proposal.

It was clear to Erickson that the project required a very competent landscape architect, one with technical skills, a nuanced spatial understanding of structures in relationship to landscape, and a familiarity with modern design. In February 1974, Oberlander received a phone call from Bing Thom, project manager at Erickson's office. Thom solicited Oberlander's opinion about the project, and he recalls, "She was very enthusiastic and honed in on some important technical questions. I asked her to present her approach the following morning. She didn't have a lot of time, but she came to the office and described her ideas. It was clear that she had the passion, the right type of thinking for the project, and as we later learned she was very keen to figure out how to install and maintain plants living on structures. I had only seen one such project, the Oakland Museum, so this was a real issue for us."[76]

Oberlander knew it would require a huge learning curve for her to succeed on this project. The scheme not only posed technical challenges but the design also had to entice people from the street into Robson Square. Experiencing this on-structure landscape, Oberlander believed people would discover "an entirely different atmosphere in the downtown core" and an integrated relationship between built structure and natural elements.[77] She also cautioned that plant material has a scale in the city as well, noting that "buildings once erected tend to be complete and fixed, whereas plant material changes with each season in a predictable cycle and thus a tree devoid of its leaves can be an asset to the winter scene in the proper setting."[78] As for programming, she advised that spaces should range in scale from "the creation of small intimate areas, with indigenous plant material and mounds, to the broad pedestrian mall or wide open space suitable for a noon concert or the viewing of special events."[79] Oberlander's concluding goal was "to achieve an integrated human experience in the pursuit of daily life and leisure activities, giving the user maximum enjoyment of an urban landscape by co-ordinating and integrating the structures with the surroundings."[80]

Erickson was impressed with Oberlander's grasp of the project. Years later he remarked that "most landscape architects I'd use before were too . . . sentimental . . . not tough enough. Not intellectually up to the challenge. But I remember Cornelia felt the potential."[81] And it was this potential that Oberlander conveyed during her presentation-interview to the design team. She was hired that afternoon, commencing a professional relationship with Erickson that would last until his death in 2009. In turn, Oberlander was inspired by Erickson. He had that rare ability to create designs that enabled people to think and live anew. This was a trait she also had found in Stonorov and Kahn — that in conceiving architecture they sought to make a new world. It was this conception of design that she herself pursued in landscape architecture.

DESIGN PROCESS From 1974 to 1983 Oberlander worked primarily in Erickson's office. Much like her experience with Stonorov and Kahn in Philadelphia, the office had a highly integrated atmosphere. The architect Nick Milkovich describes the collaborative nature of Erickson's office: "Erickson was very Socratic. He presented questions to the whole team . . . design work began as a conversation."[82] Jim Wright, another architect working on the Robson Square project, recalls how these discussions were made material. Initial studies often involved "working models made of Styrofoam, cardboard, and dried sponge (for plant material) allowing spatial ideas to be changed or scrapped as the model was pulled apart and reassembled."[83] This method enabled the designers to "rapidly develop an intimate relationship with the building and its site."[84] Although a final schematic design had been agreed upon in 1974, revisions continued to be made. In December 1975 the entire project was put in jeopardy when the Social

Credit Party, led by the former premier W. A. C. Bennett's son Bill Bennett, was voted in. However, the only major change requested was to keep the Centennial Fountain. The original plan called for the fountain to be removed and the area redesigned to blend with the rest of the complex.

OVERALL CONCEPT Intensifying the use of Vancouver's urban core was a chief goal of the Robson Square project. The three-block-long project sat at the confluence of four distinct areas in the city: residential areas to the west, businesses to the north, historic Vancouver to the northeast, and partially abandoned industrial land to the southeast. By locating a project that integrated government, judicial, public, and private uses with entertainment and cultural programming at this crossroads, it was planned that the city's core would be livelier day and night. Erickson voiced this need for an exuberant urbanity, charging, "We must think of our cities as places to live in and enjoy rather than places to work in and get out of."[85] Jim Wright argued that the creation of Robson Square was one of three crucial urban design efforts that would ensure the city's future livability. The first was the prevention of a major freeway cutting through Chinatown and the second was banning development on the agricultural lands south of the city. Both prohibitions directly involved Peter Oberlander.[86] As a third prong, the development of Robson Square was followed by numerous other projects in Vancouver that ultimately introduced "urban housing into the city at a rate unmatched in North America."[87]

A main reason for laying the fifty-five-story tower on its side was to increase the transparency between judicial spaces and plaza uses, and to link these legal and recreational uses to the activity on Robson Street. Erickson contended, "In most courthouses there is little that offers basic reassurance to the distressed or even the basic amenities for the many participants forced to spend long hours in the court precincts."[88] For Oberlander, the three-block project was a "place to see and be seen."[89] The horizontal layout also allowed the designers to break the confines of the urban grid, enabling people to effortlessly meander through the site.

On Block 61 the design team created a low-density urban complex in a park-like setting, and great effort was made to integrate interior and exterior spaces: a ceiling could be a water basin; a roof could be rich with planting; and a wall could become a waterfall. Accordingly the threshold between architecture and landscape was a permeable condition "not barricaded, but a complex boundary

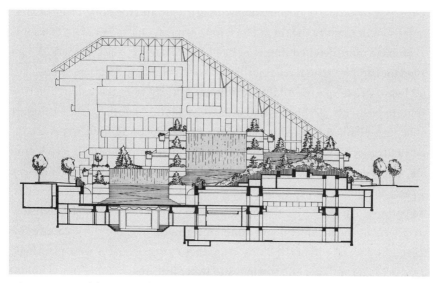

Robson Square and the Provincial Law Courts Section, circa 1975. Architect: Arthur Erickson. Landscape Architect: Cornelia Hahn Oberlander. Drawn by Daryl Plater.

between inside and outside."[90] The architect Marco Polo would later observe that Robson Square defied "the traditional figure/ground relationship between buildings and open space. Rather than treat the landscape element as mere ornamental forecourt, as does F. M. Rattenbury's courthouse of 1911. . . . Erickson, Oberlander and Robillard have integrated landscape and building, emphasizing their relationship in section over that in plan."[91]

Conceived during the oil crisis of the 1970s, Robson Square was designed to reduce the energy drain that these large complex structures put on an already taxed urban center—an emphasis that Oberlander eventually incorporated more fully into her oeuvre. Thus, Erickson ensured that water was recycled throughout, and passive ventilation and cooling systems were devised, such as the 840,000-gallon water tank in the Law Courts' basement, which cooled the building, instead of a conventional air-conditioning system. Oberlander's extensive green roofs helped to insulate the interior spaces and they were planted with low-maintenance species. She also researched and employed drip irrigation, an emerging technology at the time. Compared to spray irrigation, which increases water loss from evaporation and wind, drip irrigation maximizes water usage by hydrating the plants slowly with water distributed directly to their roots.

LANDSCAPE STRATEGY Collaborating with Erickson and the design team, Oberlander sought to unify the three-block-long project. One of her main tasks was to complete more detailed studies of Blocks 51, 61, and 71. The schematic design called for complex spatial relationships between building elevation, street level, and below grade spaces. Adding to this complexity were the wildly differing program elements. At Block 51 an at-grade sculpture court for the future art gallery was planned. This courtyard space stepped below Robson Street to connect with Block 61, which was programmed to accommodate an ice-skating rink, an outdoor dining court, connection to a future transit line, and linkages to 525,000 square feet of interior office space, restaurants, exhibition areas, and parking. These interior spaces on Block 61 were located three stories below street level at the north end and up to a maximum of three stories above the street at the south end of the block. Atop these interior spaces were plantings, paved areas for walking and seating, and water features.

In addition to this diverse programming, each block contained different architectural typologies. Block 51 contained the neoclassical former courthouse. The building on Block 61 was a low-profile structure with the architecture largely camouflaged by terraced plantings and water features. The new Provincial Law Courts on Block 71 was kept to seven stories above grade to match the height of the courthouse; however, it was still a huge structure, occupying the entire block, with a large glazed atrium designed to facilitate the growth of plants inside. Given this diverse architecture, it was clear that it was the landscape that would be the unifying experience tying the three blocks together.

As for the system that would support the plants in this landscape, during the early 1970s off-the-shelf products for on-structure planting were virtually nonexistent in Canada. Oberlander researched a number of lightweight growing mediums and a waterproofing system that would maintain the integrity of the building envelope. While she and Erickson worked together on the planting scheme he admitted that "everything is there because of her exhaustive research into growing mediums."[92] Oberlander found a mixture of peat, sand, and perlite that would solve the problem, but it took three years to convince her teammates that this medium was the best solution.[93] The growing medium, which was installed over a waterproofing membrane and a drainage layer, was kept at a constant thirty-inch depth throughout the project to echo the contour of the built structure. The depth was only changed at the twenty-five-foot-high mound at the corner of Robson and Hornby Streets on Block 61. Here, Styrofoam was stacked over the tourism office with the membrane and lightweight growing medium on top to create a veritable hill in the urban landscape.[94]

While Oberlander worked on many facets of the landscape, it was the planting design for more than fifty thousand shrubs and trees — in most cases on-structure — that demanded her greatest attention. She researched new technical areas, such as computerized irrigation and fertilization techniques, and she collaborated closely with the architects and engineers to create seamless interfaces with the building. Raoul Robillard, a horticultural expert, and Erickson and Oberlander worked together on the plant selection. She recalled Erickson's acute assessment of her monochromatic planting scheme. "We started with masses of evergreens, then he pointed out that there are many greens. I began to pay more attention to variations."[95] This can be seen on Block 61 in the planted areas around each of the two dome-shaped awnings — a shape that echoed the dome on Rattenbury's courthouse. At the street elevation surrounding each dome, Oberlander planted fifty-five Hick's yews skirted by fifty-five kinnikinnick. The upright yew, with its dark green needle-like foliage, provided a subtle contrast to the lower-growing kinnikinnick's olive-green ovular leaves.

The majority of the exterior planting was designated for Block 61. The planting plan in 1977 displayed a coherent syntax at work. Three types of on-structure planting systems were to form the basis of the scheme: the walkway plantings, the box planters, and the flying planters. Each planted areas had its own plant palette and arrangement in relation to the structure. The walkway planting areas encouraged pedestrian movement across the block. Here, Oberlander called for rhododendrons, laurel, and mugo pines with a lower planting of kinnikinnick and ivy. The evergreen foliage of the shrubs helped to define the walkway areas as corridors, while the low-growing ground cover was woven over the pavers, which were staggered on the upper elevations, evoking the sense of being on a leisurely walk.

Robson Square's box planters looked like giant balustrades, flanking the waterfalls and stramps — a hybrid born of the mating of stairs and ramps. To express the verticality of these balustrades and to counterbalance the width of the stramps, two lodgepole pines were selected for all the large planter boxes. The planters also contained a Japanese maple and a magnolia. The warm light pink hues of the magnolia in spring and the maple's fall color corresponded with the pink granite paving. This repeated planting pattern created a consistency in the spatial complexity of the landscape on Block 61, allowing for continuity across

Robson Square and the Provincial Law Courts, the box planters and stramps, Vancouver, circa 1978. Architect: Arthur Erickson. Landscape Architect: Cornelia Hahn Oberlander.

an elevation change of four stories. According to Oberlander, if each planter was installed with different plants, the design would have added more chaos to the already complex design. With the same plant selection "people's eyes are carried."[96]

The flying planters were the narrow trays that cantilevered from the façade of the provincial government building on Block 61 and the Law Courts on Block 71. These flying planters were filled with alternating bands of memorial roses and clipped laurel to create a visually striking pattern that countered the concrete

Robson Square and the Provincial Law Courts mound over the tourist offices, Vancouver, 1993. Architect: Arthur Erickson. Landscape Architect: Cornelia Hahn Oberlander.

of the building façade.[97] While the upright laurels provided a consistent green line that accentuated the horizontality of the window banding, the roses — which cascaded over the planters — broke up the long parallel lines of the building. Alternating these species in the planters, she created an interplay between a planted form that mimics the architectural lines and one that defies them.

The large mound at the corner of Robson and Hornby Streets was a special area of Block 61. Oberlander conceived this spot as a space set above street life, a place for a private lunch, quiet conversation, or sunbathing —"a place where people feel like they are not in the midst of a city."[98] Rising approximately thirty feet above street level, it was planted to resemble a small clearing in a woodland with a layering of lodgepole pines and maples underplanted with rhododendrons, photinia, and vines, and with an open lawn crowning the top of the mound.

While much emphasis was placed on planting Block 61, Oberlander also worked on the project's street edges. Twin allées of London plane trees were originally planned for all sides of the project site. Erickson selected plane trees because of their bold branching patterns, which would contrast with the horizontal lines of the flying planters.[99] In 1978, due to concerns from the city's engineering department, the city council voted that red sunset maples would

Robson Square and the Provincial Law Courts allée, Vancouver, 2011. Architect: Arthur Erickson. Landscape Architect: Cornelia Hahn Oberlander.

be used instead.[100] Oberlander planted the maples fifteen feet on-center, although the city wanted twice as much space between them. Fortunately, this was a battle she won. Combined with the planted façade, the trees, which were planted down the northwest sides of Blocks 61 and 71, have created one of the most beautiful streetscapes in Vancouver.

Another unifying element for the project was water, a feature that was particularly important to Erickson. Water began on Block 71 and was harnessed in a channel almost three hundred feet long. The channel continued from the Provincial Law Courts, bridged over Smithe Street, and connected to Block 61, where a succession of waterfalls came to rest just above street grade. Thus water movement became increasingly more active as it cascaded down from the

Robson Square and the Provincial Law Courts waterfall revealed as a window at night, Vancouver, circa 1978. Architect: Arthur Erickson. Landscape Architect: Cornelia Hahn Oberlander.

Law Courts towards Block 51. It was Erickson's thought that by designing successively smaller basins as the water approached street level, the sound of the falling water meeting the basin would increase and help mute traffic noise.[101] The falls were also part of the heating and cooling systems for Blocks 71 and 61, and they played a role in fireproofing as well.

The continuous integration of building and landscape at Robson Square was also a result of its reading as a single concrete pour. In its topography of surface features the stairs and stramps appeared to be carved from the depths of the ground and the plants and water physically part of the building and plaza spaces. This sculptural elegance noticeably contrasted with urban plazas that are cluttered with planters and discrete fountains, separating the animate features of plant life from the inanimate logic of the structure.

Oberlander collaborated with the design team on the hardscape details as well. To unify the experience of all three blocks a consistent paving material and pattern were used throughout. The pattern employed narrow pavers of lightweight concrete and pink granite, which were integrated with the drainage strips. According to Oberlander, the light color was selected so that there was a luster to the surface on Vancouver's many rainy days.[102] This paving pattern was oriented in a linear pattern to guide movement across the three blocks. To further link the three blocks, the paving extended across Robson Street, which was reduced to twenty-four feet in width and closed to vehicles other than public transit. Pavers were also laid out in rectangular patterns like large urban rugs to delineate places to gather or pause.

Also, Oberlander was instrumental in the design of the now-famous stramps that connected the terraced spaces on Block 61. A sculptural solution that permitted wheeled access and places to stop and sit, it issued from numerous studies (earlier schematics for Robson Square showed a separated stair and ramp system). Oberlander recalled that Alberto Zennaro, then working in Erickson's Vancouver office, had designed an elegant set of stairs. But when she asked him how a person in a wheelchair or with a pram might ascend them, he lacked a response. Another designer on the team had previously developed a scheme with the ramp to the side of the stair system, but Oberlander had a different solution.[103] She picked up a felt-tipped pen and drew a "goat path"—a diagonal line across Zennaro's stairs—and the stramps for Robson Square were born.[104] By the following day Zennaro had perfected the stramp design that can be seen today.[105]

All the outdoor furnishings, such as benches and lighting fixtures, were custom designed for Robson Square. According to Oberlander, "Great care was taken in designing the 'street furniture' . . . benches, trash cans, kiosks, vending carts, phone booths, and bus stops, all bear a family likeness and were designed to relate to each other and the landscape material."[106] The design team also combined furnishings in an unusual manner. For example, the pathway lights on Block 61 were designed to dual as seating. Robson Square's custom-designed benches were particularly notable. Oberlander recalled that Willy Bruegger, a Swiss-born architect, showed her mock-ups of them. While at first she thought the benches were too clunky looking, he demonstrated how their table-wide backs could serve as a ledge on which to place food.[107]

Lastly, Oberlander's work on Robson Square marked an increased use of historical references in her design process, and it may have been reinforced by her collaboration with Erickson. It was also during this time that the Oberlander family was taking trips to Italy with the UBC architectural historian Abraham Rogatnick. Like Oberlander's employment of historical references in her residential work, her use of history in the design of Robson Square differed from the École des Beaux-Arts landscape architects or later postmodern designers who sought more literal translations of history. Referencing was either subtly expressed with materials or by replicating the dimensions of historical works.

Given that the design team sought to connect the judicial programming of the project with seats of governance from antiquity, Robson Square has numerous classical references. For example, the Law Courts' lobby dimensions were based on the law courts of Pompeii. The public lobby was sized at 210 feet by 60 feet, resembling the Pompeii space, which was 220 feet by 75 feet.[108] To further this reference, Oberlander selected plants for the Law Courts' interior lobby that matched some of the vegetation that the archaeologist Wilhelmina Feemster Jashemski had identified in her excavations at Pompeii. These plants included lilies, ferns, date palms, and figs.[109] Interestingly, the plane trees Oberlander installed had a genetic reference to antiquity. Their seeds were from the collection of Dr. W. C. Gibson, professor and head of the history of medicine and science at UBC. In 1970 Gibson brought the seed collection to Vancouver from Greece. According to Oberlander, they were "taken from the original plane tree on the island of Cos (Greece) under which Hippocrates is said to have taken the oath of medicine about 400 BC."[110]

Orange trees were also selected for the public lobby of the Law Courts, but they had much humbler origins. Oberlander sourced them in an abandoned orchard in California and shipped them to Vancouver. Unfortunately they were ill fated. Days before the Law Courts' opening the trees were heavily laden with fruit, adding brilliant flecks of orange to the subtle hues of the lobby. Chief Justice Sonny Nemetz complained that the orange trees made it look like the province had spent too much money on the project and he demanded the removal of the sumptuous fruit immediately. The head gardener was able to make juice and a large quantity of marmalade from the harvested oranges. Unfortunately, the orange trees were replaced with indoor ficus trees, the ubiquitous staple of many interior landscapes.[111]

RECEPTION Block 61 opened in October 1978, hosting the new provincial government building, recreational facilities, and their related landscapes. This middle block was named Robson Square after John Robson, a nineteenth-century premier of British Columbia, although the entire three-block project is often referred to as Robson Square. The new Law Courts building on Block 71 opened a year later, and Block 51, with the historical courthouse repurposed as an art gallery, opened in 1983. The initial opening ceremony for Block 61 was quite festive, featuring the release of five thousand helium-filled balloons, a concert by the Vancouver Firemen's Band, an ice-skating show, guided tours, and of course free food. In the United States, Robson Square was praised in *Time*, the *New York Times*, and *The New Yorker*. Journalists were particularly captivated by the way the landscape psychologically removed people from the midst of the city. A *Time* magazine reporter observed, "In some green areas, traffic cannot be seen or heard over the splashing of waterfalls."[112]

In contrast, many of the Canadian newspapers were initially critical, asserting that staff working inside the building complained about light quality. In the fall of 1980 courthouse stenographers and shorthand reporters working in Block 61's lower floors held a series of protests charging that the low levels of natural sunlight were not acceptable. There was also a fear that the three-block project was too ambitious, vastly over budget, and — like any great building complex — its roof leaked.[113] One reporter noted that "to a lot of people, including Government officials, architects and environmental psychologists, Robson Square is a bit of a gamble."[114] The reporter even went so far as to claim that the free sesame chicken wings, tacos, perogies, and "100 pounds of hot corned beef sandwiches, canapés and French pastries" were the real draw for the hundreds of people attending the opening.[115]

Despite these criticisms, during the late 1970s and 1980s Robson Square proved to be extremely popular. There was ice-skating in winter and roller-skating in summer, as well as major programming events that enlivened the sunken plaza.[116] These events ranged from contemporary dance performances, to sports events, to the World's Largest Tea Party that was held to celebrate the marriage of Prince Charles and Lady Diana. Some of these programs drew between 45,000 and 50,000 people to Robson Square, with the lower levels of Block 61 serving as the stage, and the stramps and street-level areas acting as the grandstand for spectators.

The 1981 renovations that converted the courthouse to the Vancouver Art Gallery also contributed to the project's success. Oberlander reused the London plane trees, which had been rejected by the city for street trees, and arranged them in a row to visually connect Block 51 with Block 61. The gallery's main entrance on W. Georgia Street was closed and a new street-level entrance faced Block 61, further linking the three blocks. The entrance lobby and gallery shop occupied the street level, while a stepped terrace and gallery café occupied the second level.[117] Perched above the street and given a southern exposure, the gallery's outdoor café is still one of the most popular places for lunch in the city.

Spontaneous events also gave life to these three blocks in the center of the city. The stairs of the Vancouver Art Gallery became an established site for public protest and expression. For example, HIV/AIDS activists staged a "die in" in 1990. The center block was also a popular place to take lunch for people working downtown. In 1990, as Oberlander was conducting a site visit, a neatly made man in a suit and tie approached her. He thanked her for her contributions and mentioned that weather permitting he had taken his lunch at Robson Square every day since it had opened. He explained that he was an accountant and that these short visits brought an element of delight into his otherwise lackluster day.[118]

Robson Square won the 1979 ASLA President's Award of Excellence with the jury highlighting the integration of architecture and landscape architecture. Yet for decades architectural critics have debated the success of the project. Some critics found the amount of concrete excessive. Even so, the project's plantings and water features, particularly on Block 61, have been consistently identified as humanizing the concrete and glass.[119] There were also critics who found the Provincial Law Courts disconnected from the street because it lacked windows at the sidewalk edge. The architecture critic John Pastier observed that this condition did not make the legal procedures transparent to the people.[120] And Suzanne Stephens in *Progressive Architecture* adds, "While the building *appears* open and transparent, the actual system continues to operate behind closed doors and beyond securely controlled corridors."[121] Unfortunately over the years, programmatic changes have jeopardized the landscape's success as well.

A year after Robson Square opened, Robson Street was reconfigured to accept traffic and its distinct paving was eventually covered with asphalt. The entrance foyer connecting Block 71 to 61 was locked for security reasons when the courts were not in session. Combined, "these two events limited pedestrian movement north–south through the three blocks."[122] Tragically, the transit stop at the sunken plaza level never materialized. According to Erickson this area was planned to accommodate large numbers of commuters using the new subway.[123] The restaurants at the sunken plaza level failed as a consequence. Situated below street level, with no transit stop, it was difficult for them to attract clientele. Nevertheless, while the lower plaza fell into disuse, the remainder of the plaza spaces continued to be frequented by local residents, tourists, and workers on their lunch hour.

Maintenance has also been an issue. Initially, two full-time gardeners tended the vegetation at Robson Square. They also handled the annual plantings, for which they regularly consulted Oberlander. However, as budgets diminished the plants received less care and their growth began to compromise the structure. Between 1992 and 1993 the province began major repairs to address leaks caused by roots in two planter boxes that had penetrated the waterproofing membrane. On Block 61 a mature lodgepole pine, magnolia, Japanese maple, and some rhododendrons were removed to be replaced by ventilation grates.[124] In 2000 the ice rink was closed due to budget constraints — despite fundraising efforts by local groups. Many governmental offices and conference spaces on Block 61 had also been vacated. While the University of British Columbia moved some of its programs into these quarters, for almost a decade the sunken court was seldom used.

2010 Olympic and Paralympic Games

With Vancouver's hosting of the 2010 Olympic and Paralympic Games, Robson Square was identified as a prime celebratory site. However Olympic plans involved major renovations to Block 61. For example, to demonstrate the novel use of British Columbia's forest products, a mammoth wood canopy — covering both sunken areas on Blocks 51 and 61 and extending over Robson Street — was planned. Resembling the calcareous covering of a huge burrowing shellfish, it was quickly dubbed "the clamshell." Ultimately, these proposed changes incited debates concerning Robson Square's preservation and many landscape architects, planners, and architects rallied to define the significance of the project.

A noteworthy argument made during this debate was the way in which the project was conceived. Robson Square was built during a time when there was great faith in the ability of architects and landscape architects to design vital urban environments. It was a period before urban design was simply made part of the marketing apparatus of developers.

While plans to install the clamshell were dropped, by the time of the Olympic and Paralympic Games, significant changes had already been made to Block 61. The circular ice-skating rink was expanded to an oval and security railings were placed everywhere — around planters, terraces, and waterways. This overuse of railings disturbed Oberlander the most. During a 2010 site visit at Robson Square, she commented that the "plantings looked like they were in jail" — and they certainly did.[125]

Yet, there would be some redemption. Event programming was returned to the site and 1.5 million people visited Robson Square during the games. It was a venue for live entertainment, sports demonstrations, light shows, video displays, performances throughout the day, as well as free public ice-skating, and a very popular zip-line. After the Olympics and Paralympics the mound and major portions of Block 61 were stripped of their plantings to perform structural maintenance. The waterproofing installed in the 1970s had a thirty-year life expectancy. It had lasted more than thirty years, which was not bad given the technology of the times.[126] Some of the larger plant material was removed and maintained off-site during these renovations.

Robson Square marked a significant point in Oberlander's career. She not only advanced her practical knowledge of rooftop landscape design; she also brought her detailed understanding of people's movement through space to the highly volatile context of a major urban project. Architects working in Erickson's office at the time, such as Bing Thom, Jim Wright, and Eva Matsuzaki, would later open their own practices and engage Oberlander as a collaborator. Erickson also hired her on other projects while she worked on Robson Square. For example, in 1980 they began working on the Laxton Building, a ten-story office tower with planted balconies. Located along a steep escarpment in downtown Vancouver, the project built upon the intimate relationship between planted and built form that characterized Robson Square.

The Laxton Building was defined by a diagonally stepped façade that, rather than adhering to the grid of the street, echoed the northwest aspect of the escarpment's contour lines. The levels of the building's stepped façade alternated between zigzag floor plates and straight floor plates. Upright plantings traced the balconies of the zigzag floors, while cascading plants (originally English ivy) lined the balconies of the straight floors. Since the plants were brought to the structure's edges, the geometries of the building were dramatically amplified. Now called the Evergreen Building, it was nearly demolished and replaced in the mid-2000s. Fortunately, it was given heritage status, and Oberlander was consulted in 2006–7 to replant the terraces (with Hahn ivy replacing the English ivy). Today the planted edges trace the alternating silhouettes of the floor plates, creating a striking image of a green, architectonic mountain.

Robson Square was followed by work with other well-known architects in Ottawa, Berlin, and New York City. However, it was her collaboration with Erickson that she prized the most. Oberlander called Erickson "a marvel, a real inspiration to me."[127] The feeling was mutual. Erickson was later quoted as saying,

Oberlander "understands what I'm thinking about, and is the only person who understands what I am talking about."[128] Her collaboration with Erickson reinforced their shared belief that simplicity should not be confused with plainness and, in Erickson's words, "lack of detail for crudity, modesty for cheapness, structural veracity as a boring grid."[129] Indeed these ideas were bound to the transformative mythology that design could change the way people live in the world. Their convictions were tested in another Oberlander and Erickson collaboration: the Canadian Chancery in Washington, D.C.

Canadian Chancery

The site for the Canadian Chancery was 501 Pennsylvania Avenue, NW, or Block 491. It occupied a key axis in L'Enfant's 1791 plan for Washington, D.C., and the processional route between Capitol Hill and the White House.[130] Despite the lofty address and the guarantee to maintain sight lines to the Capitol in perpetuity, the surrounding urban fabric was characterized by neglect at the time of the building's design.[131] Like Robson Square in Vancouver, the development of the project was part of a larger scheme to revive downtown Washington.[132] Unlike Robson Square, its design needed to meet the aesthetic ambitions of the Pennsylvania Avenue Development Corporation's (PADC) revitalization plans. These ambitions, which stressed a very literal use of classical architectural motifs coupled with increased concerns about security, grew more demanding as the project unfolded. Early conceptual schemes were subjected to an unprecedented number of design review committees — Erickson numbered them at twenty-five.[133]

From the inception of the project Oberlander worked as part of Erickson's team, and like Robson Square they emphasized the human experience of the building and site, and its connection to its context.[134] Given the program requirements and the building's footprint restrictions, the six-story chancery could only occupy two-thirds of the site. The design team took advantage of this situation by creating a 98–foot by 197-foot paved courtyard that was accessible to people coming from Pennsylvania Avenue and John Marshall Place Park, named after the influential fourth chief justice of the U.S. Supreme Court and designed by the landscape architect Carol L. Johnson in 1983.

According to Oberlander, "the basic concept of the design is to accentuate the open space of the Chancery while addressing the park" next door.[135] Oberlander wanted people working inside the embassy to enjoy a borrowed view of the park, a view that visually linked her terraced gardens with the park as one continuous landscape. Thus, the street between the chancery and the park was closed and Oberlander extended the paving of the courtyard and a continuous berm across the former street to further connect the two sites. Additionally, in plan view, the courtyard's long dimension corresponded with Johnson's elegant grass panels for the park, adding another layer of connection between the two open spaces.

At the same time, the design team extended John Marshall Place Park into the building façade by "terracing up to the roof level to enhance and visually extend" the park.[136] Stonework, mullions, and plantings in the terraced garden and courtyard echoed the modular planning of the building. For example, the clipped hawthorns coincided with the spacing of window mullions.

The selection of plant material in these terraced roof gardens and at the building's perimeter has been attributed to sources as diverse as Pliny's descriptions of plant material at Hadrian's villa to Babylon's mythical hanging gardens.[137] Oberlander's use of evergreens and roses, as well as oak trees at the Pennsylvania entrance, evoked the plant palette admired by the ancients. However, she admits that while the entrance courtyard with its simple pool and plantings echoed classical ideas, the planter boxes also remind one of the cascading trees of Canada's mountains.[138]

Erickson would have a difficult time with PADC's intervening desire for the building to express classical motifs. To relate to the surrounding architecture, he proposed a circular cornice supported by twelve columns representing the provinces and territories of Canada. He also made sure the height of the structure related to the lower cornice of the U.S. Courthouse. Nonetheless, one of the design review committees demanded more classical columns, so he gave them six fifty-foot-high fluted columns, but he subverted their function "through a very personal take on 'modern Classicism.'"[139] The massive columns were hollow and made of aluminum — and they supported only the Plexiglas awning.

Construction began in 1986, and the embassy was officially opened on 3 May 1989. *The Spirit of Haida Gwaii,* a sculpture by the Haida artist Bill Reid, was set in the middle of the large pool in the courtyard. The Canadian Chancery won the 1986 American Institute of Architects' Gold Medal and an International Citation Award from the Canadian Society of Landscape Architects in 1991. Not only was the embassy's architecture praised but the building's connection to the adjacent park space was also identified as an important accomplishment of the design. Paul Goldberger, the architecture critic for the *New York Times*, reported, "The building itself wraps around the plaza, and it is from the plaza that the most appealing part of the façade can be seen, the series of terraced office floors hung with plantings."[140] Yet some were worried about the openness of the scheme. Administrators in the embassy, for example, were uncomfortable with the extent of public access and wanted to surround the chancery with a waist-high fence; they felt it was too inviting and too linked with the city. Regardless, the building remained open and accessible from the park.

Over the years Oberlander and Erickson worked together on numerous institutional, residential, and commercial projects. Their last collaboration was an on-structure landscape for the Waterfall Building located near the entrance to Granville Island in Vancouver. Developed by a former philosopher at Simon Fraser University, the project was to be a "lifestyle laboratory" that blurred the distinctions between home and work. In the intervening years since Robson Square, Vancouver had been attracting large numbers of professionals in the film and public relations industry and related creative trades. In fact, by the early 1980s the city was labeled Hollywood North. To accommodate this new population, the Waterfall Building was conceived to offer a mix of domestic, work, and entertainment spaces.

The building complex, designed by Arthur Erickson with Nick Milkovich, entailed five separate structures containing studios and split-level residences that wrapped around a central courtyard with an art gallery at its center. The entrance façade was defined by a dramatic 65-foot-long by 12-foot-high sheet of water pouring into an overflowing basin — hence the project's name, the Waterfall Building. The courtyard, which was also the roof of the underground parking garage, was comprised of a simple tapestry of pavers, ground cover, trees, and a small reflecting basin at the entrance to the gallery. Oberlander designed gardens on all five rooftop structures, which were deemed public amenities by the city and thus enabled the building to exceed the 40-foot height restrictions in the area. With a restrained palette of white roses at the buildings' edges and a wave of ornamental grass across the rooftop surfaces, the gardens today serve as communal patio spaces for residents. Steel spiral staircases, which surprisingly emerge from the façades of the top floors of the units provide access to these spaces. Like Robson Square, the sound of the waterfall permeates the

The Waterfall Building spiral staircases allow access to roof gardens from each residence, Vancouver, 2011. Landscape Architect: Cornelia Hahn Oberlander. Architects: Arthur Erickson with Nick Milkovich Architects.

complex, muting the noise of traffic and supporting an environment that is at once immersed in but removed from the city.

The time span between Robson Square and the Waterfall Building project marked a period when Oberlander became an internationally know expert in bringing natural elements into the urban condition. Indeed she continued to humanize the urban environment well into the first decade of the twenty-first century with the New York Times Building project.

The New York Times Building

The New York Times Building project was the first large tower development undertaken in New York City since the 9/11 terrorist attacks. It also occupied the last parcels of land to be revitalized as part of the Theater District redevelopment plans initiated in the 1980s. During the past twenty years these plans for Midtown Manhattan had ushered in projects such as the renovation of Bryant Park and later Times Square. Occupying ten properties on 8th Avenue between 40th and 41st Streets, the site had the character of the old Times Square area—a jumble of small shops, some serving legitimate enterprises and some supporting the sex and drug trade. Not without protest, the properties were acquired through the process of eminent domain.

The building's primary tenants, the New York Times Company, had outgrown its 1913 building. In 2000 it conducted a private design competition, inviting sixteen well-known architects to submit schemes for the new tower. The proposal put forth by Renzo Piano and Fox & Fowle was announced as the winner in December 2001. Oberlander and HM White Site Architects were consulting landscape architects. White and Oberlander had initially met through a mutual friend and collaborated on a proposed master plan for the Queens Botanical Garden. While they did not receive the commission, they both agreed that they were destined to work together on a project in the future. Hank White recalls that he and Oberlander "shared the same sensibilities and felt a strong personal connection to each other."[141] Thus, when White was asked to join Renzo Piano and the Fox & Fowle design team, he immediately contacted Oberlander and asked her to join him.

The team's proposal for the 1.5-million-square-foot complex emphasized transparency and lightness. The jury viewed transparency as essential to both the conduct of a newspaper and an enlightened evolution of the skyscraper typology. According to one jury member, "their design was chosen for its 'sense of humanity.' A skyscraper doesn't have to be a slick, opaque building that can be translated as arrogant. This is a newspaper. It needs to be transparent."[142] The original design entailed a five-story atrium, cantilevered tower, and an extensive rooftop garden with a reflecting pool. After three years of design reviews, a more modest configuration emerged, a tower with a meadow rooftop and a lower wing that wrapped around a 4,900-square-foot courtyard open to the sky. The courtyard, now buried behind the building, provided an extra challenge for Oberlander and White. Oberlander recalls that "originally Piano envisioned a grid of nine-foot-on-centre birch trees covering the space of the courtyard."[143] However, she knew that light would be a problem both for people and plant life

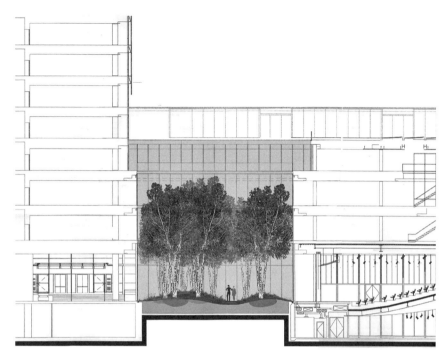

New York Times Building Courtyard Section B-B. Landscape Architects: HM White and Cornelia Hahn Oberlander. Architects: Renzo Piano and Fox & Fowle.

in this space. They commissioned Robert Brown at the University of Guelph and Robert LeBlanc of Ekistics Planning and Design to model microclimatic conditions in the courtyard and rooftop areas.

Brown and LeBlanc simulated five daily light conditions — each representing different periods of the year — that tracked the movement of the sun, resulting shade patterns, and the wind.[144] The solar studies of the courtyard proved to be particularly revealing. They demonstrated that the varying light levels would not support a uniform planting of any single species of tree. Brown and LeBlanc then predicted where the trees would survive and the type of plant material best suited for the courtyard and roof. "This information became a critical element in shaping the resulting design of the courtyard and rooftop gardens."[145] The revised design was an irregular arrangement of mature birch trees positioned where the sun was most abundant in the courtyard. Paper birch trees (*Betula papyrifera*) were selected not only because they would survive under these conditions but also because their light papery bark expressed the project's concept of transparency and lightness — as well as the natural material upon which the newspaper is printed.

Oberlander called the final scheme for the courtyard a fragment of the Hudson Valley's ecology.[146] It comprised seven birch trees planted within a series of small, moss-covered hills, and a bisecting walkway of epi wood. This building material from the Brazilian walnut tree was selected because it was particularly resistant to insects and decay. Two varieties of moss, hair cap and fern, were grown in a nursery specifically for the project. Oberlander personally supervised grading and the installation of the mosses and birch trees. Here, mature trees were essential because they needed to be tall enough to reach the sunlight penetrating the courtyard. Construction of the landscape began in 2007 with much fanfare, and the birch tree installation caused the biggest stir. It was the sight of her seven birches that caught the attention of many passing by the construction site. The 40- to 50-foot-high trees, weighing approximately 32,000 pounds, were cued up along the street resembling an oversized audience awaiting entrance to the theater.

The New York Times Building opened on 19 November 2007. Architectural critics and the public debated the success of the project. Piano had wrapped the structure with 186,000 3-inch-diameter, off-white aluminum-silicate ceramic rods that became the focus of dispute. The giant scrim helped block the sun and reduce heat gain, and it was key to the concept of transparency because it helped avoid the black box look that comes with tinted glass curtain walls. Nonetheless, Piano was not satisfied with their grey color and some critics complained that they made cleaning the glass underneath extremely difficult. In contrast, the courtyard garden became an important symbol for the project, appearing in numerous photographs of the building and even in the *New York Times*'s own promotional material. Not surprisingly it has contributed to the reading of the building's transparency. Surrounded on all sides by glass walls, and visible from the main lobby, retail area, and auditorium, the courtyard garden allows natural light to penetrate the center of the building — light rendered a vibrant shade of green.

While dark green plants in the garden would have played off the white bark of the birch trees, darker colored plants would have absorbed more light. Without a doubt the brilliant chartreuse green of the vegetation permeates beyond the glass walls and colors the spaces surrounding the courtyard. This effect is particularly dramatic at the entrance from 8th Avenue where the elevators are grouped in two banks, a positioning that allows direct views to the garden. Since the courtyard is open to the sky, snow and rain are visible at the center of the building. Importantly, those working in the building can view this changing scene. They have not, unfortunately, appreciated the auditory contributions of the courtyard. Birds have found it to be a rewarding destination and their songs can be heard throughout the building. One angry tenant called Oberlander in Vancouver and asked her to get rid of the birds because they were making too much noise.

The economic recession, which ensued a year after the project's opening, was an unforeseen event affecting the project. The rooftop installation was put on hold. Regrettably even the most well-researched plans can be foiled by plumbing problems. Shortly after installation the irrigation system for the courtyard malfunctioned. Instead of delivering a fine mist, water was distributed in large quantities over the mosses. The chlorine filter also failed, and by 2010 all the mosses had died.[147] In response, the ground plane was replanted with light green grasses and ferns that are similar in color to the mosses. Another unanticipated problem has been public access. For security reasons the courtyard has been off-limits to the public. While the nature of the security risks posed by the courtyard is unknown, the building has been climbed twice as of this writing.

Not unlike playground environments, during the last decades of the twentieth century, urban environments in North America became increasingly subjected to concerns over litigation. This anxiety was exacerbated by the transference of many former public spaces to private ownership and control, which has limited the movement of people in urban environments. Likewise, while landscape architects like Oberlander made major forays into understanding and mapping the way humans move through the environment, these studies eventually became the purview of social scientists and environmental psychologists. The creative explorations that had once defined urban design were replaced by behaviorist models that, as Sylvia Lavin points out, "under cut the value of design."[148]

At the same time landscape architects came to increasingly understand the environment as an ecological context. Ian McHarg's highly influential text *Design with Nature* (1969) increased advocacy for environmental improvement and put landscape architects at the forefront of addressing pollution and other ecological problems. Tapping into her knowledge of natural systems that began as a child, Oberlander broke new ground in understanding how the landscape could express environmental values in ways that not only mitigated pollution but also increased ecological integrity. The inclusion of ecological systems as part of Oberlander's conception of the human environment informs the next chapter, "Ecological Environment."

ECOLOGICAL ENVIRONMENT

4 This chapter begins with Oberlander's and the profession's increasing support of the environment as a "movement," which sought to stop the degradation of ecological systems. For landscape architects enlisted in the environmental cause this support went deeper than preventative measures against pollution and to the root of the design process itself. As the landscape architectural theorist Elizabeth K. Meyer has observed, the movement changed the way landscape architecture was practiced. Ecological information and analyses became primary factors in site analyses.[1] It also followed that the environment was increasingly interpreted for its nonhuman ecological attributes. While early proponents of the environment, like Oberlander, stressed their human dimension, environments eventually came to be referred to by primarily nonhuman site factors. By the late 1970s many landscape architects were engaged in the design and planning of regions and large-scale habitat areas. At the same time, however, there was an increased interest in the communicative powers of landscape design as central to its art.

Meyer posits that landscape architects working in these two veins often disagreed on the fundamental thrust of the profession: Should it be the product of art or science? Oberlander represented a middle ground by communicating environmental values to people at a human scale as the art of her practice. Starting with the Museum of Anthropology, she spearheaded the use of plant material vital to First Nation peoples as a means of representing cultural practices that elaborated a particular ecological context. She also explored the way art is experienced as a designed landscape in her gardens for the National Gallery in Ottawa. By the 1990s Oberlander would play a role in another phase of urbanism emerging in Vancouver with her design of the rooftop landscape for Library Square by the architect Moshe Safdie and Downs/Archambault & Partners. For this project she used a regional element to generate form and expression, which also contributed to the ecological functioning of the project.

An Ecological Dialogue

In the final chapter of *An Approach to Design,* Norman T. Newton concludes, "I must leave to you further pursuit of the fascinating parallels between ecology and design. . . . I urge you to follow that path as far as you can go. It will repay you in countless ways."[2] Oberlander, with other landscape architects, certainly followed these parallels. Her design work from the 1970s onward became increasingly focused on saving and enhancing the ecological integrity of natural systems, which had become synonymous with the environmental movement. While she still remained committed to the social goals of landscape architecture and the importance of human experience, her interest in natural systems greatly informed her later career as she became a leading expert in the field.

The broadened interpretation of the term "environment" to account for primarily natural systems was due in large part to public acknowledgment of their unprecedented degradation. Aldo Leopold's *A Sand County Almanac* (1949) had brought to light how modern agricultural practices, such as overgrazing, and industrial practices, such as toxic waste dumping, were damaging terrestrial and aquatic systems. His "land ethic," which held that humans are duty bound to maintain healthy ecosystems for the benefit of the entire biotic community, laid the groundwork for a generation of environmentalists. After World War II the rate of power generation, resource extraction, and suburban expansion, as well as unbridled consumption, had increased pollution to the point where North Americans were witnessing firsthand dead rivers, trash-laden highways, and sunsets obscured by an ominous red haze. With the publication of Rachel Carson's *Silent Spring* (1962), concerns over the damaged natural environment expanded from the conservationists' purview to the broader public, who overwhelmingly felt that pollution was not a justifiable fallout of economic progress.

It has been argued that given landscape architecture's work with natural systems, the profession "positioned itself as part of the environmental solution."[3]

Moreover, the materials that landscape architects worked with — plants, soil, and water — were regarded as constituting a source of public good that should be saved and enhanced. Since the founding of the profession and the coeval creation of parks in the nineteenth century, landscapes have been identified as providing a collective benefit to society. The conservation movement and consequent legislation to preserve natural areas for human enjoyment in perpetuity built upon this sentiment. Still, by the late 1960s and early 1970s the environmental movement had gained an unprecedented momentum. The environmental historian Adam Rome claims that the movement was propelled by three groups: (1) an increasingly liberal-minded citizenry, (2) women seeking to expand their roles in society, (3) and young people determined not to repeat the mistakes of their parents. For Rome, this created a diverse and powerful political force that battled to improve the public good, which had perished in the escalation of private excess. The quality of the environment — the ecological health of air, water, and soil — emerged as "a classic example of a public good, since consumers could not simply buy fresh air, clean water, or a sprawl free countryside."[4]

Many landscape architects either identified with these groups or became members. Albert Fein's 1971 survey of the landscape architecture profession, in which he attempted to map out its future goals, revealed a shift in its self-definition, adding to its mandate a "greater emphasis on scientific study and recognition of the ethical responsibility of landscape architecture in terms of stewardship of the land."[5] While Fein argued that in serving the public good landscape architects needed to be both "the physicians of the environment" as well as "artists of the land," respondents thought an important goal for the profession was "to play a more effective role in formulation and practice of public policy," particularly as it related to environmental problems.[6] An interesting finding from Fein's 1971 survey was the youthful age of landscape architects. Sixty-one percent of the reporting practitioners were under forty years old, compared with 24 percent of architects, 22 percent of planners, and 12 percent of engineers. Women, too, were growing in numbers as representative of the profession. The landscape architect Joan Iverson Nassauer found that "by the late 1970s there was an increase of women in full ASLA membership, and a quarter of the associate members were women."[7]

If Rome's thesis is correct — that young men and women were a driving political force in the environmental movement — then landscape architects were not only interested in environmental quality as public good from their historical work with natural systems; it was also because of who they were. Rome observes that women's participation in environmental activism in particular served as "a vehicle for personal growth" and a challenge to the "long-standing view of science as a male province" of knowledge.[8] This is evident in Oberlander's career. Since coming to Vancouver she has advocated for environmental causes as both a professional and a volunteer. When she first arrived in Vancouver, she and other women volunteered to work towards improving the environment. With other women she formed numerous ad-hoc committees and societies concerned with pollution and preservation, "but by the 1980s, most of them had jobs" addressing environmental issues."[9]

As Oberlander's reputation grew, she integrated this drive to save the environment within the purview of professional activities. When she was elected president of the Canadian Society of Landscape Architects (1986–87), for example, she used her office to demand — along with a growing number of environmental groups, scientific experts, and the Haida Nation — that the federal government ban clear-cutting on South Moresby Island. The saving of Moresby Island, an archipelago on the southern tip of Haida Gwaii (formerly the Queen Charlotte Islands) containing ancient forests and unique fauna, was a turning point in Canadian environmental history. After a series of fiery confrontations with local protesters and the ensuing international uproar, the Canadian government preserved the area as the Gwaii Haanas National Park Reserve and Haida Heritage Site. Inspired by this event, Oberlander became the environmental chair (1987–88) of the Canadian Society of Landscape Architects and worked to raise awareness within the profession in achieving sustainable development.

Any discussion on environment and landscape would not be complete without mentioning Ian McHarg. He was instrumental in linking the environmental crisis with the practice of landscape architecture. In his writings, lectures, television appearances, and practice he exposed the damaged condition of the natural environment and argued that landscape architects were central to its repair. A landscape architect's understanding of the ecological sciences, he believed, would not only garner a new appreciation of nature but also produce an approach to designing with it. His promotion of the overlay mapping method and his enthusiasm for science forged the field of ecological planning and fundamentally changed the profession of landscape architecture. While his actual knowledge of science and nature was flawed, his unyielding enthusiasm captured the imagination of many landscape architects, including Oberlander.[10]

The conscious integration of natural and social sciences in landscape architecture greatly expanded the scope of professional activities, but at the same time it created divisions within the field. These fissions fell along art/science lines, but they were also related to scale. Those engaged in large-scale, regional work believed that ecological inventories and systematic analyses of this information would produce a series of viable design alternatives. This approach initially characterized the work of academics, such as McHarg at the University of Pennsylvania, and later Carl Steinitz at Harvard. With access to emerging computer technologies in the 1980s, Steinitz greatly expanded the analytical powers of the overlay mapping method.[11]

This large-scale work intersected with policy development and regulations that in turn yielded its own language to describe and decipher natural systems. This shift further separated planning from smaller-scale landscape design. During the decade of the 1970s both Canada and the United States enacted a spate of environmental legislation at national, regional, and local levels to combat pollution and transformed natural systems into subjects of regulation. For landscape architects a river was no longer simply a watercourse. Understanding a river not only involved knowledge of its ecological attributes but also the complex network of governmental agencies, special interest groups, stakeholders, and disciplinary expertise for which the river was a matter of interpretation.

The realization that landscapes require long-term ecological thinking — to reduce the social and ecological costs of short-term, market-driven development — is commonly attributed to landscape architects who worked at this regional scale. However, this wisdom can also be attributed to a cadre of landscape architects, Oberlander among them, who were designing human-scaled landscapes. These landscape architects were incorporating environmental thinking at the scale of the individual site, bringing the ecological message to people through firsthand encounters with the landscape. This thread of logic has been interwoven into Oberlander's career from her early efforts in Philadelphia housing to the schoolyards designed in Inuvik in recent years.

THE LINGUISTIC TURN

The late 1970s and early 1980s also marked a time when landscape architects were becoming disillusioned with the traditional mandates of modern landscape architecture. Eckbo's contention that "landscape design is a 'conscious re-arrangement of the elements of the landscape for use and for pleasure'"[12] failed to meet changing ideas about the communicative potential of landscapes. These ideas were fueled by earthwork artists who shared similar materials with landscape architects: terrain, water, sun, shadow, plants, rocks, concrete, and manufactured objects. In the hands of these artists this material was employed to convey ideas about the site, culture, or history. As the idea that landscapes were not simply experienced perceptually but interpreted cognitively took hold, a number of landscape architects designing at the human scale began considering the reading of their own work by others. Landscape architects attempted to make their landscapes and gardens mean and communicate something to those using them.[13]

This interest in the communicative powers of landscapes was also influenced by the idea that meaning itself was culturally constructed. While landscape architecture scholarship did not embrace postmodern critiques with the voracity of architecture, this thinking brought a new criticality to discourse. Some critics writing about landscapes borrowed from Marxist critiques that revealed landscapes as concealing class interests, but they also looked to art historians and cultural geographers. In his influential article "Form, Meaning and Expression in Landscape Architecture," Laurie Olin drew upon the interpretive methods of the art historians Erwin Panofsky and Rudolf Wittkower.[14] Olin posited that similar to the communicative properties of nonverbal arts, such as painting and sculpture, landscapes could be decoded and thus deliver messages. For example, linguistic devices, such as metaphors, could serve as the design strategies Olin proposed. His emphasis on the semantic reading of landscapes, in turn, unlocked a range of expressive approaches to landscape design — from referring to a site's history to evoking a bygone vernacular practice to revealing hidden natural processes at work.

Early in Oberlander's career she made references to dimensions or typologies of historical precedents as a generator of form. By the 1970s however she had expanded this approach by attempting to communicate ideas about culture, nature, and their interrelationship in the formation of the environment. She would find her first inspiration for this approach in her design for the landscape at the Museum of Anthropology at the University of British Columbia. Here, she would provide an emblem of a First Nations landscape and select plant material that they used for food, clothing, and well-being. This association between First Nations culture and their use of natural elements helped generate the form and content of her landscape. It represented an ecological relationship and one that was little known by most people outside the First Nations.

Museum of Anthropology

Audrey and Harry Hawthorn, both professors of anthropology at the University of British Columbia, initiated the idea for a Museum of Anthropology (MOA) in 1971. During the previous decades, the Hawthorns had amassed one of the most extensive collections of First Nations artifacts in Canada. Rather than selling these objects to dealers, many Haida, Kwakwaka'wakw, Coast Salish people, and other First Nation groups had entrusted them to the Hawthorns with the understanding that they would be placed on display and studied for educational purposes. By the end of the 1960s the Hawthorns' acquisitions had outgrown the cramped basement museum in the university's Main Library; totem poles and other large pieces were stored in a farm shed off-site.[15] With funding secured from the government and the university, Arthur Erickson was hired to begin design work on the new museum. In addition to the Hawthorns' holdings, the new facility was to include the Marianne and Walter Koerner collection of First Nations artifacts, and other works from Innuit, Asian, and European cultures.

MOA was an important first step in redressing the Western treatment of First Nation peoples in British Columbia. Since the nineteenth century, Western settlers had systematically displaced them; there was little recourse to reclaim their lands or benefit from their natural resources. Anti-potlatch laws — legislated in 1884 and repealed only in 1951 — prohibited First Nation peoples from celebrating their traditional festivals. The deeply flawed residential schools, which separated children from their parents in order to assimilate them into Canadian culture, almost guaranteed the complete erasure of their traditions. By the 1970s a delegation of First Nation peoples and Canadians had begun to demand that the government change its policies. It was during this period that MOA was conceived.[16]

Educating a public audience to the universal value of aboriginal art was a key goal for the museum's organizers.[17] In the past, the art of First Nation peoples had been treasured for its anthropological significance, or it was displayed in a cabinet of curiosities as testimony to a lost culture. MOA was planned to redefine this relationship between art, culture, and anthropology. Audrey Hawthorn conceived a novel approach to this redefinition — what she called "visible storage." Typically anthropologists studied artifacts in isolation, away from public view. Hawthorn's idea was to blur the boundary between academic study and the public viewing of art. Her approach changed policies regarding the public's accessibility to artifacts. It also influenced Erickson as the idea of making the artifacts visible "as art" became an important point of departure for the design team.

The ten-acre MOA site, situated between NW Marine Drive and Tower Beach on the UBC campus, was also Musqueam First Nations land. Perched on the cliffs high above the beach, the site afforded views of the North Shore Mountains, Howe Sound, and the Strait of Georgia. This prominent point had been a post for the Canadian military during World War II, which left behind one of the site's most interesting relics: three gun emplacements. An aerial view taken in 1943 shows these emplacements aligned in a row on the top of a long berm that traversed the site. Until the 1970s the site had accommodated student dormitories called Fort Camp. In addition to the residences were sports fields, mature stands of trees, and a rhododendron/woodland garden designed by the horticulturalist John Neill.

DESIGN PROCESS Oberlander was immersed in the design of Robson Square at Erickson's office when he approached her about working on MOA. He unfurled a preliminary sketch for the building and asked, "What would you do, Cornelia?"[18] Her response, "to express First Nations culture in the landscape," both intrigued Erickson and set her career on a new course. While Erickson's contribution would be a modern interpretation of First Nations West Coast architecture, Oberlander conceived the landscape as a place to offer visitors experiences with plant specimens valuable to the livelihood of the First Nations — a concept she would nurture over time and in many future projects. As Erickson later remarked, "Her idea of turning the forest into an ethnobotanical museum extended the museum into the landscape. It was a brilliant idea."[19]

In preparation for the project both Erickson and Oberlander attended an exhibition of Haida Nation art, organized by Audrey Hawthorn and the Haida artist Bill Reid. Although the Haida lived along the coastal bays and inlets of Haida Gwaii, a considerable distance north of Vancouver, Erickson and Oberlander decided early on that the project would take its inspiration from their art. Many attributes of Haida art appealed to their modern aesthetics. For one,

Aerial view showing gun emplacements at the UBC Museum of Anthropology site, 23 February 1943.

they admired the Haidas' robust handling of material. The rawness of the hewn wooden totem poles and the bold abstraction of figures contrasted with other examples of First Nations art, which tended to be more literal and fastidiously executed.

The Museum of Anthropology provided another opportunity for Oberlander to increase her knowledge of plant material and First Nations culture, as well as how the landscape might communicate ideas important to this culture — values deeply tied to the land. The project also presented a huge challenge since her design idea had entered uncharted territory in landscape architecture. Ethnobotanical gardens were practically unheard of in Canada at the time. Oberlander consulted the UBC archaeologist Charles Borden, who suggested she read *This Is Haida* (1968) by Anthony Lawrence Carter. The book featured colored photographs of Haida Gwaii, a landscape of abandoned villages, windswept shorelines, and dense dripping forests. Oberlander immediately focused on the vegetation in the photos, which contained long grasses, sand dune flowers, and golden spruce trees. While she was able to identify many of the plants, the grasses were unknown to her. It was highly unlikely that they could be found at a local nursery. Vernon "Bert" Brink, a UBC plant science professor, identified them and from there she created a custom seed mix for the MOA grass, a mix still used today. Oberlander also read Erna Gunther's *Ethnobotany of Western Washington: The Knowledge and Use of Indigenous Plants by Native Americans* (1945), which revealed how the different aboriginal cultures used vegetation in their daily lives. For example, "common fern were boiled to make cough syrup, and the pitch of the Douglas Fir was used on sores."[20] And she consulted Dr. Nancy Turner, who was conducting groundbreaking research on the use of plants by First Nation peoples on Vancouver Island.

Plant research was only one facet of the project; the site itself was to play a major role in determining the structure of the MOA building. As at Robson Square, the design team worked with 1:500 models, which included contours, major existing trees, neighboring buildings, roads, and parking. They decided that the building would be a low structure to maintain the dramatic vistas from the site and to preserve the view from NW Marine Drive, and that it would be set back 250 feet from the cliff edge. They also elected to save the gun emplacements that lined the site and to incorporate these elements into the overall design.[21] Referring to these artifacts, Erickson later noted, "We turned this obstacle into an opportunity, having worked out the size and relationship of the museum's various spaces."[22]

OVERALL CONCEPT The main goal of the MOA project was to give visitors an idea of life in the province before it was occupied by British and European settlers. In Erickson's words, they sought to "convey the idea to all of those who visit the Museum, and those who study in it that at one time, on this coast, there was a noble and great response to this land that has never been equaled since."[23] The seventy-thousand-square-foot museum was to be a modern interpretation of a Northwest Coast First Nations longhouse but given a green roof. The wooden post and lintel system associated with traditional longhouses was translated into a series of monumental precast-concrete columns and beams that terminated in the museum's Great Hall. The forty-five-foot-high glass room housing the largest of the First Nations carvings — giant mortuary totem poles, elegant canoes, and eating trains — allowed visitors to view the works under natural light, enhanced by a borrowed view of the landscape.[24]

LANDSCAPE STRATEGY The original landscape plan embodied two key features of the Northwest Coast First Nations culture — a coastal inlet and the plants important for cooking and medicinal use. A large reflecting pool and pebble beach represented the coastal inlet. The shoreline was an important landscape feature to First Nation peoples because it was the ideal location for their villages and totem poles, and the primary site for cooking.[25] Importantly, the reflecting pool also played a visual role. Views from the Great Hall melded the pool with the Burrard Inlet beyond. Outside, the landscape was mirrored in the glass façade while the pool's surface captured the building's image.

Given the museum's proximity to the busy NW Marine Drive, a series of large mounds planted with the Haida seed mix were configured to block roadway noise. Examples of the economy of Oberlander's work, these mounds and others in the project were realized by diverting soil excavated as part of the construction of Robson Square.[26] The mounds also syncopated people's movement through the site by revealing portions of the path and elements in a sequence intended to spark curiosity — a technique that she would more fully develop on the site later in 2009.

Oberlander designed a self-guided tour that brought together both Haida references and the site's more recent history. Starting at the west side of the building, a path of loose crushed stone, with simple split-log benches set along the way, leads visitors to one of the most endurable remnants of the site: the first of the three massive gun emplacements and a reminder of how close Vancouver was to the threat of war. The path continues through the ethnobotanical area, which features plants used for medical and nutritional purposes. Here mature maples, hemlocks, and cedar were preserved, trees vital to First Nations livelihoods. Ferns and mahonia were planted in the undergrowth of this area. First Nation peoples used the spores of ferns to make powders from which to heal wounds; the berries of the mahonia shrub were consumed raw or used in jellies and jams.[27]

This area opens to an area marked by the Haida complex, comprised of six totem poles and two Haida cedar-plank houses. Created by Reid and the Namgis artist Doug Cranmer between 1960 and 1962, these works replicate Haida dwellings of the nineteenth century. From the Haida complex the path leads visitors around the large reflecting pool, over a large grass mound — planted with Oberlander's seed mix — and to the third emplacement. The second emplacement is inside the museum and serves as the foundation for Bill Reid's sculpture *Raven and the First Men.*

While construction began later that year, the biggest hurdle for acceptance was the proposed water feature. Beginning with the first presentations of the project in the 1970s there were concerns that the reflecting pool would put added pressure on the eroding cliffs that loomed over Tower Beach below. Geologists were consulted however, and they attested that if erosion control was provided, the water would present no problems. The reflecting pool was, in fact, designed to lessen the conditions of the slope as it would capture rainwater and mitigate erosion from runoff.[28] Unfortunately neither the pool nor a majority of the ethnobotanically significant plants were realized in the first two decades of the project. Likewise, schemes for a planted roof were deemed too risky.

RECEPTION   The Museum of Anthropology opened on 30 May 1976 and attracted an international audience of politicians, artists, and scientists, including First Nation artists, then–prime minister Pierre Trudeau, and the celebrated anthropologist Margaret Mead. While many visitors and critics stood in awe of the architecture and the art it housed, they were unaware that the landscape lacked the reflecting pool and plantings. The realization of the landscape continued to plague Erickson and Oberlander over the next thirty years, prompting the art historian John Beardsley to call it the "thwarted masterpiece."[29] The university conducted further studies of the reflecting pool, and the threat of impending earthquakes was brought into the equation.[30] Despite these problems, MOA became one of Vancouver's primary tourist destinations, attracting approximately 180,000 visitors each year and offering programs to 15,000 schoolchildren."[31]

Over the years architectural critics debated the artistry of Erickson's building. There were concerns about the use of natural light in the museum and its low profile from NW Marine Drive.[32] However, many felt that the grand scale of the structure made it the first museum to begin "to do justice to the monumental aspects of Northwest Coast carving and spatial design."[33] Yet it was the museum context itself that incited most of the debate in anthropological and curatorial discourse. As a museum dedicated largely to First Nations cultures, the entire project was drawn into discussions that questioned the ethical implications of recontextualizing native cultures within the Western museum format.

On the one hand, critics viewed the creation of the museum as a paternalistic move that treated First Nations cultures as historical phenomena rather than living cultures. "Predicated on the concept of a dead or dying people whose culture needs to be 'saved,' those doing the saving choose what fragments of a culture they will salvage. Having done this, they become both the owners and interpreters of the artifacts."[34] On the other hand, some were impressed with the role that First Nation individuals and groups had played in the museum's conception. One UNESCO publication, for example, applauded MOA for working directly with the First Nation artists and representatives, emphasizing "a dynamic and the changing, rather than the definitive, situation."[35]

However, the most salient critique came from the Musqueam Band, who resented the emphasis on Haida art and culture. While MOA sat on traditional Musqueam land, a Haida dwelling and non-Musqueam totem poles featured prominently in the landscape, and Gitxsan artists had carved the museum's front doors. For the Musqueam Band, this not only demonstrated a disregard for their traditional land but also exemplified the collective grouping of First Nation peoples as "other" to Western culture. Oberlander's landscape was not drawn into this controversy; however, by 2010 when she returned to create the pool, she also revised the planting scheme to address the concerns of the Musqueam Band.

2009–10 EXPANSION During the intervening years Oberlander returned to the museum to consult on planting and the reflecting pool. Since its opening she has overseen the temporary filling of the pool three times — for the 1993 filming of the movie *Intersection,* for the Asia-Pacific Economic Cooperation leaders' summit in 1997, and for Erickson's eightieth birthday in June 2004. Twenty-one years after opening its doors, MOA expanded its display area and created a cafeteria and the new Centre for Cultural Research, containing staff offices and laboratories; the Audrey and Harry Hawthorn Library and Archives; and a new courtyard. These additions brought an extensive revamping of the landscape, which had fallen prey to university maintenance practices. It also resulted in the construction of a permanent reflecting pool. Under Oberlander's daily supervision, excavations, regrading, and sealing of the pool began in the summer of 2010. The original subsurface was removed and filled with sand and gravel, and coated with bentonite, a natural material that expands when wet and self-seals when punctured. The shape and depth of the pool matched those

Wosk Reflecting Pool echoing
Haida Village and totem poles at
the UBC Museum of Anthropology,
Vancouver, 2011. Landscape
Architect: Cornelia Hahn Oberlander.
Architect: Arthur Erickson.

specified by Oberlander in the original 1975 drawings. In honor of its benefactor, it was named the Yosef Wosk Reflecting Pool, and it officially opened on 9 September 2010.

The museum also made an effort to incorporate the local Musqueam Band into its daily operations. For example, Musqueam leaders now officiate at the openings of new events and exhibits on a regular basis. Likewise the new Reciprocal Research Network, which involves both First Nation communities and researchers, has created an online database of the collection, enabling objects to be virtually viewed and researched. Oberlander also addressed concerns of the Musqueam Band in her revised planting plans. She expanded the self-guided tour from the pool by wrapping the main path around a series of mounds culminating at the new courtyard. Here, Oberlander paid tribute directly to the Musqueam Band. Musqueam, or m-uh-th-kwi, means people of the river grass. Thus at the courtyard and surrounding the new additions she planted horsetail, a plant found in wet forests and on the peripheries of lakes, rivers, and ponds common to the Musqueam territory. The Musqueam people used the tips of the plant in their basketwork and the plant's long vascular stems, which have a high silica content when dried, were used for polishing.[36] While her ethno-botanical garden was never part of the official research or educational agenda of the museum, the framing of the horsetail in the central courtyard draws attention to this unusual-looking plant and to the people to whom it refers.[37]

The Museum of Anthropology set a new course in Oberlander's career as she began to use the composition and materials of her landscapes to express ideas about culture, art, and the environment. The National Gallery of Canada presented another opportunity where she explored the communicative potential of gardens and how the Canadian landscape has shaped and elaborated ideas about contemporary art. The project also invited a greater scrutiny of her work as the gallery was a part of the highly volatile context of civic projects undertaken in Ottawa, the nation's capital.

National Gallery of Canada

Since its inception a succession of directors of the National Gallery of Canada have lobbied for a permanent home. For most of the twentieth century the gallery was housed in temporary quarters, often in spaces designed for other purposes and unsuitable for viewing art. Architectural competitions were held in 1954 and 1976; however, they did not yield a building. After numerous wrangles over the need for a national gallery, its artistic direction, and where it should be situated in Ottawa, a new building and location were approved in 1982.[38] The site was a parking lot for the National War Museum, but it was also adjacent to a cliff-top open space overlooking the Ottawa River called Nepean Point.[39]

Despite the banality of its former use, the art critic Douglas Ord noted that the site completed an "architectural round" between the Notre Dame Cathedral Basilica to the northeast and Parliament Hill to the southwest — a position between the orders of the law and those of the spirit.[40] The gallery's site also lay on the ceremonial route (called The Mile of History) passing from the prime minister's and the governor-general's residences to the Houses of Parliament, past the Chateau Laurier, Major's Hill Park, the United States Embassy, and the Notre Dame Cathedral Basilica. This iconic location further established the public presence of art at a national scale.[41]

Between 1982 and 1983 funding for construction was secured from Trudeau's government, and the Canadian Museum Construction Corporation was formed to oversee its construction. The former National Gallery director Jean Sutherland Boggs chaired the corporation. After a limited competition, Moshe Safdie was selected as architect, in association with John Parkin and Associates, who had won the competition for the gallery in the 1970s. Oberlander was selected as the landscape architect. The Safdie and Oberlander team was an interesting choice given the gallery's latest acquisitions. Under the directorship of Boggs, the National Gallery steadily amassed a major collection of contemporary art, from paintings by Picasso to Andy Warhol's *Brillo Boxes*. In some ways Safdie was an odd choice as the building's architect because he did not consider Picasso's or Andy Warhol's work to be art.[42] His taste for painting and sculpture resided in eras before the twentieth century. Oberlander, in contrast, eagerly embraced twentieth-century modern art. These diverse attitudes would shape their individual design responses to the gallery project.

DESIGN PROCESS As he had been for the Canadian Chancery project, then–prime minister Trudeau was directly involved in the initial stages of the gallery's development, a participation that would have unfortunate consequences in the building's realization.[43] The design was fast-tracked due to the growing "climate of anti-intellectualism and neo-conservatism" and the project's association with the Trudeau Liberal government, which lasted only until September 1984.[44] Fast-tracking meant a rapid design-development process, with construction beginning before the design and documentation phases had been fully completed. According to the architectural journalist Trevor Boddy, fast-tracking was injurious to the design process and ultimately the built result because it broke the process down into discrete segments of design work that constrained the ability to address the project as a whole.[45]

This segmented approach is reflected in the project drawings that record the process at the Cornelia Hahn Oberlander Archive in the Canadian Centre for Architecture. Most drawings depict only portions of the building and landscape, as if they had been conceived in isolation. Despite this limitation, the drawings indicate an important change in Oberlander's practice. During the early 1980s Oberlander began to hire landscape architects to work in her office. In 1983 she hired Elisabeth Whitelaw, who would become Oberlander's long-time associate. From this point onward, Whitelaw's delicate hand drawings, often rendered in color pencil, represented an aesthetic that complemented Oberlander's own distinct black-and-white drafted drawings.

Changes in both the federal government and the economic recession of the mid-1980s erected extra hurdles for the design team. In 1984 the conservative government was voted in and the National Gallery project was chastised as a symbol of Liberal excess and a waste of public tax dollars. As a consequence Boggs was fired, the Canadian Museum Construction Corporation was dissolved, and the management of the museum's construction was handed over to the Department of Public Works.[46] These shifting power struggles incited additional reviews, budget cuts, and, in some cases, extensive revisions. Oberlander's design for the entrance garden, for example, received extra scrutiny as it did not resemble landscapes typical of Ottawa's urban landscape.

OVERALL CONCEPT The overall design concept for the National Gallery sought to reinforce Trudeau's desire for a national capital where "the institutions of culture and art have been given equal importance to the institutions of governance."[47] Given the gallery's privileged position along the ceremonial Mile of History, and Safdie's dislike of modern art, the building reflected the Gothic Revival of the parliament buildings, particularly its library.[48] In contrast, Oberlander gravitated to the gallery's contemporary works, which she thought better expressed the character of a modern nation. In addition to its official mandate, the National Gallery was also conceived as part of the social and leisure life of Ottawa. Thus the building's internal organization attempted to reflect "the organizational pattern of a city" with a sequence of street-like galleries and piazza-like spaces, courtyards, and gardens.[49] Oberlander's landscape extended this concept outdoors by creating a pathway system that connected the front of the National Gallery to Nepean Point behind the gallery. She also took the concept a step further in her landscape strategy by relating to the modern art that the gallery housed.

LANDSCAPE STRATEGY Oberlander designed three major exterior areas for the National Gallery and one interior courtyard. Each area evoked a subject of the twentieth-century art displayed immediately indoors. Given the nature of the fast-track process this helped unify her design. Oberlander also took advantage of the fact that construction was taking place during the design phase. This situation informed her concept for the main entrance garden, later called Taiga. Her initial reaction to the construction site was that "it was a found landscape." She goes on, "I discovered when digging for soil depth that the area was covered with flat rocks, so I exposed them and repositioned others — some weighing as much as 10 tons — that had been excavated during the construction."[50] Using the existing bedrock, like chunks of the Canadian Shield, required some convincing before it was accepted. As Oberlander notes, "For four years, the National Capital Commission said 'How do you know there are rocks down there?' And I took the hose from the fire hydrant and exposed them. And they were exactly where I said."[51]

This rock provided the literal and figurative foundation for the Taiga Garden. Taken from the Russian term *taiga*, the Taiga Shield is located between the country's tundra and temperate forests. It is dominated by conifers, mainly spruce and fir, and represents a major forest ecozone in North America. Oberlander also selected plants from this northern terrain. She consulted Friedrich Oehmichen, a landscape architect, horticulturalist, and honorary professor at l'Université de Montréal, regarding species selection. With poetry, he recommended that she select vegetation that would entice people to inspect plants closely. In 1986 he wrote to her: "I may even say enchanted beauty is only revealed to the searching eye at a close-up position, forcing the observer literally on his knees to get the appropriate perspective."[52] In response to this invitation, Oberlander selected bog cranberry, wild strawberries, Canadian cinquefoil, and kinnikinnick — a ground cover whose tiny but colorful flowers and berries demand closer attention. Tatarian dogwood, blue iris, rosemary, wild red-leaf rose, wild grasses, and Austrian pines and mugo pines completed the palette. Oberlander was directly involved in the installation of vegetation on-site. Plants such as the dogwood, blue iris, and kinnikinnick were planted in the cracks and veins of the carefully laid rock. Mugo pines were installed at an angle to give a windswept appearance.[53]

The Taiga Garden flanks the gallery's interior glass-and-concrete colonnade that leads to the Canadian and Aboriginal Art galleries. Oberlander sought to express Canadian art in this garden. She looked to the Group of Seven artist A. Y. Jackson's *Terre Sauvage* (1913) in particular. This oil-on-canvas painting depicted a cloudy sky and coniferous trees arising from a rocky ground. The Group of Seven, whose paintings are featured in the National Gallery, painted the rugged terrain of Canada's wild landscapes to both challenge the genteel art informed by older European tastes and cultivate a national identity.[54]

What would become the minimalist garden, located between the National Gallery, National War Museum, and Sussex Drive, looked quite different in

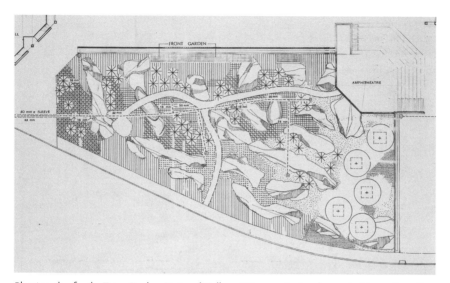

Planting plan for the Taiga Garden, National Gallery, Ottawa, 1985. Landscape Architect: Cornelia Hahn Oberlander. Architects: Moshe Safdie, Parkin/Safdie Architects Planners.

the initial drawings released to the public in November 1983, which depicted a rectangular grass area whose formality was more reflective of the baronial war museum.[55] Later designs demonstrated a greater affinity with the gallery's modern art collection. Oberlander's final scheme, the Minimalist Courtyard, referred to the art of Donald Judd and Carl Andre featured inside. Her design, employing only one type of tree and ground surface, featured twelve flowering crab apples positioned twelve feet on-center and set within a court of crushed grey gravel. Minimalism, with its emphasis on effacing the author's interpretation, invited the spectator to construct the meaning of the work and to see everyday elements "anew."[56] Thus, it was Oberlander's goal to distill the basic phenomena of the landscape and direct people's attention to their own experience of the trees and their changing form, light, color, and texture — as they did with the art in the gallery.

A pedestrian sequence, which also expresses the art that surrounds it, connects Sussex Drive to the spectacular views afforded by Nepean Point behind the gallery. Oberlander's Pin Oak Allée starts at Sussex Drive, passes between the National War Museum and the new gallery, and emerges at Nepean Point as the Op-Art Path. The shape of this path witnessed numerous iterations in form, from angular to sinuous, with the final incarnation taking shape as a zigzag.

Path alternatives, National
Gallery, Ottawa, 1985.
Landscape Architect:
Cornelia Hahn Oberlander.
Architects: Moshe Safdie,
Parkin/Safdie Architects
Planners.

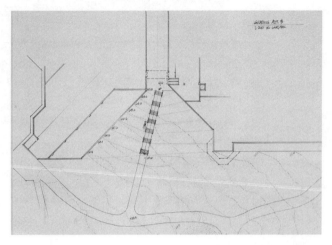

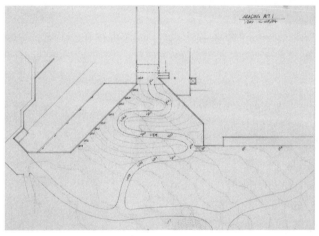

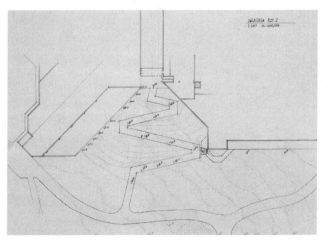

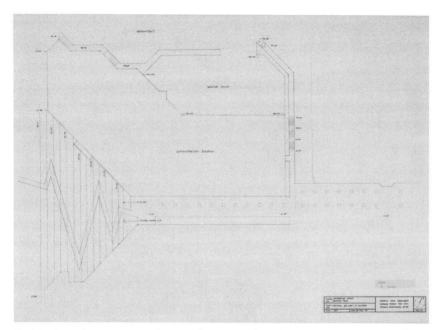

Final Op-Art Path, circa 1985. Landscape Architect: Cornelia Hahn Oberlander. Architects: Moshe Safdie, Parkin/Safdie Architects Planners.

The zigzag path directs views with different lines of vision to the gallery and eventually across the Ottawa River. Underscoring the play of mental representations and bodily movement during encounters with op-art, the path makes tangible how appearances change with one's vantage point.

Oberlander's design for the interior courtyard was a departure from the exterior gardens inspired by genres of modern art. The courtyard served as a forecourt to the restored nineteenth-century Rideau Chapel that was relocated inside the National Gallery. Here, Oberlander planted fig trees and ferns on a diagonal in contrast to a mass planting of red geraniums. Illuminated by natural light from the skylights above, the courtyard provided a reflective space that echoed the "monastic simplicity" of early churches in Canada.[57]

RECEPTION The National Gallery opened on 21 May 1988; a year later Oberlander's design received a Regional and National Award from the Canadian Society of Landscape Architects. Safdie's interpretation of gothic architecture in glass and steel stimulated heated debates by both architectural critics and the public. At the same time it was noted that the National Gallery's fractured fast-track design process led to a gallery that felt more like a series of separate buildings. There was also controversy over the collection as well. While acquisitions made under Boggs's term raised alarm, there was also a concern that recent acquisitions were now too safe. Indeed, many artists thought the gallery's role as an educator was limited to "those works safely historical with a cast iron integrity bestowed by the art historian."[58]

Oberlander's entrance garden caused debate as well. Douglas Ord proposed that the Taiga Garden provided "the National Gallery's first art reference."[59] While Charles Oberdorf expressed in the *Toronto Star* that Oberlander's landscape design *was* art, remarking that the garden "captured the mystic essence of the taiga. Hers is as much a work of art as any in the building next to it. As visitors on those concrete stairs look out to that rugged, indomitable terrain, she reveals to them this country's soul."[60] Other critics were skeptical about the appropriateness of the Taiga Garden or the idea that any garden could be art. Ord also thought the interpretation of *Terre Sauvage* was too loose, with pines replacing the painting's black spruce trees, and limestone replacing the granite shield.[61] Likewise, the architectural critic Lisa Rochon noted that A. Y. Jackson's trees were "permanently bent" in the painting, a feature difficult to replicate in the three-dimensional garden in Ottawa.[62]

However, it is important to remember that Oberlander's gardens are not literal references — something her critics often miss. Never drawn to historical fantasy, at the National Gallery Oberlander made reference to the *way* these art genres work. The Group of Seven's images of uncultivated Canadian wilderness challenged traditional European art that had been imposed on Canadian culture. The Taiga Garden works in the same way. Oberlander's refusal to design a prescribed path in the garden is an invitation to wander through its craggy recesses and pause on the exposed rock that serves as informal seating. Indeed, its wildness starkly contrasts with Ottawa's neat and tidy lawns and floral displays — another European tradition. Thus the Taiga Garden works the *way* the Group of Seven art does, by challenging the conventional landscapes commonly found in North American capital cities.

POSTCONSTRUCTION The National Gallery attracts thousands of visitors every year and it is a rite of passage for many Canadians visiting Ottawa. The landscape around the gallery has received numerous sculptural interventions over the years. In 2005 Louise Bourgeois's spider sculpture *Maman* was installed at the gallery's entrance, and in 2010 Oberlander was consulted to site Roxy Paine's *One Hundred Foot Line*, a stainless steel sculpture reminiscent of a soaring tree trunk that reaches ten stories. The work was originally slated for the Taiga Garden, but Oberlander found a better location — on the grassy slope leading to Nepean Point, between the Op-Art Path and the statue of Samuel de Champlain. This was an ideal location because the sculpture creates a single vertical line that counterbalances the vast horizontal expanse of the Ottawa River. Oberlander is currently in preliminary discussions with the National Gallery to design a permanent sculpture garden.

In 1989 Oberlander returned to Ottawa to design the landscape for the Ottawa City Hall, with Moshe Safdie as architect. And in 1990, with the architect Richard Henriquez and the sculptor Jack Harmon, she won the competition to design the UN Peacekeeping Memorial, situated between the National Gallery and the United States Embassy. Completed in 1993, the memorial commemorates Canada's longtime commitment to peacekeeping efforts around the world. The memorial comprised a trio of bronze cast figures poised atop slabs of granite with inscriptions attesting to the Canadian commitment to peace. Oberlander not only provided the planting scheme for the main monument area but also designed an oval grove of twelve oak trees representing Canada's ten provinces and two territories (Nunavut would not become separate from the Northwest Territories until 1999).

With four publically funded major projects completed — Robson Square, the Museum of Anthropology, the Canadian Chancery, and the National Gallery of Canada — and with her growing interest in the ecological and communicative potential of landscape architecture, Oberlander returned to public work in Vancouver. By the 1990s Vancouver's intensive tower development in the downtown core had produced an urban enclave of high-density housing with ample open spaces and civic amenities, described by American planners as "Vancouverism."

For Oberlander, however, this planning model did not live up to its potential. From her perspective, dense building and ample open spaces were insufficient. The building and landscape needed to function together ecologically — and landscapes could accommodate and express this relationship. Certainly at this point in her career she was well poised to incorporate this idea into Vancouver's urban fabric, and she began with Library Square.

Library Square

Established in 1887, the Vancouver Public Library occupied several locations until 1957, when Semmens & Simpson designed a new facility at Burrard and Robson Streets. By the late 1980s the library, which was designed to hold 750,000 volumes, was overflowing with more than 1 million. A flood in 1988 and the structure's failure to meet seismic standards further exacerbated the need for a new building. In the summer of 1989 the Vancouver Public Library Board commissioned a $300,000 study that assessed community needs, which led to a November 1990 referendum in which 69 percent of voters supported the construction of a new central library.[63]

This tremendous public support, coupled with Vancouver's dot-com growth in the early 1990s, compelled the city to build not only a library but also a major mixed-use development with office spaces for the provincial and federal government. Like Robson Square, the project was to serve as a catalyst for further development in the eastern sector of Vancouver's urban core. Unlike Robson Square, this project would not be a skyscraper turned on its side. Vancouver's recently adopted density bonus transfer system permitted buildings to be constructed above the current zoning restrictions in exchange for the development of parks, community centers, and other amenity projects. The architect Chris MacDonald points out that Library Square represented an early example of the city block–scaled, mixed-use development approved under this system.[64]

The board studied forty-four sites and selected Block 56, a parking lot owned by the federal government. Located between W. Georgia, Robson, Hamilton, and Homer Streets, it was ideally situated between the downtown core and the new and planned sports and entertainment complexes to the south. In September 1991 the City of Vancouver launched a three-stage competition for the selection of the project's designers. The competition brief challenged competitors to integrate a major civic structure with a large office building that was "inviting and transparent."[65] The short-listed teams were interviewed and asked to submit a written proposal and make a formal presentation to the selection committee.[66] The three finalists were invited to create conceptual designs presented in drawings and three-dimensional models that would be shown to the public.

DESIGN PROCESS Oberlander was instrumental in forming the team with Moshe Safdie, faxing him a copy of the call for qualifications, and writing in capital letters — WE MUST ENTER! Safdie asked that she work exclusively with him, to which she agreed, but this precluded her working with Arthur Erickson.[67] Oberlander was very familiar with the site and knew there was a grade change of 20 feet across the block. Any solution would need to address this slope. According to Oberlander, an important formal and technical problem was devising a building footprint that gracefully accommodated this significant grade change.[68] They comprised one of eight teams shorted-listed, and eventually they ranked among the top three. Initially Oberlander and Safdie sent ideas to each other by fax, but eventually they worked in person, collaborating with the local architectural firm Downs/Archambault & Partners. At the time, the computer had just come to play an important role in the design process. The team's working method produced drawings that alternated between sketches on trace and computer renditions of various schemes. Once a design on trace reached a definitive stage, one of Safdie's associates would model it in the computer to produce different perspective views. The printouts of these views were then traced over to make changes, with corresponding adjustments made to their digital renditions.[69]

As on the National Gallery project, the design for the library was to expand the public realm within the structure. In response Oberlander broadened this basic idea by bringing the publically accessible spaces to the rooftop.[70] And as they did on the National Gallery, the design team considered the communicative potential of the built work. Given that library use provided the main program, they explored the architectural language of structures housing resources for public use. After the team had devised eighteen different designs, they settled on a concept that entailed an elliptical colonnaded wall wrapping a core structure that gracefully handled the change in slope. Atop this structure they proposed an amphitheater and public garden.[71]

For five weeks the conceptual drawings and models, accompanied by public questionnaires, were on display at various locations throughout the city. The three short-listed projects were mandated by the Architectural Institute of British Columbia guidelines to remain anonymous; thus the schemes were labeled A, B, and C.[72] While public input was not binding, the outcomes were shared with the professional jury who made the ultimate decision.[73] Proposal C clearly captivated the public's imagination and received the most attention from the press. While many critics chided the proposed building for resembling the Colosseum in Rome — or as "somewhere between a joke and a folly"— it was the only design to generate any enthusiasm.[74] A writer for *Canadian Architect* underscored that "the result of the vote shows how precise is the architects' understanding of the city's Zeitgeist; Vancouver is a branch plant town with head office aspirations."[75] People were particularly captivated by the rooftop garden, which "promised an outdoor gathering space, and offered views of the city for all."[76] Proposal C "emerged as the clear public favorite, with the support of 70 percent of the more than 7,000 public ballots submitted."[77]

Public input was accompanied by reviews conducted by the city's Urban Design Panel, the Library User Advisory Committee, and a technical advisory committee. The evaluations helped inform the jury to make recommendations to City Council, which would make the final decision on the winning scheme. On 14 April 1992 Proposal C was declared the winner and described as "not just a repository for books but also a place for people."[78] Oberlander's team had won but there was a substantive battle ahead. Like most competitions, changes ensued once further design work commenced. These changes included relocating the tower and reducing the extent of the rooftop garden. The team met throughout the spring and summer of 1992 at Downs/Archambault & Partners, which was charged with the design development and preparation of construction documents.

OVERALL CONCEPT A key goal of the design was to link the main branch library, federal office tower, childcare facilities, rooftop garden, and retail and service facilities with a major public interior space. A five-story public concourse would house these diverse programs and give a civic identity to the city. The public concourse would accommodate the grade change between Robson and W. Georgia Streets and also provide a route for pedestrians cutting across the block, thus connecting the project to the urban fabric.

Given the relationship between the public library as a source of knowledge and a dependency on civic knowledge to keep society just, transparency was a major theme that informed the design of Library Square. Particular attention was paid to the visual exchange between the library and the retail spaces, using glazing that enabled library patrons to look down to the retail spaces below, and from the concourse to the library. There was also an attempt to make the building's infrastructure — air ducts, sprinkler piping, cable trays, and wiring — visible from the main concourse.[79]

The act of collecting written documents and records for borrowing can be traced back to Mesopotamia and this history prompted consideration of architectural forms appropriated, quite literally, from classical idioms. According to Safdie, Library Square was "to give 'a tradition-less Vancouver a sense of memory tied to classical ideas of learning and scholarship' by creating a sense of civic identity."[80] The library's exterior shell was designed with a four-tiered precast-concrete colonnade that coiled around the main building. Initial schemes for the rooftop garden explored classical forms, such as the amphitheater, but by 1992 the rooftop garden itself was in jeopardy.

GARDEN CONTROVERSY While the public garden and amphitheater had been integral to Proposal C's concept from the beginning, major changes to the building design affected the size and program of the roof. The addition of a two-story shell space for future expansion drastically reduced the garden's dimensions and the realization of an amphitheater an unlikelihood. There was growing concern over maintenance and particularly supervision of the garden if made public. The librarians feared that patrons would leave books outside in the garden only to be damaged by the elements, or throw the books from the roof, potentially killing someone. The fact that federal offices occupied the upper tower floors also put public access to the roof in jeopardy. Some critics even thought that given Vancouver's rainy weather, a rooftop would rarely be used.

Citing these misgivings, the Vancouver City Council voted unanimously that the roof garden would be off-limits to the public. Safdie and Oberlander wrote letters contesting the vote. In a letter to the Facilities Development manager, Safdie wrote, "Given the enormous public interest in the roof garden its deletion signals a lack of credibility in the public process."[81] But the council's decision prevailed and the director of the library confessed that she "did not regret its loss other than sympathizing with Moshe and Cornelia's vision of what could have been."[82] These alterations to the garden did not go unnoticed by the public, who were informed that the council would not revisit the prospect of an accessible rooftop garden for at least twenty years.[83] As one *Vancouver Magazine* journalist disparaged, "It's a fair guess that the rooftop garden so invitingly displayed on Safdie's original model played a role in winning the hearts of Vancouverites," but it was not to be.[84]

LANDSCAPE STRATEGY Oberlander began her redesign of the roof garden with a twofold objective: to create an ecological model for greening tower structures and to express this in a design visible from the adjacent buildings and provincial government offices that rose above it.[85] Initially there was little recognition of the roof's contribution to the ecological functioning of the building in relationship to the urban environment. However, "Oberlander was quick to point out that green roofs are more than just nice things to look at. They compensate for the hole that urban development creates."[86] She conceived the thirty-three-thousand-square-foot roof as a water retention vehicle that stored and delayed storm water, and at the same time reduced the building's heating and cooling requirements.[87] Oberlander had pioneered Canadian on-structure plantings at Robson Square; years later Library Square now gave her the opportunity to use new membrane systems, root barriers, and lightweight soil mixes. These technical improvements enabled her to grow fifteen-foot-tall maples in only fourteen inches of growing medium.

In her redesign Oberlander avoided heavy-handed classical imagery. While Safdie's office proposed a "tartan pattern" of planting for the roof, Oberlander instead made reference to the Fraser River — British Columbia's longest watercourse.[88] The river's alluvial plains feature in the region's history as the site of one of the earliest recorded First Nation settlements. During the nineteenth century it was the primary route between the lower mainland and the interior when lands south of the 49th Parallel were made part of the United States. In reference to this hydrological system, Oberlander composed sixteen thousand blue and green fescue grass plugs in a meandering swath around the central light well. The blue fescue referred to the river while an outlying band of the green fescue referenced the Fraser's alluvial grasslands. A third band consisted of twenty-six thousand kinnikinnick ground cover plants representing higher ground.

Oberlander also consulted on Library Square's street-level spaces. To differentiate the threshold between the south-facing plaza and the intersection of Robson and Homer Streets, curving lines echoing the arcade were designed for greater social use. The wall circling the plaza also provided a ramp and stairs that facilitated access for those in wheeled vehicles — and doubled as an impromptu amphitheater. At the building's southeast edge one can discern iterations of Robson Square: terraces with integral plantings of cascading roses. Along the streets bordering the site, Oberlander selected tulip trees, except on W. Georgia Street where the city required maples. The library's northwest entrance was less successful as Oberlander's planting scheme for the area was drastically reduced due to budget constraints.

RECEPTION On 26 May 1995 more than 1,300 people attended the official opening of Library Square. While speeches and music were appreciative of the finished work, UBC architecture students dressed in togas to protest the emphasis on classical motifs in lieu of West Coast architectural traditions.[89] A hardhat tour and Operation Bookworm preceded the opening with 7,000 volunteers parading the last of the ten thousand books relocated from the old library on Burrard Street to the new building. There followed a weeklong celebration of events including author readings, children's story time, and a gala benefit for the library's capital campaign.

The public was clearly disappointed that the roof garden was deemed off-limits. As one journalist observed, "The only disappointment for those taking Wednesday's first non-hardhat tour of the building is that the small roof garden will be off limits to the public — at least for the next 15 years. That's when the provincial government's lease on the top two floors will run out and the library can expand upward."[90] In fact the only public knowledge of the garden was the erection of a small information board inside the library that tells part of the garden's story: "Here it is what it looks like, but you can't see it."[91]

Unlike at Robson Square's Block 61, people seemed to like working in the new Library Square, particularly the librarians who had played a central role in the project's development. Five years after its opening, the chief librarian and staff stressed their satisfaction with the building.[92] Although the library's collection was essentially unchanged from the old central branch, after Library Square's opening patronage more than doubled, averaging well over 10,000 people per day. Vancouverites also seemed to be profiting from the transparency of the building. According to one librarian, "People race to get desks along the walls so they can look out over the city."[93]

Architectural reviews of the project focused largely on the exterior of the building and "its Coliseum-like form which was seen as an inapt trope" that ignored its location in Vancouver.[94] Architects cringed at its historical literalism, and its uncanny resemblance to the Roman icon.[95] Yet, as Rhodri Windsor-Liscombe pointed out, "There exist significant iconographic variations between the Roman original and the Vancouver edifice."[96] However Witold Rybczynski, visiting in 1996, confessed that "the first impression that the building makes is unmistakable: the Roman Colosseum."[97] Safdie would spend the rest of his career maintaining that the resemblance was unintentional. But there were more serious critiques regarding the structure's disconnect between the internal workings of the building and its external appearance. In *Architectural Review* it was noted that "the library itself, which is a comparatively simple, modest, rectangular building[,] is completely concealed from the outside by the over-blown cardboard stage set. Perhaps there is something to be said for working from the inside outwards after all."[98]

There was even less agreement on the success of the project's relationship to the urban context. While *Canadian Architect* found the "failure to integrate the components of the architectural parti accompanies the failure of the project to integrate with its context,"[99] architectural journalists, such as Trevor Boddy, observed that the "social logic of his bridge-like entrance walkway made sense to me for the first time. By limiting space, by pushing people together inside the city's largest single room, the architect makes Vancouverites interact."[100] Approaching Library Square from Robson Street, the large aperture created by the wrapped colonnade is inviting and in warm weather throngs of people occupy the impromptu amphitheater. Yet, from W. Georgia Street the building casts a deep shade over a large expanse of undifferentiated ground plane, giving quite the opposite effect.

SECRET GARDEN The rooftop garden that has thrived during the intervening years remains off-limits to the public. Despite concerns about maintenance, the grasses require no fertilization or extensive care. They have been raked once a year at the end of the winter.[101] The garden also fulfilled many of Ober-lander's goals. The plants matured and have taken form as a tapestry of color and texture enjoyed from the surrounding office towers. The garden has also contributed to the building's energy efficiency. Ten years after its completion a one-year storm-water-runoff monitoring program of the garden was completed; it revealed a "48% reduction in runoff volume" and a reduction of peak flows during summer storm events.[102]

Inconveniently accessed only by a ladder and trap door from the building's upper floors, the garden eventually became a secret garden. Oberlander has in-spected it regularly and has led tours with small groups of people — often other landscape architects, architects, or visiting journalists. Travis Dudfield, stand-ing "ankle-deep in wind-whipped grass," was particularly taken with the rooftop garden's carelessly romantic feel: "After spending over an hour on the roof and seeing Vancouver from this elevated vantage point, I realized the roof's real purpose and why those who know about it are so enamoured with it: It is only when you are standing in something alive that the sublime vistas we often take for granted become truly accessible."[103]

By sheer word of mouth people began to take note of this hidden treasure. Aerial views of the garden began to appear in advertising about Vancouver. In a 2004 essay for the *New York Times Magazine* Jane Jacobs declared that "there is no better place to look than Vancouver, where a partnership with nature is altering the urban skyline," and she mentioned both the Robson Square and the Library Square green roofs as examples of this partnership.[104] The year 2005 marked the garden's tenth anniversary. Carrying a cake in one hand, Oberlander ascended the ladder to the roof to celebrate the garden's success with a small group of friends. While it might not be a popular sentiment, the garden's prime appeal may be due to the fact that it is secret. The uninterrupted field of blowing grasses lends it a wild quality, a condition that, given the roof's size, would be difficult to attain with paving, benches, and the other accouterments conventionally demanded for public spaces.

Plans are afoot to redesign the garden, however. Yosef Wosk, who funded the filling of the Museum of Anthropology reflecting pool, has begun fund-raising for a "Literary Sky Garden." For Wosk, the new garden would celebrate the multicultural aspect of Vancouver by creating individual gardens that showcase each cultural group. For example, the English would be represented by a rose garden with a passage from Shakespeare displayed nearby. While Oberlander has not publically commented on this idea, it will certainly be a challenge to represent all the mixed and diverse cultures of Vancouver in garden form. The literalness of the concept will surely invite criticism — the essential or genuine character of a culture is not always easy to ascertain.

Most salient, Library Square added another layer to Oberlander's career, one that emphasized the ecological and infrastructural function of the landscape. This is paramount in the decades following Library Square as a growing awareness of climate change and other environmental crises shape the design and discourse of landscape architecture. Ultimately, this awareness has increased the need for measuring the ecological performance of landscapes. Oberlander would bring this thinking to the C. K. Choi building project, and then to Northern Canada with her design work for the Northwest Territories Legislative Assembly in Yellowknife, and a combined primary and secondary school in Inuvik.

Ecological Infrastructure

The decades of the 1990s and 2000s witnessed crises caused by numerous natural disasters, energy shortages, terrorism, and war, as well as global economic recession. These events sharpened political disputes over the fate of the natural environment. Numerous studies, as well as a film and world tour by the former U.S. vice president Al Gore, warned how the planet's climate was changing at an unprecedented rate. Awareness of global warming has a noteworthy history in Canada. During the nineteenth century the British tried to ameliorate Canada's cold climate by burning its overbearingly vast forests. This decision was based on the theory of "climatic progress," which held that cold temperatures could be moderated by burning the forests. Unfortunately, the haste to warm the country had devastating consequences. In 1825 one-quarter of the province of New Brunswick was burned to the ground by a runaway fire. Nonetheless, as late as 1862 the *New York Evening Post* enthusiastically reported that this destruction of the province's forests had abated the severity of cold temperatures and that winters had been shortened by two months.[105]

Without doubt this attitude has changed. The increased awareness of the global environment has also led to a renewed interest in the metropolis as a locus for ecological design. While Ian McHarg vilified the city and endorsed low-density housing as the desired vehicle for his ecological method, by the 1990s low-density single-family housing had become increasingly associated with sprawl and greater car dependency. Moreover, the diffusion of the single-function infrastructure — highways and power lines among them — generated by suburban sprawl created increased ecological disturbances.

Although many of the projects designed under the aegis of New Urbanism were not located in cities, the reduction in car-dependent settlement patterns and the increase in networked open spaces produced potent ideas for rendering existing urban centers more livable. Architects, in particular, began to see buildings not as discrete, isolated objects but as units tied to the larger systems governing energy, water, air, and light. Landscapes provided the ecological infrastructure. Using their knowledge of natural systems, landscape architects designed landscape features with high ecological value, such as wetlands, as a functioning component of the urban ecosystem.

While landscape architects have been more environmentally aware since the 1960s, the rise of a global ecological consciousness has directed every decision in the design process towards reducing impacts. Terms such as "ecological footprint" and "carbon neutral" became concepts central to designing and evaluating the performance of a designed landscape. Likewise, green rating systems and best practices manuals, such as LEED and the Living Building Challenge, were adopted from architecture to calculate the energy and environmental performance standards of landscape architecture projects. Moreover, landscape architects developed their own toolkits, assessment packages, checklists, and modeling software to predict the impact of their designs.

Implicit in these measures was the goal to create landscapes that enhanced ecological functioning. These tasks supported and improved ecological processes, such as water filtration, nutrient recycling, wildlife movement, and food sources for human and nonhuman life. Since ecological functions are the underlying building blocks of natural habitats, this knowledge expanded the concerns addressed by each design task. Likewise enthusiasm for the ecological contribution of landscapes gave birth to a wealth of subgroups, such as native plant societies and xeriscape associations, who pledged to uphold the ecological merit of new designs and existing environments.

CHANGES IN LANDSCAPE AESTHETICS

Ultimately these shifts in practice also affected the appearance of landscapes. Ornamental shrubs and imported vegetation selected primarily for their color, texture, and form were increasingly replaced by plants identified as more fully contributing to habitat, water filtration, or low water use. Thus ecological performance trumped plant selection based only on appearance. As we know, function was a hallmark of modern landscape architecture. Half a century ago Norman Newton predicted that only if biological, mechanical, assigned, and affective functions were included in landscape architectural design did "our approach deserve to be called functional design."[106] Consequently, our reading of this function was equally important.

In her influential article "Messy Ecosystems, Orderly Frames," Joan Iverson Nassauer asserts that the reading and interpretation of ecologically valuable landscapes posed challenges. The visual appearance of many ecologically important landscapes and wildlife habitats often violated cultural norms, which tended to place high value on neatness and conformity. Hardstem bulrush plants, for example, are of high ecological value. They provide stream bank stabilization and habitat for wetland birds, salamanders, and muskrats. Yet the plant's uncontrolled appearance, and the muskrats they might harbor, most likely defies what many people think is an appropriate planting for a residential garden. Coupled with this conundrum, the environmental philosophers Glenn Parsons and Allen Carlson note that there is a translation problem. Even if hardstem bulrushes are accepted into the plant palette of a garden, their ecological functioning may not be perceptible.[107]

This aim — helping people see and understand the ecological functioning of a landscape as integral to its aesthetic appreciation — would become an important feature in Oberlander's work. It can be seen in her constant battle with University of British Columbia maintenance crews at the Museum of Anthropology who care for the Haida grass mix; it requires no spraying or mowing, but to some visitors looks too wild and insufficiently manicured. While the ecological message may not always be readily apparent to those experiencing her landscapes, Oberlander has taken every opportunity to point out this feature of her work. In fact, by the close of the twentieth century she was becoming known worldwide for her ecological landscapes; in 1990 she was the first landscape architect to receive the Order of Canada, one of the country's highest honors.

With successful on-structure landscapes in Vancouver; Ottawa; Washington, D.C.; New York; and Berlin, Oberlander also became an international expert on the topic of green roofs. With Elisabeth Whitelaw and Eva Matsuzaki she wrote *Green Roofs* for Public Works and Government Services Canada in 2002. Oberlander has regularly reminded landscape architects that they possess the knowledge and skills to address the ecological and social problems of our times. In her address in 2009 to the Canadian Society of Landscape Architects at their seventy-fifth anniversary celebration, she charged: "Landscape architects today have at their disposal the experience and technical ability to enhance our contacts with nature in an infinite variety of ways on the ground as well as on roofs. . . . If we want landscape architecture to become the Art of the Possible we must discover new aesthetically pleasing solutions, ecologically and technically sound ones, while satisfying social and economic goals."[108]

Oberlander is more than a spokeswoman — she continues to practice and refine her ecological ideas. Moreover, her drive was given great momentum in the late 1980s when Peter gave her a report by the Brundtland Commission, called *Our Common Future.* The report gave evidence of the critical need to realize a sustainable future at a global scale and the necessity to involve all sectors of society in this quest. He placed it in her hands and said, "Cornelia, this document will change the way you practice."[109] In Oberlander's design for the C. K. Choi building she made these words true.

The C. K. Choi Building

During the 1990s the University of British Columbia was in the midst of a ten-year capital expansion program, yet it had neither a sustainability agenda nor environmental guidelines.[110] This lack of policy changed with the new C. K. Choi facility, which would house the Institute of Asian Research and the Centre for India and South Asia Research. In early 1992 the C. K. Choi project was identified as a potential model for sustainable design and building practices on campus. As proposed, the research center would have no connection to the university's storm-water or sanitary sewers, and no air-conditioning. Heating for the new building would be solar generated and construction would utilize recycled materials.

DESIGN PROCESS Oberlander, Matsuzaki/Wright Architects, and Keen Engineering were selected as the design team, and in 1992 Oberlander, the architect Eva Matsuzaki, and the mechanical engineer Jeanette Frost began their unique collaboration. Early in the process they agreed to not only meet the challenges presented by the project brief but to expand the mandate. Both Oberlander and Matsuzaki had worked in Erickson's office on Robson Square. They were eager to adapt for this project the collaborative methods gleaned from Erickson. Oberlander recalled that a collaborative approach was absolutely necessary to conceiving the entire project as one ecological system.[111] From 1992 through 1995 they worked together every Tuesday to address the issues of site and structure, and the interrelated natural systems that affected their design. Some Tuesdays Oberlander led the discussion; other Tuesdays it was Matsuzaki or Frost who directed the conversation. Every decision was considered in light of its environmental impact. However, this collaboration was not merely an exercise in comparing calculations. It was intuitive as well as rational. For Matsuzaki, "the team had the passion at a very emotional level that lasted three years."[112]

One of Oberlander's first tasks was to analyze the site, which contained an unassuming parking lot on its eastern side and a gently sloped area containing Douglas fir trees to the west. The mature trees occupied 70 percent of the land

and they were also part of a larger stand that linked the building site to the Japanese-styled Nitobe Garden nearby. During one Tuesday meeting, Oberlander suggested that restricting the building footprint to only disturbed terrain — the parking lot — could save the trees. This was a challenging idea: to confine the footprint of a thirty-thousand-square-foot building to the outline of a parking lot that occupied only 30 percent of the site. Despite the restrictions, the team was up to the challenge, and today the three-story building's plan matches the shape of the former lot.

LANDSCAPE STRATEGY As the design process evolved Oberlander, Matsuzaki, and Frost worked collectively to ensure that the ecological systems of architecture, engineering, and landscape architecture were synchronized. Since the building could not connect to the sewer system, composting toilets were specified. The solid material from the toilets was mixed with wood chips and red wiggler worms to create topsoil that could be used by the university's ground staff. The liquid from the toilets was combined with the building's grey water and rainwater from the roof. This water was channeled to subsurface trenches located between the building and the sidewalk. It was important to the design team to make these trenches visible to people, so that the public could see the functioning of the landscape. Oberlander researched plants that could filter runoff in the grey water trenches, a task that would lead her to consult with Bill Wolverton, formerly a senior research scientist with NASA's John C. Stennis Space Center in Bay St. Louis, Mississippi. Based on his advice, she selected irises, sedges, and reeds to best filter the water. She also planted a line of gingko trees between the C. K. Choi building and the street's edge. Highly valued in traditional Chinese medicine, the trees were also excellent absorbers of air pollutants.[113]

The effect of shadows from the existing stand of trees and the building's solar needs were also assessed. If the trees remained, would they shade the building and potentially block the path of sunlight to the planned solar panels? Oberlander consulted an expert arborist on-site, who pruned the trees to ensure that light would penetrate the building. Later a solar analysis revealed that the trees would not hinder the light needs of the new building.

The C. K. Choi building relied on an assortment of secondhand fixtures, such as handrails and electrical conduits, and the structure itself was made of recycled materials. Large timber trusses were taken from the 1930s armory building

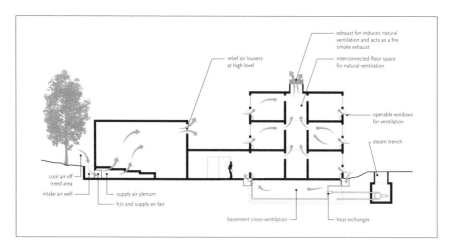

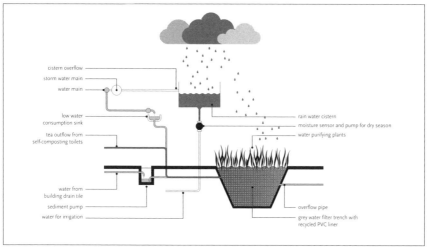

Diagrams of the C. K. Choi building infrastructure (*top*) and water system (*bottom*), 27 April 2012. Landscape Architect: Cornelia Hahn Oberlander. Architects: Matsuzaki Wright.

across the street, which had been condemned. Similarly, the bricks used to clad the building's exterior were in their third life.[114] They were first used as ballast in nineteenth-century ships sailing between Asia and North America; thereafter they paved the streets of Vancouver's Gastown; and today the bricks cover the façade — with a beautiful patina that hints at their extended lives.

Yet, recycling did not stop with building materials. Bringing the construction process into the ecological equation was also crucial. The design team instructed the contractors to recycle all materials used during construction.

With makeshift containers labeled for every conceivable item, such as old nails, scraps of wood, and discarded metal, everything was recycled — even the contractors' lunches. Oberlander also investigated ways to prepare the soil for planting that would minimize the impacts on the environment. Instead of importing new soil for the ferns destined for the west side of the building, she used knowledge gleaned from a lifetime of gardening. Worms were used to loosen the existing earth. Using these long soft-bodied invertebrates, which aerate the earth by eating their own weight in soil each day, rich humus was produced for the plantings.

RECEPTION The C. K. Choi building opened on 7 October 1996. Along with the standard opening speeches, guided tours explained how the building and landscape functioned together to minimize energy consumption. The composting toilets drew the most controversy. With the commencement of monitoring, the design team could finally determine if the project really met the high standards established at the beginning of the collaboration. They found that the project used half the water consumed by the average campus building. This was due in large part to both the building and landscape performing as a single water recycling system.

In 2000 the C. K. Choi building was designated by the American Institute of Architects Committee on the Environment as one of the ten best green buildings in North America. Off both the electrical grid and the university's storm-water and sewer systems, ecological degradation was minimized. The building and landscape have also continued to serve as an educational source for architects, landscape architects, and engineers, as well as local high school students, who are particularly fascinated by the water and air systems, and above all, the composting worms. Walking by the C. K. Choi building today, one immediately notices the grey water trench teeming with the irises that are markedly noticeable in spring. Upon closer inspection it is evident that the storm drains from the building are feeding this planted area. This symbiotic relationship between landscape and architecture is a rare moment in the built environment, yet it is the subtle hallmark of Oberlander's work.

The C. K. Choi project, with its acute dedication to environmental impacts, was a turning point in Oberlander's career. It gave her command of how site and structure could function together to enhance ecological conditions, and how the construction process itself was a vital point in the project where

Planted water filtration trench at the
C. K. Choi building, 2005. Landscape
Architect: Cornelia Hahn Oberlander.
Architects: Matsuzaki Wright.

environmental damage could be minimized. It was during this same time that
she began to direct her attention to the North, where environmental degradation was extreme, and where a rich and diverse culture was beginning to
achieve self-governance.

The Northwest Territories Legislative Assembly Building

Northern Canada is a protean geography, where inhabitants speak many different languages and cultural practices vary as much as its changing temperatures. Given its location, the effects of climate change have been exacerbated
in the North, with dramatic alteration of ice formation and thawing, melting
permafrost, and increased toxins in the water, ice, and soil. Oberlander was
one of the first landscape architects to address the needs of those feeling the
repercussions of this change — communities in the extreme north of Canada.
Building upon an approach she first developed in Philadelphia many years before, Oberlander started listening to people who had been routinely ignored.

The Northwest Territories, Nunavut, and the Yukon comprise Northern Canada. Occupying almost half the surface area of Canada, it is the size of the Western, the Central Western, and the Southwest regions of the United States combined. Without doubt, the idea of the North is unique to Canada. While the United States promoted expansion with a Manifest Destiny that drove settlers westward during the nineteenth century, Canadian claims to the North were never followed by large-scale nonaboriginal habitation. Its limited access from the south, extreme weather, vast scale, and acres of Shield made colonization difficult and for decades Northern Canada was governed remotely from Ottawa.

There are as many myths about the North as there are cartographic truths. Centuries of literature and art have created what the English professor Sherrill Grace calls its "discursive formation." Within this discourse, Grace cites numerous fictions: the homogeneity of the northern aboriginal people, that Northern Canada is empty, and that it exists outside history.[115] Glenn Gould's groundbreaking radio documentary *The Idea of North* (1967) exposed these discursive projections on Northern Canada. His polyphonic program contained musical excerpts interlaced with five voices giving simultaneous accounts of Northern Canada, shifting in volume and perspective. The documentary revealed actual and imagined life there, and also the fact that many Canadians were still considered outsiders. That same year the Canadian government enacted legislation enabling people living in the North to begin governing themselves. This move sought to decentralize civil service from Ottawa and to promote self-governance within the territories.[116] Ottawa designated Yellowknife as the capital of the Northwest Territories and it was the first territory to create a fully elected legislative council, which took office in 1975. The Yukon followed in 1978 and Nunavut in 1999.

The Northwest Territories occupies more than 450,000 square miles of Taiga Plains and Shield, and has been the ancestral land of native populations for more than five thousand years. In 1870 the British government transferred control of the land to Canada. For almost a century Ottawa established towns and schools in the territories, as well as partnerships with private companies to extract their resources.[117] While the Legislative Assembly was formed in 1975, for fifteen years its members conducted "the public business of the Territory in school gymnasia, banquet halls and other temporary facilities."[118] In 1990 the council agreed to establish a permanent assembly in Yellowknife.

Known as the "Diamond Capital" of Canada — where extracting this hard crystalline carbon and a little luck could bring substantial wealth — Yellowknife was a small but rapidly developing city in the early 1990s. Innovative plans for funding were devised to realize the assembly project and to encourage local participation among the twenty-two communities scattered across the jurisdiction. One goal was to acknowledge the diverse population of these communities, which had largely developed autonomously.[119] The assembly's form of governance was also significant. All members of the legislature were independents and together they operated under a consensus system rather than party politics, which was thought to garner only rivalry rather than cooperation.

Pin/Matthews Architects of Yellowknife teamed with Matsuzaki/Wright Architects and Ferguson Simek Clark Engineers to submit a proposal for the new legislative building and landscape. When devising the team, Jim Wright immediately thought of Oberlander. He had worked with her on Robson Square and Eva Matsuzaki had collaborated with her on the C. K. Choi building.[120] Given their past experience in municipal design work and their sensitive handling of natural processes, the team was a likely choice and they won the commission. A main goal of the council was securing a design team who would "respectfully work with the land."[121] Despite its rugged appearance the Northwest Territories possessed a fragile ecology, one that was increasingly vulnerable to climate change. It was against this backdrop of political, cultural, and climatic transformation that the project was conceived and ultimately realized.

DESIGN PROCESS Shortly after receiving the commission Oberlander traveled with the project architects Jim Wright and Gino Pin to Yellowknife. The site, located on the outskirts of the city, was relatively undisturbed. Situated beside Frame Lake, it featured stands of mature black spruce, tamarack, and white birch trees, and an eleven-acre peat bog that delayed runoff before it reached the lake. On a much larger scale the bog was an integral element of an expanse of boreal peat land that was absorbing carbon from the atmosphere. The team decided to locate the forty-six-thousand-square-foot assembly building on the edge of the lake, anchoring it to the volcanic rock of the Canadian Shield. As she had approached the National Gallery design five years earlier, Oberlander considered the spatial sequence between the orders of law and the quotidian life of the city. Thus, the team decided to conceive the bog as a transitional space between the new assembly and the city of Yellowknife.

LANDSCAPE STRATEGY Oberlander was keen to take an active role in preserving the site's trees and peat bog, and restricting the impact of the building on the site. As the design team toured Yellowknife they encountered a recently constructed hospital. Oberlander immediately noticed that the landscape was planted with viburnum and potentilla plantings, "and they were sick."[122] Their poor health was due to the fact that they had been imported from Edmonton. The city was more than nine hundred miles south of Yellowknife, three plant hardiness zones away, and a benign climate compared to Yellowknife. Oberlander's discovery prompted her to think about the assembly site as a generator for its own plant life. Unlike the C. K. Choi building, the Yellowknife site was largely untouched and site disturbance would be unavoidable. In response she planned to collect seeds from the building site and incubate them in local greenhouses.

At the time no nursery in Yellowknife was willing to grow plants from seed. This did not stop Oberlander's plans however, and she returned to Yellowknife with the horticulturalist Bruce McTavish. Together they collected kinnikinnick, rose hips, and cuttings from vaccinium and other plants from the site for the landscape design. For the rooftop of the assembly building they collected tissue cultures of locally growing saxifrages, enough to produce ten thousand plants. Oberlander and McTavish transported the seeds, clippings, and tissue cultures to Vancouver and cultivated them in greenhouses there. When planting in Yellowknife began, she returned with the vegetation — genetic progenitors of the plants that had been growing on the site. These were planted using a technique she called "invisible mending."[123] Borrowed from sewing, the goal of invisible mending is to attract as little attention as possible to the stitch itself. Applied to the landscape, plants were not installed in defined planting beds, but instead interspersed in disturbed areas and bare patches — an approach that made the planting process invisible but the result highly effective.

The Yellowknife project shared the fast-track method used for the National Gallery, and construction was already under way as the design was still unfolding. When Oberlander arrived at the site to oversee the installation of plants she discovered that portions of the peat bog had been destroyed by fire.[124] Although peat bogs are extremely difficult to reestablish, their valuable contributions to water and air quality as well as the unique habitat they afford made their restoration at the Yellowknife site critical. In response, Oberlander devised what she called "the cookie tray technique." Instead of bulldozing the bog for the

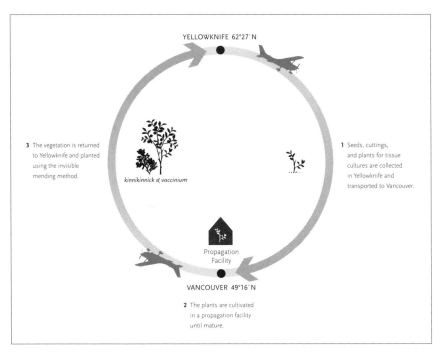

YELLOWKNIFE 62°27′N

3 The vegetation is returned to Yellowknife and planted using the invisible mending method.

kinnikinnick & vaccinium

1 Seeds, cuttings, and plants for tissue cultures are collected in Yellowknife and transported to Vancouver.

Propagation Facility

VANCOUVER 49°16′N

2 The plants are cultivated in a propagation facility until mature.

Plant cultivation scheme for the Northwest Territories Legislative Assembly building, Yellowknife, 27 April 2012. Landscape Architect: Cornelia Hahn Oberlander. Architects: Ferguson Simek Clark/ Pin Matthews with Matsuzaki Wright.

roadway entrance, she instructed the contractor to use the earthmoving equipment like a giant spatula. Similar to lifting cookies off a tray, the plant material in the bog was scooped up and transferred to the disturbed areas of the existing bog. By salvaging the bog material Oberlander saved a valuable organic material that may have been in gestation for thousands of years.

Other aspects of the site design also demonstrated Oberlander's growing sensitivity to the ecological integrity of the North, recalling Kiley's advice "to walk lightly on the land," given to her half a century earlier.[125] Rather than paved paths on grade, boardwalks that floated above the landscape became the standard walkaways. This not only guaranteed minimal contact with the ground but also allowed animals to pass beneath the paths undisturbed. This boardwalk system was connected to a segment of the four-and-a-half-mile-long Frame Lake Geological Trail, which enabled direct encounters with the lake's rock, flora, and fauna, as well as providing a complete running circuit.

RECEPTION The Northwest Legislative Assembly building opened on 17 November 1993 with its elected assembly members as well as other territorial representatives and former prime minister Chrétien in attendance. Today tours are given of the assembly building and its grounds. Inside, visitors view the circular chambers where the territories' nineteen members sit; outside they are reminded of the uniqueness of the site and perhaps even the sensitivity of the designers' response to the landscape. As of this writing the plant material has matured. The bog serves a critical ecological purpose and with its low flat expanse creates a poignant transition space between the Legislative Assembly building and the city. The project also embodies the wisdom of Oberlander's advice to Arthur Erickson ten years earlier at the Bagley Wright site: "Plant what you see." At the Northwest Legislative Assembly building the genetic material of the site itself became the generator of its future landscape. Oberlander built upon this method in her design work for Inuvik's East Three School, also located in the Northwest Territories.

East Three School

The town of Inuvik is a relatively young community, conceived in 1954 as a replacement for the ancestral settlement Aklavik, which had suffered from decades of flooding and erosion. One of the first planned towns close to the Arctic Circle, by 1961 it featured a government dock, temporary school, airport, water and sewage systems, Royal Canadian Mounted Police post, and nursing station. With the discovery of oil in the Beaufort Sea, employment diversified, bringing further economic development to this small community. However the town has remained small, with a population of 3,586, largely comprised of Nihtat Gwich'in, Inuvialuit, Dene, Métis, and nonaboriginal people.[126]

For many resource-dependent communities in remote regions, oil and gas extraction has done little to generate local wealth or a sense of community that reflects traditional aboriginal life. However, the people of Inuvik have been able to consistently realize projects that link their unique context to community programs and infrastructure. For example, they founded the first Great Northern Arts Festival in July 1989, galvanizing numerous art traditions through community participation. Originally hosting artists only from the Northwest Territories, over the years the ten-day festival has grown to include artists from all over the Canadian North, Alaska, the Orkney Islands of Scotland, and the Yucatan in Mexico.[127] In 1998 residents created a nonprofit society to raise funds to transform the hockey rink of a defunct residential school into the Inuvik Community Greenhouse.

Inuvik is situated on the Taiga Plains of the Northwest Territories, farther north than Yellowknife and 2 degrees above the Arctic Circle. It is a climate of extreme temperature changes, which can range from 70 degrees below zero to 90 degrees Fahrenheit.[128] Oberlander has called Inuvik "the land of the sky," where light plays a dramatic role in annotating seasonal changes. In December the night lasts for thirty days, while during the summer months there can be sixty days of continuous daylight. This prolonged day prompts a brief and intense growing season of approximately four months on average. The town lies along the East Channel of the Mackenzie River, which borders the largest delta in Canada, the Mackenzie River Delta. This delta plays a crucial ecological role in the region. It provides habitat for polar bears, whose food sources are rapidly diminishing with climate change, and moderates the hydrology of the region. The Mackenzie River Delta's marble-like pattern of alluvial deposits is laden with vegetation. Functioning much like a giant sponge, the delta retains water coming from north-flowing rivers to the Beaufort Sea.

Like other Northern communities Inuvik was feeling the effect of climate change in tangible and directly measureable ways. Impacts have been documented in the migration of trees and animals as well as in the stability of the town's physical foundation. Most of the surface of Inuvik is comprised of a thick blanket of permafrost — where the earth's crust has remained below 32 degrees Fahrenheit for two or more years.[129] Permafrost affects almost every aspect of life in Inuvik, from its transportation (the city is only accessible by road in the winter and summer) to its water supply, agriculture, hunting, and building construction. It also influences the engineering of sewage and water lines, which are constructed entirely above ground in a series of utilidors.

Since the 1960s scientists have recorded the melting of permafrost in the Mackenzie Delta region. Melting is one of the most critical environmental factors in the arctic deltas as it affects ground and surface water, and the limits of the delta edges.[130] Oberlander has observed firsthand the changes to the permafrost. During a site visit in 2009 she reported that she walked in mud up to her knees. The permafrost, which is typically six inches in depth, had decreased to a mere one to two inches in depth.[131] In turn, the melting permafrost has increased the depth of the active layer, soil that regularly thaws in the spring and summer months, and provides the stratum for root growth. With increased snow runoff and rains, water percolates through this layer, but is unable to penetrate the permafrost below. The oversaturated active layer creates pools of standing water on the surface, killing plants that thrive in dryer soils, impeding new construction, and damaging existing structures. The physical structures that housed Inuvik's 1959 elementary school, Sir Alexander Mackenzie School (SAM), and its 1969 high school, Samuel Hearne Secondary School (SHSS), were failing due to the extreme climate changes in the region. In 2004, Inuvik secured funding through the Northwest Territories government infrastructure acquisition plan for a new combined K-12 school.[132]

DESIGN PROCESS In 2005 D. K. Consulting of Yellowknife carried out an extensive planning and visioning study with teachers, staff, parents, and students at both schools. There was significant interest in joining the two facilities, with a maximum capacity of 1,050 students. The formerly separated schools would share resources and programming, and combine their two gyms to form a double-size gymnasium. The most prominent concern expressed by parents was a separate playground for the new school's youngest children.[133] When the architect Gino Pin was commissioned to design the school the following year, he immediately invited Oberlander, who was both an expert in the design of children's environments and a specialist in the design of Northern landscapes.

The prospect for a new school inspired Inuvik teachers, staff, and parents to think about ways it might express their cultures. For example, they decided that the school would offer second-language instruction in Gwich'in, Inuvialuktun, and French. They also envisioned a building and landscape that embraced the different art and cultural practices that had been in development since the end of the last ice age. In addition to the standard request for display cases showcasing awards and trophies, parents also requested artwork, such as painted murals, sculptures, traditional tools, and pictures of elders, community leaders, and students. Participants gravitated towards symbols relating to their unique setting, such as the Northern Lights and the Mackenzie River Delta, which they thought expressed the interconnectedness of water and sky, land and town, old and new, community and school.[134] Indoor and outdoor gathering spaces for use by school and community members were to become the town's hub and community center.

Both parents and students stressed that they wanted more on-the-land and cultural activities created for the students and the community.[135] According to the visioning report, "one of the most imaginative responses" was to have "no ceilings." If we look at the intent of the suggestion, it speaks to the desire to "bring nature and the environment indoors."[136] There was also a strong sentiment to build the newly combined school on the SAM site. Its location between the commercial district and residential areas to the north and east was central. The site was also adjacent to Jim Koe Park, named after Chief Jim Koe, who was an avid promoter of curling, a Scottish sport where players slide stones across a sheet of ice with the aid of brooms.

LANDSCAPE STRATEGY The building plan was conceived as a wide "V" with the high school on one side and the elementary school on the other. At the angle of the "V" plan was a double-size gymnasium and congregation space to be used by both schools. Oberlander described three guiding principles shaping the design response: embracing the cultural uniqueness of the community, working with (not against) the climate of extremes, and adjusting the design to accommodate the fragile ecology of the area by employing the same methods used at the legislative building site in Yellowknife.[137]

Early European settlers in the North built conventional structures directly on the permafrost; in time the heat from these buildings melted the ice below and caused many of them to sink. Today buildings and walkways in Inuvik are constructed on piles and gravel pads approximately three to six feet deep. The new Inuvik school was raised over a bed of gravel with pilings driven thirty feet into the earth. The raised structure served a dual purpose. It allowed for the heaving that comes with the permafrost freezing and thawing and it also enabled wildlife to cross underneath. Unfortunately, the raised structures also posed challenges to entering and leaving the building, particularly given the kind of direct access to the outdoors that parents and teachers had envisioned. With careful handling of the grades around the building, Oberlander created access to the main entrance and the playground egress points while maintaining a clear space around the remaining sides of the building for air to flow.

Inuvik's shifting winds and snowdrifts also provided an additional challenge for a project that was to accommodate small children. In speaking with local residents, Oberlander found that "in Inuvik the wind used to go over the town, but now it blows at three feet and sweeps the ground, hurting children and making it impossible to open exterior doors."[138] Her observation corresponds with findings published in the 2012 *Arctic Report Card,* which recorded stronger

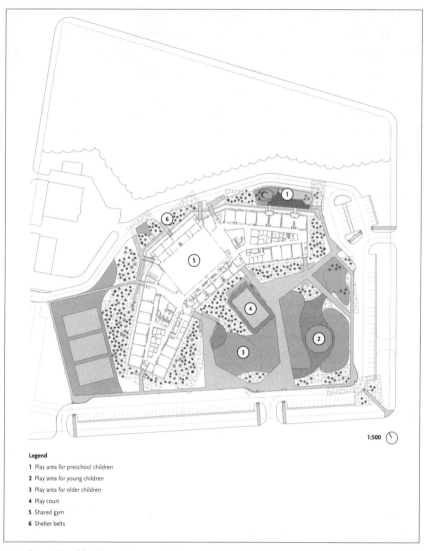

Legend
1 Play area for preschool children
2 Play area for young children
3 Play area for older children
4 Play court
5 Shared gym
6 Shelter belts

1:500

East Three School landscape plan, 27 April 2012. Landscape Architect: Cornelia Hahn Oberlander.
Architect: Pin Taylor Architects.

winds and blowing snow closer to the ground in 2011 and 2012.[139] The pattern
of drifting snow was also a factor, and a condition unique to the North. The
Coriolis force, movement caused by the rotation of the earth, is at its greatest
at the poles.[140] Pin modeled the movement of snow to determine the location of
the building, its height, length, and angle to insure that wind scoured the snow
away from doorways instead of piling it in front of them.[141]

Another element of the plan that sought to minimize the impact of the wind was the retention of a large stand of trees to the north of the building and the construction of a large continuous berm. These features served as a shelterbelt while extending the children's play and exploration opportunities. A play area specifically for preschool children corresponded to their classroom space, and its location east of the building captured the morning sun. Building upon her fifty years of experience in play space design, Oberlander created an environment that combined small hills with logs removed from the Mackenzie River. Given the extreme temperatures of the region, metal was not an option. In front of the school a large multipurpose space, defined by Oberlander's signature grass circle, provided an outdoor venue for the school and community to play some of their most cherished games. These include spear throwing, knuckle hopping, and blanket throwing.

Since there were no plant nurseries in the far North, Oberlander again used the method she had developed at Yellowknife — harvesting the local site and surrounding area for plant material and propagating it in British Columbia.[142] After receiving permission from the Inuvik elders, plants and seeds were collected in 2009 and 2010. These plantings included edible berries such as cloudberry, bearberry, and soapberry.[143] The design team also selected plants used in preparing traditional cuisine to be used as part of the home economics courses and by community members.

Trees, too, were transplanted with the approval of Inuvik elders. In 2009 Oberlander and the arborist Norm Hol inspected trees in a nearby woodland. Together they identified mature specimens of birch, spruce, and larch to be relocated to the school site. The height, girth, and foliage of these mature trees would contribute to wind deflection starting from the opening day of school. Hol performed root pruning approximately three to four feet around the base of the trees to prepare them for transplanting. In 2012 Oberlander returned with five thousand plants to be installed at the school site. Upon her arrival she discovered that a summer storm had saturated the soils. The rains produced a series of water pools at the soil's surface, indicative of water trapped in the active layer. This prompted immediate adjustments to the planting plan. The mature trees were transplanted to the school site.

RECEPTION East Three opened for students in September 2012. In addition to Oberlander's culturally and ecologically sensitive landscape design, the school's

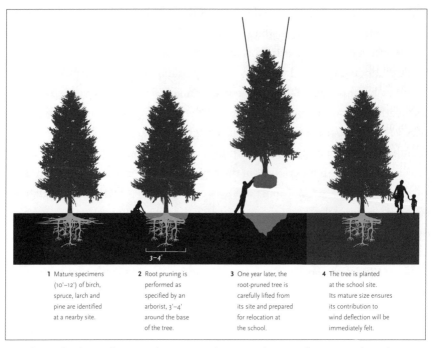

1 Mature specimens	2 Root pruning is	3 One year later, the	4 The tree is planted
(10'–12') of birch,	performed as	root-pruned tree is	at the school site.
spruce, larch and	specified by an	carefully lifted from	Its mature size ensures
pine are identified	arborist, 3'–4'	its site and prepared	its contribution to
at a nearby site.	around the base	for relocation at	wind deflection will be
	of the tree.	the school.	immediately felt.

East Three School tree relocation scheme, 27 April 2012. Landscape Architect: Cornelia Hahn Oberlander. Architect: Pin Taylor Architects.

architecture also provides numerous references to life in the Arctic, such as images of seals, bears, and moose painted in bright colors on the hallway walls. The school also features three polycarbonate panel canopies at the high school and elementary school entrances and the main entryway. Since the school is home to a number of different cultures, these canopies reference natural and cultural phenomena witnessed by all. These references include fracture seas, air streams from overhead jets, light passing through prisms, meandering delta rivers, and sun dogs (an atmospheric occurrence producing bright halos of light in the sky on either side of the sun).

In summary these three chapters, "Housework," "Human Environment," and "Ecological Environment," describe the strata that have formed the foundations of Oberlander's landscape architecture. The next chapter, "Invention," moves beyond these foundational ideas to explore the exact methods she used and, in several instances, invented to design the modern landscape.

INVENTION

5 The following describes some of the design inventions that Oberlander has devised over the years. Given the scope of new projects available to landscape architects after World War II and the new design vocabulary emerging in the profession, Oberlander was often pressed to invent her own details, techniques, and design approaches.

Marc Treib commented at a panel discussion in 2009 at the annual conference of the Council of Educators in Landscape Architecture that we are still trying to understand the types of design approaches used by modern landscape architects. Those landscape architects designing at the human scale were not always forthcoming about the subject. This was a reason why Ian McHarg was so appealing — he had a clear method. While the techniques and methods I describe are rarely as prescriptive as McHarg's map overlay method, and they certainly have not all been invented by Oberlander, they do shed light on how she has practiced, information that may be useful to designers as well as historians.

As Ron Williams reminds us, landscape architects working in the decades immediately after World War II could not rely on the plethora of manufactured landscape materials and technologies available today. Some wartime materials and fabrication systems were adapted to civilian use, but other elements, such as light standards, benches, or play equipment, were often designed by landscape architects. Williams himself designed a light standard with the industrial designer Jean-François Simard at Lumec. It became a common fixture used in American and Canadian cities for decades.[1] Custom-designed site details were typically created for one project; if successful, they were put into production. In 1953, for example, Oberlander designed a series of streamlined, reinforced-concrete flowerpots for the Philadelphia International Airport designed by Carroll, Grisdale & Van Allen Architects. She later used these same pots in residential projects, such as the Wongs' garden, and at her own houses in Vancouver.

Oberlander's details for children's environments were particularly ingenious. In 1958 she devised a combined seesaw and merry-go-round apparatus for her daughter Judy. Sitting on the seesaw-like plank, children could swivel vertically up and down as well as move horizontally in a circle. Likewise, for a Vancouver play environment in the 1970s she recycled a fallen tree by securing its trunk upright in a foundation and attaching a tire swing to its branch, creating what she called a "vertical climbing tree." She also devised numerous technical details for her green roof projects and even developed innovative construction techniques, such as the grid method for the application of bentonite, which she originally employed at the British Columbia Institute of Technology Discovery Parks in 1981 — and later used for the reflecting pool at the Museum of Anthropology in 2010.

Modern Methods

Landscape architects have also fashioned design methods. I do not claim here that Oberlander invented all the methods described, but her work over the past half century gives us an insight into their nature.

STRUCTURE AND LAND

Oberlander will tell you that a fundamental approach to her design work is what she calls the "fit between land and structure." We know that many modern landscape architects had abandoned the École des Beaux-Arts conception of landscape design as an unfolding of symmetrical geometries extending in axial lines from the house.[2] For modern landscape architects, the formal qualities of design — its spaces, lines, and forms — often came from the site itself. Oberlander stressed this as early as 1954 in her lecture at the Vancouver Housing Authority's Houses for All conference. Here, she reminds the audience, "In designing new communities, it is not possible just to provide houses and put them like little wooden blocks on the land, regardless of contours, soil conditions, and exposure."[3] While property lines and the flow of contour lines on

Spinning seesaw invented by Oberlander, circa 1960.

a site plan might inspire the lines and shapes of landscape plans, the slope of the site yielded vertical consequences regarding building configurations. For Oberlander grading was the landscape architect's most important tool, and slope and soil were the first features she studied.

Together with Arthur Erickson, she perfected an approach to fitting structure and land, particularly on sites with extreme slopes and rocky outcrops. Reminiscent of the Oberlanders' approach to their Ravine House, Erickson often employed columns or other support systems to elevate the structure above the land. Raising a building over the landscape on pillars was one of Le Corbusier's tenets of modern architecture and numerous North American architects adopted this idea. Certainly elevating the structure might allow for circulation underneath. Unfortunately, the park-like landscape beneath the building, which was often promised in the planning stages of such designs, rarely materialized. In his analysis of Le Corbusier's pilotis-inspired projects in France and India, Jan Woudstra argued that the interface between Le Corbusier's architecture and landscape at the moment of the pilotis was vague and probably more politically driven; appealing to bourgeois sentiments favoring pastoral parks.[4] Erickson, fortunately, relied on Oberlander's expertise and determination to preserve the existing features of the site, and to design a new landscape in sympathetic accord with Erickson's architecture.

Oberlander's site plan for the Monteverdi housing estates (1979–82), designed with Arthur Erickson and Eva Matsuzaki, exemplified this idea. Located on the steep western slopes of Caulfield in West Vancouver, the Monteverdi site featured outcrops of some of the oldest rock formations in the area, Caulfield gneiss. This coarse-grained metamorphic aggregate posed a challenge to fitting the site and structure. In addition to the bedrock and nearly vertical grades, the site was covered with mature western red cedars, Douglas firs, and maple trees. Oberlander, Erickson, and Matsuzaki worked together closely to position the roadway and structures in consideration of the trees, slope, and orientation. Like Cherokee Village that Oberlander designed with Oskar Stonorov, the width of the main road was reduced as it weaved through the established stands of trees. The rock and columns supported Erickson's twenty residences, which floated above the steep slopes, preserving the land below and making the houses appear as part of the forest architecture. Erickson and Oberlander's approach is very poignant today. A comparison of Monteverdi Estates with housing recently developed around it is striking. Many of the newly constructed houses are oriented to the street and constructed on standard building pads, two decisions that have tragically resulted in extensive grading and the subsequent removal of the trees.

DESIGNING AND DRAFTING

While fitting the land and structure was important to Oberlander, so too were other design methods employed. One obvious question is: How did Oberlander's design method influence what she designed? We know that she has always conducted exhaustive background research for each commission and she pioneered collaboration with children and community groups. In the end, however, it was Oberlander who designed the landscape. According to Elisabeth Whitelaw, Oberlander still uses some of the basic drafting tools she acquired in the 1940s, such as the T-square, triangles, and tracing paper. Although Oberlander often worked in model form at Erickson's office, in her own atelier she has relied to a large degree on numerous iterations of drafted plans, sometimes with colored-paper cutouts and sections where needed.

Alberto Perez-Gomez and Louise Pelletier have argued that the tools of representation not only influence the generation of architectural form; they also convey the belief systems of the architect. This notion underscores how representational tools are fundamentally linked to how a project is conceptualized. In *Representing Landscape Architecture*, Marc Treib noted how the evolution of the plan in the profession of landscape architecture distinguished the designer's approach from that of the gardener's. William Robinson, for instance, who

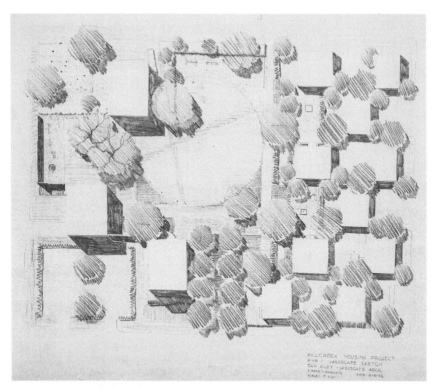

A rare freehand and drafted schematic drawing by Oberlander of Mill Creek Public Housing, Philadelphia, 1952.

conceived of the garden as the result of the act of gardening, "wrote little of the totality of the garden that would issue from native or exotic plants of which he wrote."[5] The plan was the provenance of the designer, and when well done "a short-hand for complex social and spatial thinking."[6] Indeed, plans abound in Oberlander's archive at the Canadian Centre for Architecture.

Oberlander's plans are accompanied by notes, charts, an occasional doodle, and written ideas for projects — often scribbled on the backs of envelopes and other scraps of paper that attest to the often frenetic pace of her life. There are some examples of perspective sketches, but these illustrations were typically drawn by another member of the design team. Oberlander jokingly remarked that learning to sketch during her studies at Harvard was sidelined by her greater desire to ski. Nonetheless, she eventually excelled at drafting, and her plans were almost always drafted rather than sketched, even conceptual studies. Oberlander admits that the drafted plan enabled her to unify the larger site

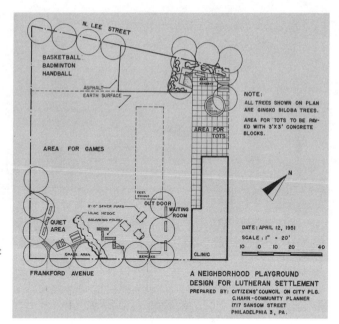

Playground for the Lutheran Settlement House, Philadelphia, 1951. Landscape Architect: Cornelia Hahn Oberlander.

issues and the project's spatial needs.[7] Thus, hers are not the loose and flamboyant sketches characteristic of Lawrence Halprin or the axonometric studies that are a Garrett Eckbo signature. Instead Oberlander's process resonates more closely with the early graphic work of Frank Lloyd Wright.

The art historian Eileen Michels has observed that despite working at the eminent offices of Sullivan and Adler, Wright did not gravitate towards freehand perspective sketches. Instead his architecture was related "in a fundamental way to his creative, inspired utilization of the instruments of the drawing board."[8] The role of drafting tools is evident in Oberlander's design response to flat, urban sites in particular. For example, the 1951 plan for a playground in Philadelphia, a project she designed for the CCCP and the Lutheran Settlement House, demonstrates the role of a T-square and triangle. Many of the spaces in this plan, such as the quiet area and play apparatus areas, are formed by the opposing angles of the 30/60–degree triangle.

THE LOGIC OF THE MODULE

Drafting also lent itself effortlessly to the rubric of the module. In modern architecture the module played a significant role as both a method and a symbol of organization. "The universal space associated with the steel frame and the planning grid was assimilated into a finely modulated field. This modularity, and the flexibility that it implied, became the very image — and the instrument — of the organizational complex."[9] Moreover, the production of architecture aligned itself with industries and businesses connected to the building process, favoring labor-saving methods, industrial standards of construction, and pre-fabricated materials. Thus, the use of the module offered a plausible approach to construction methods.

The coherent arrangement afforded by the module was also emphasized in the design of single-family homes and gardens in the postwar years. The Oberlanders' Tick-Tack-Toe House employed a nine-square module. Originally conceived in steel and masonry for a competition in Chicago, the Oberlanders changed the construction material to wood when the house was built in Vancouver.[10] Wood reigned as the primary building material in Vancouver, particularly for modest-size houses that were in such demand at the time.

Oberlander frequently used the module in her residential landscapes, often echoing the building module in the paving and dimensions of exterior spaces. In her description of the Friedman garden in *Western Homes and Living* in 1955, she notes that the house and garden were integrated "through the paving tiles which match up directly with the dimensions of the house."[11] Architectural modules were also a feature of her public work. Oberlander utilized the glazing module of Erickson's Canadian Chancery building to guide her planting plan, locating the hawthorn trees "five feet on-center with five-foot trunks to co-incide with the spacing of window mullions."[12]

In the 1970s John Ormsbee Simonds recommended that landscape architects look to the Japanese use of the module. The Japanese architectural module system, or *ken,* provided a standard building unit that roughly measures three feet by six feet. For Simonds, in Japan if a space or object did not fit the mea-surements of the module, "it is not distorted to fill the module, rather it is set free within the module and composed within the modular framework. The fact that an object is smaller or larger than the module is not concealed but is artistically revealed and elucidated."[13] He added that the Japanese employment of the module also helped the designer to avoid symmetry. This method can be seen in Oberlander's 1959 design for the Cook residence in Alberta, where the patio modulation of pavers is interrupted by a tree placed in an asymmetrical relationship to the ground plane pattern.

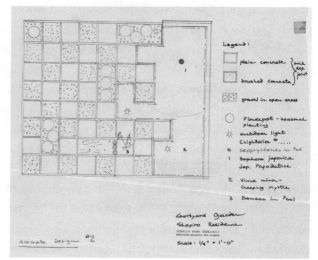

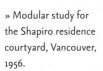

» Modular study for the Shapiro residence courtyard, Vancouver, 1956.

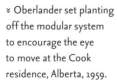

» Oberlander set planting off the modular system to encourage the eye to move at the Cook residence, Alberta, 1959.

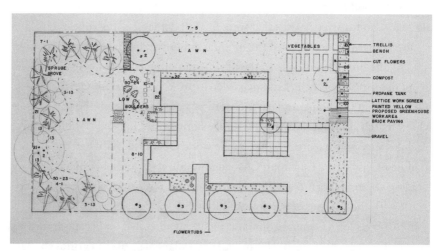

Oberlander was still employing the module in the 1990s when she was commissioned to design a garden for Linda Yorke and Gordon Forbes's midcentury house in Vancouver. In the late 1940s, Ned Pratt of Sharp, Thompson, Berwick & Pratt designed the house, which launched Pratt's modular approach to architecture. The Yorke/Forbes hired André Rowland to design an addition and Oberlander to redesign the entire yard, including a play area for their children. They stressed that they wanted to keep the original design intent of the architecture. Oberlander's site analysis and memo to her associate Elisabeth Whitelaw are telling, requesting that she take measurements of not only the house's floor-to-ceiling window mullions that ran the full rear of the structure but also the distance between fence posts.[14]

THE PROCESS OF ABSTRACTION

While use of the modular helped unify the landscape with the architecture, the process of abstraction enabled the landscape architect to explore alternative relationships between mass and space in a landscape design. By distilling design elements into discrete units, Oberlander possessed a syntax of infinite arrangements driven by principles of composition, such as occult balance, and the way the landscape was intended to be used. The endless possibilities of abstraction can be seen in Oberlander's conceptual collages from the 1950s of the University of British Columbia Faculty Club outdoor terrace.

Located on the northern edge of the campus and overlooking the Burrard Inlet and the North Shore Mountains, the new faculty club was a gift from Mrs. Thea and Dr. Leon J. Koerner. The split-level structure with a large rear yard was planned as the main social center for university faculty—a place for reading, playing music, recreating, and dining. The architect Fred Lasserre designed the first phase of the building in 1956. Oberlander designed the parking area, viewing terrace, and garden. Looking at the design studies for the terrace, one can see the abstract design process unfold.

Oberlander began with a plan view using square construction-paper cutouts sized on the module of the building. Reminiscent of both Froebel's seventh gift that used paper cutouts and the Bauhaus design methods translated in the Harvard curriculum, the squares were used to represent a range of elements, such as planters, benches, or trees. Oberlander tested different variations, eventually pasting down four versions. The squares were then translated into seating, planting, and paving in a second set of three schemes.

The Faculty Club and Social Centre opened on 15 July 1959 with a visit from Queen Elizabeth and Prince Charles. The facility also contained a water feature designed by Oberlander. Using a series of square basins, she created a cascading water fountain in the northeast corner of the garden—a design element that later was the inspiration for a second phase of design work by Arthur Erickson in 1963. Erickson connected the water feature with a much larger pool that was edged by concrete decking and a new pavilion for faculty dining. Oberlander replanted areas around the faculty club in 2008 when the pavilion was converted into classroom spaces.

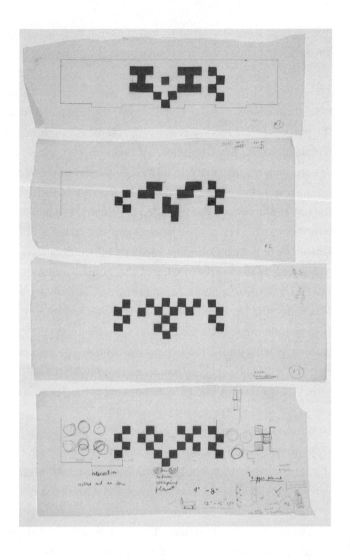

During the late 1950s Oberlander also collaborated in the design of the Rose Garden directly east of the Faculty Club. While the process drawings are no longer extant, the built work tells of a similar approach. Here, the traditional garden beds associated with roses have been recast as an orthogonal circuit of roses, grass, and walk set within a large amoebic shape. The garden once contained nine hundred roses (including three hundred rare varieties), and while it existed it was extremely popular with rose enthusiasts and featured in historical images of the campus.[15] The meandering pattern allowed people to weave among the roses for closer inspection and smelling, and it accommodated the

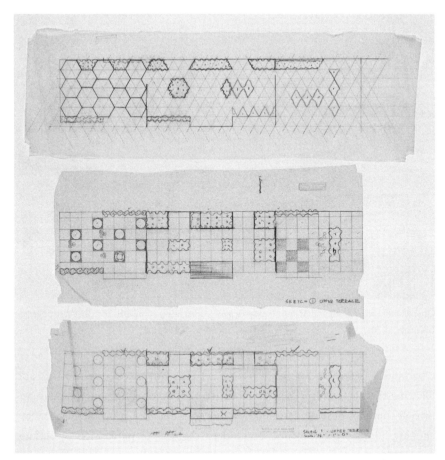

« ↑ The process of abstraction starts with paper cutouts that are transformed into landscape elements for the UBC Faculty Club terrace, Vancouver, 1956.

slope. Alas the Rose Garden was destroyed in 1997 with the construction of a new parking garage in its place. The replacement garden designed on top of the garage contrasted starkly with the former scheme. Paying tribute to the traditional notion of a rose garden it features a geometrical layout of beds outlined with neatly trimmed boxwood hedges, walkways, and grass panels whose carpet-like surface appear to be clipped from a lawn bowling field.

TREE LAYOUT

While abstraction provided a method to compose and ultimately locate landscape features, Gestalt theory guided Oberlander's approach to tree layout.

Oberlander's water basin and Arthur Erickson's pool (added later) at the UBC Faculty, Vancouver, circa 1969.

Oberlander is known for her work with trees—preserving, relocating, and planting them. Yet, rarely discussed is her method of laying out trees, an approach that can best be described as a Gestalt-inspired process. Gestalt psychology laid the groundwork for modern theories of perception by linking color, form, and the configuration of objects to our ability to interpret them as something—a figure or line of movement. Developed in Germany, Gestalt theory was an interest of the early Bauhaus faculty. In 1927 the Gestalt psychologist Rudolf Arnheim visited the school and Peter Behrens and Marcel Breuer later designed a house for the Gestaltist Kurt Lewin.[16]

Oberlander was exposed to this theory in her basic design course taught by George Tyrrell LeBoutillier at Harvard. Gestalt analyses appeared in LeBoutillier first lecture. Showing the students a grid of square dots he states, "We do not need the lines to still be able to see the rectangle. Our eyes (and hence our total reaction) record the relationship of the dots and we supply lines in our imagination."[17] Two dots in a diagonal formation, he argues, this is "visual directionality," our eyes will follow the trajectory of the imaginary line between the dots. Lastly, he shows one dot and notes that for a "bull's eye, our eyes are drawn to it and it remains there." He concludes however, that this static visual experience was to be avoided, for "the notion of movement is particularly significant in modern design expression."[18]

In the following exercise, "Point and Line," LeBoutillier guided students through a seven-sheet assignment using dots and lines to suggest movement. Students start by drawing a four-and-a-half by six-inch rectangle and locating three points or dots within the space and trying "to select points which appear to you to best relate to the rectangle." By the seventh sheet students begin to connect the points with ruled lines, studying the arrangement produced and trying "to discover the tensions exerted by the dots." As LeBoutillier observes, after all, "it is the movement of the observers' attention; not illusional, but actual movement."[19]

Oberlander remembers these exercises very well and she used a variation of this method in a planting design course in 1946. The course was co-taught by Lester Collins and Stephen F. Hamblin, and Collins, who was interested in modern design, may have encouraged this technique.[20] Interestingly, Oberlander reversed the process in her planting layout for trees. She first established the borders of the site but then drew many lines across the land; where the lines intersected she put a dot, which located the position of the tree. On-site, people will sense these lines by visually connecting the trees. She used this method to plan the layout of birch trees for Jim Everett Memorial Park and at East Three School, where this process was brought into the digital field.

DESIGNING FOR EXPERIENCE During the 1960s Oberlander's understanding of human experience was significantly deepened by her design work for children. For their play environments she developed a matrix to categorize their actions as they developed and as they encountered different elements of the design. For her playground at the Inuvik School, for example, she classified the age of a child from infant to preschool against the types of play characteristics of each age, the types of spaces that supported this play, design principles, site program, and comments. The infant row noted sensory types of play, such as tactile, smell, form, light, and shadow. In turn the spatial types included "stimulation of senses," "away from active areas," "UV protection," and "adult supervision." In the design principles section under infants, the landscape was "to provide visual and sensory stimulation at baby's level" and a "separate area for infants but visual contact with older children." Likewise, the site program listed grass, glider swings, places that feel different, places to crawl, roll, watch, discover, and

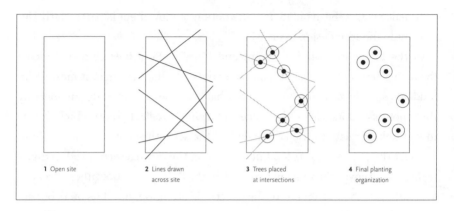

1 Open site   **2** Lines drawn across site   **3** Trees placed at intersections   **4** Final planting organization

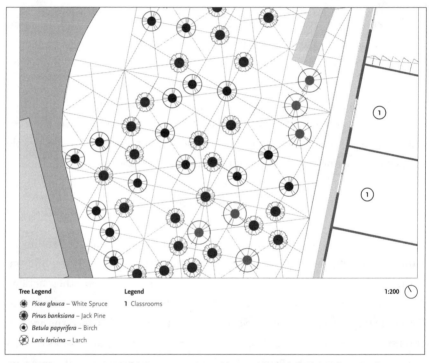

Tree Legend
- *Picea glauca* – White Spruce
- *Pinus banksiana* – Jack Pine
- *Betula papyrifera* – Birch
- *Larix laricina* – Larch

Legend
1 Classrooms

1:200

Oberlander's interpretation of the process (reversed by starting with the lines) for a tree layout technique, and applied in the planting plan for the East Three School sixty years later, 27 April 2012.

be diapered. By incorporating the consideration of children's development — physical and psychological — Oberlander enhanced her understanding of human experience in space and over time.

In 1974 at Robson Square this approach was broadened to anticipate human action and design features at various levels that spanned forty-eight feet — from below street grade to several stories above. During the 1960s and 1970s, when it was believed that urban landscapes could tap into our primeval selves, many landscape architects, architects, and environmental designers used matrices, notational systems, and scores, which attempted to model the varied layers of human experience over time and space. With the choreographer and his wife, Anna Halprin, Lawrence Halprin, for instance, developed a staggering array of approaches to understanding human experiences and their relation to group dynamics. They conducted Experiments in the Environment workshops in the 1960s, episodes that inspired much of his work. Borrowing the concept of scores from her choreography work, he developed a complex symbolic language to represent movement through space and time. Using these "motation" scores and RSVP Cycles, he attempted to design, in collaboration, an arrangement of experiences that unfolded as a unified sequence.[21]

Halprin's notational drawings exuded a fervor and comprehensiveness that are undeniably rich and interesting in their own right; however, they are often difficult to interpret. Oberlander, in contrast, developed a more legible system. When she joined the design team at Robson Square, she immediately recognized that understanding the project's section and its relation to human experience were of the utmost importance. In response she created a level matrix for all of the outdoor spaces. Avoiding a roster of symbols that would demand translation, she used descriptive text instead. The vertical depths listed in the matrix represented different levels, from 173 to 221 across the three-block project. The corresponding columns contained the headings Water, Sound, Plant Material, Pavement Treatment, Wall Treatment, Furniture, Smell, and Activities. The matrix was completed by listing how the design modified existing site conditions and contributed to new sensations and activities at each of the levels. Thus, running water in the Restaurant Courtyard level on Block 61 not only muted traffic noise; it also contributed sounds of gushing, spilling, and spraying water, which in turn encouraged or discouraged certain types of activities. This connection with elevation, design, and the sensations and activities that they

Level	Activities	Street furniture	Planting	Surface
Level 56 Georgia street	Entrance	Flagpoles Lighting Wastebaskets ?	Double row of Planetrees 9 m. o.c. both sides of the street Flowerpots	Granite ±50 m square
Level 53 Homer Robson	Walking	Lighting Wastebaskets	Single row of Planetrees 9 m. o.c.	Granite .50 m square
Level 53 53+ includ. roof tops Hamilton to Park 58 (Street below) 54 interconn. by stair + ramps.	for all citizens from 0-80 Passive areas Active Areas individuals/groups Entrance (a) walking (b) sitting (c) viewing watching (d) listening (e) watching Active Areas Sand Play 0-5 H₂O Play 3-18 slip + run Games areas 3-18 Chess Checkers 10-80 9 man Morris Picnic Area	Aeolian Harp (sheltered from wind) Benches in sunny areas with backrests wastebasket Sculpture - Focal Pt. Aeolian Harp Waterfall Sandpit - sand waterfall H₂O Pool earthmounds (earth Gameboards granite in floor or on table Benches + Tables Barbecue Pit Drinking Fountains	General Plte with Trees Shrubs gr.c. + grass groundcovers Shrubs Trees	Granite walks Granite walks earth
Level 50 Plazalevel	Performing Arts Stage for all ages Viewing Skating Watergames	Stage + Stairs (seating for viewing) waterdiscs (non-sinking)	On slope from Hamilton Park - Shrubs and ground-covers	granite (slip proof) H₂O
Entrance to ch's ctre.	Conservatory on learning about Plants	Conservatory	indoor Plants	Granite
Pod #2 Level 66	Receptions	Benches + Tables	Potted Trees in Flowerpots	granite in patterns
Levels 54 58 62 , 66	Viewing		Shrubs in street in ornate planters	5/74 c.H.O.

⌃ » Level matrix for Robson Square by Oberlander in May 1974 and its final content, 27 April 2012.

MAJOR LEVEL		STREET LEVEL +185 TO +191 BLOCKS 51, 61, 71	LEVEL +197 BLOCKS 51, 61	LEVEL +209 BLOCKS 51, 61
WATER		jetting	running sprinkling rainwater simulation	trickling
SOUND	Quality	noisy traffic	less noisy traffic	light traffic
	Instrumentation Possibilities	gongs	percussion wall orchestra	vibrating strings
PLANT MATERIAL		hardy plants avenues of trees seasonal color grass	shrubs hanging plants vegetable garden	shrubs hanging plants

PAVEMENT TREATMENT
(*in addition to general paving*)
		street and sidewalk
		  graphics (intersections
		  and crosswalks)
			pits and platforms
			  (children's theatre)
			hopscotch, marbles ring
			sand area
			wading pool or sprinkler
			  basin
			giant checkers
			horseshoe pitching
				tennis court
				volleyball court
				handball court
				shuffleboard court

WALL TREATMENT (*in addition to general wall texture*)		some graphics (directions and names)	fun murals fun textures	fun murals fun textures
FURNITURE		benches street lamps trash cans drinking fountains phone booths bird baths kiosks bike stands vending carts bus shelters	play structures outdoor play shelter tables and chairs for old people benches street lamps trash cans drinking fountains phone booths	benches street lamps trash cans drinking fountains phone booths
SMELL	Exisiting Additional Smells	traffic smells general city smells	general city smells plant material	general city smells plant material

ACTIVITIES		walking
		meeting
		catching buses
		running
		talking
			children's play, active
			  and passing
			  (including day care)
			old people's recreation
			lots of sitting and
			  watching
				active recreation for
				  office workers and
				  passers-by
				casual watching

afforded helped the design team to make major design decisions regarding the outdoor spaces at Robson Square.

SYNCOPATION

What Oberlander calls syncopation is another method used to position human experience as central to the design process. Borrowed from music, syncopation displaces expected beats with anticipation or delay.[22] During in the first decades of the twentieth century the use of syncopation in music intensified, most likely because it was a common feature of jazz.[23] Transferred to the landscape or garden, syncopation involves manipulating what people can see, usually with grading or plants, as they move through the space. By concealing and revealing views, anticipation and delay are brought into the experience of the landscape.

Lester Collins introduced syncopation to landscape architecture students at Harvard as a technique he borrowed from Japanese garden design. Collins and John Ormsbee Simonds developed a deep interest in the relationship between experience and design after traveling to Asia. Perhaps inspired by Tunnard's writings, their itinerary included gardens in Japan, as well as less familiar landscapes and gardens in Borneo and China. After the war, when Collins was an assistant professor in the landscape architecture department, he showed the students slides from their trips, explaining the unique handling of space in Japanese gardens, and how their syncopation conjured an element of mystery and surprise.[24] In later years, Collins studied the ancient Japanese gardening handbook *Sakuteiki* (Sensai Hisho). The wisdom gleaned from this study is most evident in his design for the Innisfree landscape in Millbrook, New York.[25]

Oberlander first experimented with syncopation in her design of children's environments. Creating winding paths and what she calls a series of child-size "hills and dales," her intent was to trigger children's curiosity — to entice them to explore the environment on their own accord. Syncopation later appeared at Robson Square both on grand and human scales. For example, the three main stramps on Block 61 are staggered. Ascending from the plaza one sees water features at the top of the first two sets of stramps; only when reaching the water do the next stramps come into view. The final set of stramps leads to Oberlander's meandering walkways where plants and the curve of the path prompt interest and movement. Syncopation at a smaller scale modulates the experience of the mound area where the height of the hill and the walkway that climbs it keep people in constant anticipation. Oberlander again employed syncopation in her 2010 design of the landscape for the new addition to the University of British Columbia's Museum of Anthropology. Here, large mounds and a winding path lead visitors from the reflecting pool, around the building, and to the new courtyard. Carefully adjusting the vertical height of the grades as metered by the horizontal lengths of the curving path, she created a sense of anticipation and delay that prompts movement between these two main spaces.

These design methods, borrowed and invented by Oberlander, give us further insight into her design process. They also reveal approaches, such as her elevation matrices for Robson Square, that have served as design vehicles for collaborating with other design professionals. This is just a start to understanding the design methods used by modern landscape architects, but it is hoped that future research will explore approaches used by other practitioners.

CONCLUSION

I opened *Cornelia Hahn Oberlander: Making the Modern Landscape* with the claim that Oberlander's narrative is also a story of modern landscape architecture. Given that her practice has spanned more than half a century, her life work has provided detailed accounts of modern landscape architecture's unfolding. Bracketed by the "Identity" chapter and the "Invention" chapter, I described three layers within her oeuvre: the social, psychological, and formal qualities of modern landscapes (in the "Housework" chapter), the human experiential qualities that landscapes afford (in the "Human Environment" chapter), and the ecological potency that landscapes can bring to a project (in the "Ecological Environment" chapter). While the nature of the written text has meant that these layers must be presented in a linear fashion, for Oberlander they are overlapping. One does not trump the others; rather, they build upon one another to form a stratum, which renders a thick conception of the profession.

As historians of landscapes have tried to chronicle the people and projects instrumental to modern landscape architecture's development, it has become apparent that they must look beyond the practicing, licensed architect and to the constellation of people, including writers, artists, gardeners, horticulturalists, activists, and community designers, who have also informed the field. Historically women have played these roles more often than that of licensed landscape architect. Oberlander's narrative poses an interesting question: Do professionals designing and building public landscapes occupy the same spotlight in the history of landscape architecture as do people designing their own backyards, writing about landscapes, or organizing a community garden? Do we miss addressing specific challenges faced by professionals, negotiating with contractors for example, when both landscape architects and nonprofessionals share the profession's history? I do not have the answer to these questions, but hopefully other scholars will probe them in the future.

Oberlander's story is not only pertinent because of her gender. The way she has approached her work is germane to current landscape architects, architects, designers, and students. Her willingness to experiment and invent has enabled her to realize design solutions that challenge conventional approaches, providing an alternative vision of practice. This is especially apparent in her daring command of projects that others would allow to be shaped by risk aversion. The fear of taking risks and its evolution as a core value in society is based on what the sociologist Frank Furedi calls the "precautionary principle," when *perceived* dangers of risks are greater than not taking risks. According to Furedi, the precautionary "principle has caused an institutionalization of caution. It offers security in exchange for lowering expectation, limiting growth and preventing experimentation and change."[1]

While the precautionary principle makes sense for the security industries, it is an inadequate principle for the design of landscapes. This is particularly true for children's outdoor play spaces, where the designed landscape should prompt curiosity and provide that vital element of challenge, but where all too often the false hope of a risk-free environment prevails. From her first experiments in Philadelphia at the 18th and Bigler Street Playground to Expo 67 in Montreal and her numerous other play spaces in Canada, Oberlander has designed landscapes for children that have resisted the conventional North American playground, which is largely shaped by fear. Planted rooftop sites are another case in point. If installed properly, planted roofs can help insulate the building, and even reduce sound penetration from the outside. Unfortunately, insurance companies are wary of green roofs because they are perceived as potentially compromising the building envelope. This perceived risk, however, has never stopped Oberlander. In fact it has prompted her to perfect her craft and perform what she calls "extreme research" regarding on-structure plantings.

There are, of course, cases where Oberlander intended public access to her landscapes, but fear prevailed. Her courtyard for the New York Times Building and the green roofs of the Waterfall Building and Library Square are examples where concerns for safety limited the design to either private use or, in the instance of the New York Times Building, reduced the project to mainly a visual space with limited access by anyone.

Oberlander giving a walking tour of Robson Square to landscape architecture students, Vancouver, 2011.

One surprisingly simple, yet important idea that has emerged in my study of Oberlander and her work is the role of time. Since landscapes change with time, and in some instances dramatically, they participate in the historical developments that shape them. For those charged with their design, this can result in decades of design work on a single project. Oberlander began Robson Square, for example, in 1974. While the project officially concluded in 1983, she was hired back six more times for adjustments and pruning, and between 2005 and 2011 she supervised the removal and storage of the plant material in order to replace the waterproofing membrane. The Museum of Anthropology landscape is another example of four decades of involvement by Oberlander. Many of her projects have also resulted in longtime collaborations with architects, arborists, other landscape architects, and clients. Oberlander and the architect Nick Milkovich, with whom she worked in Erickson's office in 1974, have realized a built project together every decade since the 1970s. In 2007 they completed the Stuart residence, a renovated midcentury house in Vancouver.

Interestingly, Oberlander has been summoned back to the Friedman residence, her first residential project in Vancouver. Designed with the architect Fred Lasserre, it was also an early example of a modern house and garden in

Vancouver. At this writing, plans are under way to restore the house and garden for an artist-in-residence program. The plant material has grown substantially, but vestiges of Oberlander's plan from 1953 are clearly legible. As a steadfast modern landscape architect, this project will present Oberlander with some fascinating questions. What will she retain and what will she remove? How will she bring the garden back to its original condition while transforming it to reflect the needs of the present?

Phyllis Lambert, founding director of the Canadian Centre for Architecture in Montreal, notes, "Cornelia's gentle but dogged persistence overcomes the bureaucracy and many needless hurdles in her way."[2] Perseverance is a character trait that surely can be traced back to her upbringing in Germany and the numerous challenges she faced after moving to North America. In fact her steady persistence took her back to Germany, lending an unexpected symmetry to her life story. In 1999 Oberlander was invited to join Kuwabara, Payne, McKenna, Blumberg Architects of Toronto in the design of the Canadian Embassy in Berlin. As the first Canadian embassy in this city, the project marked a significant moment in Canada's diplomatic ties with unified Germany. The embassy site, located on the octagonal Leipziger Platz, was noteworthy as well. The Platz was laid out in the 1730s (as one of the main entry points into the city), and in the following century it was designed to be a "people's park" by the landscape architect Peter Joseph Lenne as part of his work with the architect Frederick Karl Schinkel.[3]

During Oberlander's childhood this part of Berlin was a resplendent scene of commercial activity featuring some of the city's early experiments with modern commercial architecture. Leipziger Platz featured not only the luxurious Wertheim department store designed by Alfred Messel but also Erich Mendelsohn's high-rise office and commercial building, Columbushaus, which had been completed on the eve of Hitler's rise to power. Due to the labyrinth of intersecting transit systems at the Platz, its reformulation had also been a source of speculation by architects such as Martin Wagner.

After World War II and in the wake of a divided Berlin, Leipziger Platz lay at the very edge of the Russian zone, which bordered the British sector. With the erection of the Berlin Wall in 1961, Leipziger Platz became a no-man's land between East and West Berlin and was thus completely severed from both cities. The architect Alan Balfour recalls that for decades after the wall's erection, the vacant Platz was a source of reflection. Ascending a viewing platform on the western side, "people stared into this void, trying to derive meaning from the overlay of what this place had been and what it had become."[4]

Thus, the location of the embassy on Leipziger Platz signaled not only the mending of diplomatic relations between nations but also of the divided ambitions of a formerly segregated city—for which Oberlander served as an apt ambassador. Atop the embassy she designed a rooftop landscape. Like Library Square, this on-structure landscape was connected to the drainage infrastructure of the building and its composition also referred to a great watercourse, the Mackenzie River. Yet unlike Library Square, Oberlander's simple palette of plants was accompanied by 325 black-glass panels representing water. As the garden critic Cordula Hamann observes, "Oberlander did not succumb to the temptation of having the glass stained turquoise"; rather, the lustrous black glass captured a more profound version of the river, one that reflected the changing sky of Berlin in its image.[5]

Portraying a version of a Canadian river on a green roof in Berlin also brought Oberlander recognition by German artists, landscape architects, and architects. In 2005 the Goethe Institute and the Canadian Centre for Architecture (CCA) organized an exhibit displaying Oberlander's landscapes. Curated by Robert Desaulniers, CCA's head archivist, the exhibit featured photographs of her work taken by the German photographer Etta Gerdes. Between 2006 and 2012 the exhibit traveled from cities in Canada to several locations in Germany, including the Deutsches Architektur Zentrum in Berlin, and Switzerland.

Oberlander's return to Berlin held personal significance as well. She convinced Peter Oberlander to accompany her. In 1938 Peter's family, whose ancestors had lived more than nine generations in Austria, was forced into exile and Peter was eventually placed in an internment camp in rural Quebec. While he initially entered Canada as an enemy alien he would later adopt the country, making substantial contributions to the planning of its cities. However, in the intervening years he refused to visit Austria or Germany. Cornelia persisted, and in 2005 they toured Neubabelsberg, Wannsee, and Berlin.

They also visited Potsdam to see the Einstein Tower designed by Erich Mendelsohn. Completed in 1924, the structure was erected to prove by astronomical observations Einstein's theory of relativity and to simultaneously express his groundbreaking theory.[6] During the Weimar period the structure became a subject of debate in both public and professional architectural circles. According to the architectural historian Kathleen James (Chakraborty), it was "a lightning-rod for discussion about what contemporary architecture should look like, and in particular about the balance to be struck between individual expression and functional form."[7] The Einstein Tower had inspired both Peter and Cornelia before they had even met. Certainly the integration of the architecture and landscape was striking. Mendelsohn's Bejach house, where Cornelia played as a child, stressed a horizontal integration of landscape and structure, with building walls tracing the site's property lines. In contrast, Mendelsohn's tower emphasized sectional integration. Much of the below-grade laboratory was covered with turf and the tower appeared to emerge from the ground plane, seemingly relieved of earthbound perceptions of light, time, and gravity.

Five years later, Oberlander's experience of Weimar Germany would shape a Canadian landscape, the new Visitor Centre at the VanDusen Botanical Gardens in Vancouver. This project also marked a turning point in Oberlander's work—where her knowledge of plant form began to influence architectural form. Consulting to Sharp and Diamond Landscape Architects and Architects Busby, Perkins + Will, the design team's primary charge was to communicate to visitors how plants support our livelihood. For the architects, there was no better way to express this idea than a building whose very structure recalled plant life.

Oberlander originally intended to focus on planting the roof, but given the goal of the project, she broadened her role by assisting in the generation of the entire roof form. She did this by introducing the design team to the photographs of Karl Blossfeldt in *Urformen der Kunst* (Art forms in nature) from 1928. Using his camera like a microscope, Blossfeldt magnified our view of plants and plant parts in stark black-and-white images that revealed their elegant architectural structures. The photographs solidified the team's commitment to explore plant form for the roof structure and they researched native plants as the source of its exact language.[8] Both Oberlander and the landscape architects consulted the work of Archibald Menzies, a Scottish botanist who had accompanied Captain George Vancouver in his expeditions. His book *The Journal of Archibald Menzies* (1794) represented one of the first examinations of vegetation in the coastal area now called Vancouver. The design team selected the white bog orchid described by Menzies. The plant's structure and white color was reminiscent of Blossfeldt's images, and the architects translated its petals into an elegant roof form.

This approach yielded a dramatic overhead structure for the gardens' Visitor Centre. Opening in the fall of 2011, the public was immediately greeted by the undulating roofline, a virtual building-size corolla with a single petal raised above the others to signal the building's entrance. At the back of the center one of the giant petals almost touched the ground, and transported water to Oberlander's rainwater garden. The underside of this roof was made of wood beams, which despite their usual tendency toward straightness, had been shaped into curving forms that appeared to float above the exterior and interior spaces. The top of this roof was the underside's verdant corollary — a rolling lanceolate-shaped topography that could be seen from high points in the garden as well as Oak Street, one of the main entryways into the city.

Designed more than thirty years after Robson Square, the VanDusen Botanical Gardens Visitor Centre signaled a transformation in Oberlander's green roof collaborations. At Robson Square, excluding the mound and the horizontal curves of the upper walkways, the majority of the landscape was determined by the geometric logic of its interior structure. Vegetation was located on top of this system, greatly enhancing the experience of the rooftop spaces, but the forms still obeyed the rubric of the architecture. In contrast, at the Visitor Centre, the living algorithms of a plant found in the regional landscape guided the architectural form of the roof, providing an elegant interplay between external appearances and internal structure.

Given the trajectory of events that have shaped North America since Cornelia Hahn Oberlander joined the profession, it is fair to say that landscape architecture matters more now than ever, and that Oberlander's contributions will not be forgotten. Certainly the chief direction of the profession might be summed up as sustainable design or green design. Yet, she would surely incorporate the human dimension as part of this direction. For Oberlander there is no fission between ecological and social needs or division between the necessity of pragmatic thought and aesthetic experience. As she attests, "They are unified, they are one."[9] Without doubt Oberlander's lifetime of work has given us numerous instances of this unified vision, rendered in landscapes of hush beauty.

NOTES

Unless otherwise noted, all interviews with Cornelia Hahn Oberlander were conducted by the author, from 2008 to 2012 in Canada and the United States, and are cited as "CHO interview" with the designated date and place.

Introduction

1. CHO interview, 20 June 2009, Vancouver, Canada.
2. Ellis, *History and Biography Panel.*
3. Schenker, "Feminist Interventions in the Histories of Landscape Architecture," 108.
4. Ellis, *History and Biography Panel.*
5. Meyer, "The Post-Earth Day Conundrum," 199.
6. Williams, *Landscape Architecture in Canada.*
7. Windsor-Liscombe, *The New Spirit,* 26.
8. CHO interview, 27 October 2009, Vancouver, Canada.
9. Morris and Sakai, "Modern," 219.
10. Treib and Imbert, *Garrett Eckbo,* 27.
11. CHO interview, 4 March 2010, Vancouver, Canada.
12. CHO interview, 17 February 2011, Cambridge, Massachusetts.
13. Scarry, *On Beauty and Being Just.*
14. See the Marc Treib entries in the bibliography.
15. Proctor, "The Architect's Intention," 296.
16. Ibid., 305.
17. Herrington, "A Model Modern," Women and Modernism in Landscape Architecture, 18 February 2011, Graduate School of Design, Harvard University.
18. CHO interview, 22 March 2010, Vancouver, Canada.
19. For example, Oberlander readily admits that while the 18th and Bigler Street Playground, which she designed in the 1950s in Philadelphia, did provide a new place to play, it did not solve the formidable social and economic problems that people faced there.

1 | Identity

1. Gerdes et al., *Bilder Kanadischer Landschaftsarchitektur,* 58.
2. Stinson, *Love Every Leaf,* 9.
3. CHO interview, 26 April 2010, Vancouver, Canada.
4. Stinson, *Love Every Leaf,* 10.
5. Gundula Proksch kindly forwarded to me a list of Beate Hahn's books and translated the titles.
6. Kindergartens were banned in Germany in 1851, and the use of the gardens in Froebel's pedagogy was largely forgotten. See Herrington, "Kindergarten."

7. This is the abbreviated title. See Keatinge, *Great Didactic of Comenius.*
8. CHO interview, 11 August 2010, Vancouver, Canada.
9. Stinson, *Love Every Leaf,* 15.
10. CHO interview, 26 August 2010, Vancouver, Canada.
11. Anderson, *Women, Design, and the Cambridge School,* 112.
12. Oberlander, "Reflective Moments," 3, an unpublished essay for English IIIa at Smith College, 1941, Cornelia Hahn Oberlander estate.
13. Ibid., 4.
14. Oberlander's account supports Daniel Horowitz's thesis that the second wave of feminism, which Friedan helped start in the 1960s, began with her writings on justice for working women in the 1940s. See Horowitz, *Betty Friedan and the Making of the Feminine Mystique.*
15. CHO interview, e-mail exchange, 3 February 2011.
16. Wellwood, "Making Top Grades," 21.
17. Larivée, "City Art," 26.
18. Oberlander's grandfather Ignaz Jastrow helped to found the Berliner Handelshochschule. Her great-grandfather Albert Hahn founded a seamless pipe factory (Hahnsche Werke in Mülheim/Ruhr) and started a pension and health insurance plan for his workers that evolved into the general health and pension insurance plan for all of Germany (Gerdes et al., *Bilder Kanadischer Landschaftsarchitektur,* 57). Kurt Hahn, her uncle, founded Schule Schloss Salem in the 1920s and, with Lawrence Holt, Outward Bound in the UK in 1941.
19. Offen, *European Feminisms, 1700–1950,* 22.
20. Graham, *Managing on Her Own,* 25.
21. Erickson quoted in Leccese, "Canadian Modern," 66.
22. CHO interview, 23 July 2010, Seattle, Washington.
23. Jim Wright interview with the author, 5 August 2011, Vancouver, Canada.
24. Way, "Social Agendas of Early Women Landscape Architects," 187.
25. See Cautley, *Garden Design* (1935).
26. Museum of Modern Art, "Modern Gardens and the Landscape," 2.
27. Eckbo, *The Landscape We See,* 25.
28. McLeod, "Undressing Architecture," 324.
29. Alofsin, *The Struggle for Modernism,* 213.
30. CHO interview, 18 July 2009, Vancouver, Canada.
31. Oberlander, "Women and the Idea of LEISURE," 1.
32. Anderson, *Women, Design, and the Cambridge School,* 94.
33. Hudnut, *Report for the Academic Year 1941–42,* 292.
34. Frost, "School News," 166.
35. Oberlander had been notified by Joseph Hudnut on 5 March 1943 that she was eligible to apply to the GSD, Cornelia Hahn Oberlander estate.
36. Hudnut's memo to Oberlander described a new curriculum, 26 April 1943, Cornelia Hahn Oberlander estate.

37. Hudnut, *Report for the Academic Year 1943–44.* Elizabeth Bird Barnes died on 11 February 2010.

38. *School History,* 39.

39. Pearlman, *Inventing American Modernism,* 102.

40. Hudnut, *Report for the Academic Year 1943–44,* 205.

41. Hudnut, *Report for the Academic Year 1950–51,* 561.

42. Halprin was Oberlander's carrel-mate in the fall of 1943. According to Simo and Walker, Halprin enlisted in the navy in December 1943. See Walker and Simo, *Invisible Gardens,* 150.

43. CHO interview, 13 May 2008, Vancouver, Canada.

44. Ibid.

45. Pearlman, *Inventing American Modernism,* 203.

46. Gropius "Teaching the Arts of Design," 160–61.

47. CHO interview, 23 July 2010, Seattle, Washington.

48. Breuer, unpublished lecture to Yale University, 1.

49. Bayer, Gropius, and Gropius, *Bauhaus,* 32.

50. Brosterman, *Inventing Kindergarten.*

51. CHO interview, 23 July 2010, Seattle, Washington.

52. CHO interview, 13 May 2008, Vancouver, Canada.

53. CHO interview, 11 August 2010, Vancouver, Canada.

54. CHO interview, 13 May 2008, Vancouver, Canada.

55. CHO interview, 11 August 2010, Vancouver, Canada.

56. Unfortunately they failed to mention her name as the landscape architect.

57. CHO interview, 23 July 2010, Seattle, Washington.

58. This data was obtained with the help of Mary Daniels, Frances Loeb Library Special Collections librarian, and Norton Gerenfeld, GSD Alumni Office.

59. Heinz Peter Oberlander and his family fled to England from Vienna. While the rest of the family left for the United States, Peter stayed in England. He was later arrested and sent to an internment camp in Canada for approximately two years. After his release he entered McGill University's architecture program in 1941.

60. Pearlman, *Inventing American Modernism,* 206.

61. Newton, *An Approach to Design,* 88.

62. CHO interview, 22 March 2010, Vancouver, Canada.

63. Pond, "50 Years in Retrospect," 66.

64. Oberlander, "Parks, Playgrounds and Landscape Architecture," 10.

65. Erickson quoted in Preston, "An Affinity for Natural Beauty," 19.

66. Alofsin, *The Struggle for Modernism,* 188.

67. Oberlander, "Good Land Use + Good Architecture = Long Earning Life," 164.

68. CHO telephone interview, 16 February 2011.

69. Bremer Pond's recommendation letter for Oberlander, 10 July 1947, Cornelia Hahn Oberlander estate.

2 | Housework

1. Lester and Gillespie, *Landscape Architecture.*
2. Pond, "Foreword," 5.
3. Orland, "Book Review," 1218. For an analysis of the first, 1932 edition of *Architectural Graphic Standards,* see Emmons, "Diagrammatic Practices," 4–21.
4. Stevenson, "A Transitional Year," 127.
5. Berrizbeitia, *Daniel Urban Kiley,* 27.
6. Oberlander, "Housing and Landscape Architecture," 12.
7. Treib, "Axioms for a Modern Landscape Architecture," 53.
8. Deforest, "Opportunity Knocks!" 10.
9. Oberlander "The Professional Practice of Landscape Architecture," lecture notes, 1955, Cornelia Hahn Oberlander estate.
10. Eckbo, *Landscape for Living,* 23–24.
11. Ibid., 73.
12. Bottomley, "Landscape Design in a Modern Manner Based on the Controls of Common Sense and Good Taste," 49. Landscape architects discussed forms and space as early as 1918. See Lay, "Space Composition."
13. Forty, *Words and Buildings,* 174–95.
14. Downing, *A Treatise on the Theory and Practice of Landscape Gardening,* 327.
15. Newton, *An Approach to Design,* 113.
16. Collins, "Of Landscape Architecture," 13.
17. Newton, *An Approach to Design,* 122.
18. Thompson, *Rethinking Landscape,* 93.
19. This concern for use functions eventually led to the formalization of a design process that started with a bubble diagram, a series of circles whose size and labeling symbolized different activities, and the creation of a functional diagram that situated the relationship of these activities to the site.
20. Larivée, "City Art," 26.
21. Ruskin, *The Seven Lamps of Architecture,* 39–40.
22. Ibid., 48.
23. Robinson, *The Parks, Promenades and Gardens of Paris,* 61.
24. Modern architects, for example, condemned the architect who attempted to conceal the towering height of a commercial skyscraper with a series of Greek orders. See Goff, "Honesty in Architecture," 119–20.
25. Tunnard in Pearlman, *Inventing American Modernism,* 102–3, see also 254n. Pearlman notes that this quote was on a placard from the GSD Exhibit of 1942. The placard was re-exhibited in 2000 for the department's centennial exhibition.
26. Tunnard, *Gardens in the Modern Landscape* (1938), 103. Also see Tunnard, "Modern Gardens for Modern Houses."
27. Tunnard, *Gardens in the Modern Landscape* (1938), 103.
28. CHO interview, 30 July 2010, Vancouver, Canada.

29. Garrett Eckbo to Cornelia Hahn, 24 July 1947, Cornelia Hahn Oberlander estate.

30. Dan Kiley to Cornelia Hahn, 13 December 1949, Cornelia Hahn Oberlander estate.

31. Oberlander to Peter, 22 October 1947. She obtained the bulbs from Jan de Graaff, who brought them when he fled Holland in 1940. He later established a successful bulb business in Oregon.

32. Oberlander to planner Frederick P. Clark, 6 December 1949. She writes that she was looking to "combine practical work with the Community," Cornelia Hahn Oberlander estate.

33. CHO interview, 30 July 2010, Vancouver, Canada.

34. Shanken, *194X*, 39. See also Stonorov and Kahn, *Why City Planning Is Your Responsibility* and *You and Your Neighborhood.*

35. Progress Report for the Planning Board of the Township of Mendham, New Jersey, 1948, Cornelia Hahn Oberlander estate.

36. Ibid.

37. CHO interview, 11 August 2010, Vancouver, Canada.

38. Clendenin, "Preserve Philadelphia!" 2.

39. Heller, "Salesman of Ideas," 28.

40. Cornelia Hahn, "Germantown Gardens Exploration Trip," 2:30 p.m., Sunday, 19 February 1950, Cornelia Hahn Oberlander estate.

41. Citizens' Council on City Planning Annual Report, 1950–1951, 2, Cornelia Hahn Oberlander estate.

42. Spencer-Wood, "Turn of the Century Women's Organizations," 124.

43. Clendenin, "Preserve Philadelphia!" 11.

44. CHO interview, 23 July 2010, Seattle, Washington.

45. Ibid.

46. Ibid.

47. Dev, Gelfand, and Herrington, "Typology as Policy," 42.

48. Mumford, "The 'Tower in the Park,'" 36.

49. Clendenin "Preserve Philadelphia!" 14.

50. The exhibit also went to Mexico City, New York, and Los Angeles. See Storrer, *The Architecture of Frank Lloyd Wright*, 386.

51. Chambers, "Contracts and Specifications for Landscape Architects," 153–56.

52. Richard Haag interview with Thaïsa Way and Susan Herrington, 23 July 2010, Seattle, Washington.

53. CHO interview, 23 July 2010, Seattle, Washington.

54. Ibid.

55. Ibid.

56. Lecesse, "Canadian Modern," 67.

57. CHO interview, 27 October 2009, Vancouver, Canada.

58. Kahn, *Mill Creek Redevelopment Area Plan*, 18.

59. Spirn, "Restoring Mill Creek," 398.

60. Tyng, "Number Is Form and Form Is Number," 134.

61. Kahn, "Toward a Plan for Midtown Philadelphia," 20.
62. See Gutheim, "Piano di transformazione della zona di Mill Creek," 137–141; and Tentori et al., "Il piano regolatore di Philadelphia," 4–25.
63. "Apartments in Philadelphia," 108.
64. Ibid.
65. See Gast, *Louis I. Kahn: Works, 1944–99*.
66. Kahn, "Toward a Plan for Midtown Philadelphia," 20.
67. Mumford, "The 'Tower in the Park.'"
68. CHO interview, 31 July 2008, Vancouver, Canada.
69. Spirn, "Restoring Mill Creek," 396.
70. See Hopkinson, "Designation Letter," 1.
71. Kahn, *Mill Creek Redevelopment Area Plan*, 6.
72. Contosta, *Suburb in the City*, 115–16.
73. Oberlander, "Good Land Use + Good Architecture = Long Earning Life," 164. McHarg also lived at Cherokee Housing, See McHarg, *Quest for Life*, 136.
74. CHO interview, 30 September 2008, Vancouver, Canada.
75. Clendenin, "Preserve Philadelphia!" 14.
76. "Up, Down, and Over," 119.
77. Williams, *Recreation Places*, 250.
78. Oberlander, "Parks, Playgrounds, and Landscape Architecture," 7.
79. "Related Design Fields," 102.
80. Ledermann and Trachsel, *Creative Playgrounds and Recreation Centers*, 102.
81. She also began her problematic relationship with Creative Playthings. In an undated promotional catalog, *Play Sculptures*, Oberlander's plan view drawing of the 18th and Bigler Street Playground was published without giving her credit, Cornelia Hahn Oberlander office files.
82. Oberlander, "Parks, Playgrounds, and Landscape Architecture," 6.
83. Ian McHarg to Cornelia Hahn Oberlander, 23 April 1958, Cornelia Hahn Oberlander estate.
84. Oberlander, "Spaces for All Seasons," 6.
85. Leccese, "Canadian Modern," 68.
86. Windsor-Liscombe, *The New Spirit*, 10.
87. Windsor-Liscombe, *Historic Context Statement Post-1940 Register Update and Statements of Significance*, 13.
88. CHO interview, 26 August 2010, Vancouver, Canada.
89. Adams, "Catherine Mary Wisnicki."
90. Windsor-Liscombe, *Historic Context Statement Post-1940 Register Update and Statements of Significance*, 10.
91. CHO interview, 22 March 2010, Vancouver, Canada.
92. Waymark, *Thomas Mawson*, 143–46.
93. Archives Canada, *Justice, Webb and Vincent Landscape Architects fonds*.
94. Oberlander, "Landscaping the Single Family House," 21.
95. Oberlander, "Parks, Playgrounds and Landscape Architecture," 6.

96. Oberlander, proposal to Fred Lasserre, 14 July 1960, Cornelia Hahn Oberlander estate.

97. Oberlander, "Women and the Idea of LEISURE," 1.

98. Ron Williams interview with the author, 22 February 2011, Montreal, Canada. Canada's development was smaller and slower compared to the United States. In British Columbia landscape architects were titled as licensed professionals in 1968, and in 1972 the first Canadian Society of Landscape Architects annual conference took place in Vancouver. See Clark, "A Pocket History/Histoire de poche," 13.

99. Oberlander and Oberlander, "The Spirit of Architecture in the Canadian Northwest," 130.

100. Oberlander, "Parks, Playgrounds and Landscape Architecture," 6.

101. Windsor-Liscombe, *The New Spirit*, 26.

102. McKay, "Urban Housekeeping and Keeping the Modern House," 12.

103. Ibid., 11.

104. Gustein, *Vancouver LTD*, 158.

105. Oberlander, "Housing and Landscape Architecture," 12.

106. Windsor-Liscombe, *The New Spirit*, 69.

107. Oberlander, "Housing and Landscape Architecture," 13.

108. Gustein, *Vancouver LTD*, 158.

109. Harcourt, Cameron, and Rossiter, *City Making in Paradise*, 52.

110. Windsor-Liscombe, *The New Spirit*, 71.

111. Martin Lewis interview with the author, 7 March 2009, Vancouver, Canada.

112. Moir, "Sculptured in the Play of Tomorrow's Child," 23.

113. Luxton, "The Rise and Fall of West Coast Modernism in Greater Vancouver, British Columbia," 56.

114. Portland Hotel Society, *Shared Learnings on Homelessness*.

115. Nick Milkovich interview with the author, 30 September 2011, Vancouver, Canada.

116. Elisabeth Whitelaw interview with the author, 18 August 2010, Vancouver, Canada.

117. Ibid.

118. Dietz, "Butler Sturtevant," 234.

119. Luxton, "The Rise and Fall of West Coast Modernism in Greater Vancouver, British Columbia," 55–56.

120. Cole and McKay, *Access to Architecture: Intentions and Products*, 1.

121. Luxton, "The Rise and Fall of West Coast Modernism in Greater Vancouver, British Columbia," 56.

122. Colomina, *Domesticity at War*, 8.

123. Moir, "Sculptured in the Play of Tomorrow's Child," 23.

124. "Tick-Tack-Toe House," 16.

125. CHO interview, 22 March 2010, Vancouver, Canada.

126. Harris, "Making Your Private World."

127. Smiley, "Making the Modified Modern," 47.

128. Sketchley and Clowes, "A Gravity Survey of the Igneous Body at Little Mountain, Vancouver, B.C.," 74.

129. Milton Wong interview with the author, 12 January 2010, Vancouver, Canada.

130. "Tick-Tack-Toe House."

131. Oberlander, "A Need for Green Streets," 37.

132. CHO interview, 23 July 2010, Seattle, Washington.

133. Church, *Gardens Are for People*, 3.

134. Lavin, *Form Follows Libido*, 4.

135. Eckbo, *The Landscape We See*, 194.

136. Oberlander, "Landscaping the Single Family House," 22.

137. Ibid., 21.

138. Lavin, *Form Follows Libido*, 38.

139. Adapted from Roeckelein, *Elsevier's Dictionary of Theories, Laws, and Concepts in Psychology*, 308.

140. Jarzombek, *The Psychologizing of Modernity*, 65.

141. Tunnard, *Gardens in the Modern Landscape* (1948), 118.

142. Ibid., 121.

143. Eckbo, *Landscape for Living*, 67.

144. Mallgrave, *Modern Architectural Theory*, 203.

145. Oberlander, "Landscaping the Single Family House," 22.

146. Colomina, *Domesticity at War*, 165.

147. Quoted in Harris, "Making Your Private World," 194.

148. Oberlander correspondence with the Keevils, 1977, Cornelia Hahn Oberlander files.

149. Eckbo, *Landscape for Living*, 10.

150. Oberlander, lecture notes, 9, 1954, Cornelia Hahn Oberlander estate.

151. Oberlander, "Landscaping the Single Family House," 22.

152. Morgan, "The Enchantment of Art," 322.

153. Harris, "Making Your Private World," 198.

154. Church, *Gardens Are for People*, 21.

155. Oberlander, "Planned for Leisure Living: The UBC Home of Dr. and Mrs. Sydney M. Friedman," 15.

156. Erickson, *The Architecture of Arthur Erickson*, 106.

157. Iglauer, *Seven Stones: A Portrait of Arthur Erickson*, 75.

158. Ibid., 73.

159. Shapiro, *Arthur Erickson*, 12.

160. Erickson, *The Architecture of Arthur Erickson*, 106.

161. CHO interview with Marc Treib and Thaïsa Way, written documentation, 23 July 2010, Seattle, Washington.

162. Erickson, *The Architecture of Arthur Erickson*, 111.

163. Johnson and Frankel, *Modern Landscape Architecture*, 85.

164. CHO interview with Marc Treib and Thaïsa Way, written documentation, 23 July 2010, Seattle, Washington.

165. Tunnard, "What Is Happening to Modern Architecture?" 13.

166. Eckbo, *Landscape for Living,* 10–18.

167. Goldhagen, *Louis Kahn's Situated Modernism,* 102.

168. See Kiley and Amidon, *Dan Kiley in His Own Words.*

169. Milton Wong interview with the author, 12 January 2010, Vancouver, Canada.

170. Tunnard, *Gardens in the Modern Landscape* (1948), 91.

171. Milton Wong interview with the author, 12 January 2010, Vancouver, Canada.

3 | Human Environment

1. Koss, "On the Limits of Empathy," 141–42.

2. Eckbo, *The Landscape We See,* 196.

3. Simonds, *Landscape Architecture,* 142.

4. Also, the Norwegian architect and historian Christian Norberg-Schulz, in *Existence, Space and Architecture* (1971) and later *Genius Loci: Towards a Phenomenology of Architecture* (1979), connected philosophical meditation with experiences of environments. While Norberg-Schulz never identified a specific phenomenological method, he was able to effortlessly link vernacular and contemporary environments through experiences with them that we share as humans.

5. Newton, *Design on the Land,* xxiii.

6. Jellicoe and Jellicoe, *The Landscape of Man,* 8.

7. Marcuse, *Eros and Civilization,* xi, xiii.

8. See Jacques, "Art and Instinct," 95–96.

9. Jellicoe, "Jung and the Art of Landscape," 124.

10. Ibid.

11. Eckbo, *The Landscape We See,* 40.

12. Ibid., 191.

13. Oberlander, *Space for Creative Play,* 1, brochure, 1967, Cornelia Hahn Oberlander estate.

14. Woudstra, "Danish Landscape Design in the Modern Era (1920–1970)," 237.

15. Bengtsson, *Environmental Planning for Children's Play,* 18.

16. Woudstra, "Danish Landscape Design in the Modern Era (1920–1970)," 237.

17. Kozlovsky, "Adventure Playgrounds and Postwar Reconstruction," 187.

18. Allen quoted in Bengtsson, *Environmental Planning for Children's Play,* 8.

19. Bengtsson, *Environmental Planning for Children's Play,* 149.

20. See Passantino, "Adventure Playgrounds for Learning and Socialization."

21. CHO interview, 18 August 2010, Vancouver, Canada.

22. Stanton, *Expo 67 — Architecture.*

23. Canadian Corporation for the 1967 World Exposition, "Pavilion of Canada," 5.

24. Ibid.

25. Hill, "Children's Creative Centre at Canada's Expo 67," 261.

26. Ibid., 259.

27. Larivée, "City Art," 26.

28. Alice Borden fonds, Box 6, File 10, University of British Columbia Archives.

29. Ibid., Box 6, File 14.

30. 15 February 1962 Minutes, 2, Child Study Centre Management Committee, Alice Borden fonds, Box 6, File 17, University of British Columbia Archives; and an undated clipping "Kindergarten Take University in Stride," Canadian Press, Box 6, File 22.

31. Hill, "Children's Creative Centre at Canada's Expo 67," 259.

32. Ibid., 262.

33. H. L. Brown, "1968 Evaluation of the Children's Creative Centre."

34. Hill, *Habitat*, 13.

35. Dingman, "Expo 67," *Toronto Daily Star,* 53.

36. Herrington, "EXPO 67 Revisited," 13.

37. Hill, *Habitat*, 13.

38. Herrington, "EXPO 67 Revisited," 13.

39. Hill, "Children's Creative Centre at Canada's Expo 67," 259.

40. Adolph et al., *Learning in the Development of Infant Locomotion,* 22.

41. Conway in 1982, quoted in Herrington, "EXPO 67 Revisited," 13.

42. "The Viewpoint Early Childhood Education Child Study Centre Faculty of Education," 1.

43. CHO interview, 25 June 2009, Vancouver, Canada.

44. Acadia — Stage II — Married Student Housing Program, September 1969, Box 1, File 1, Department of Facilities Planning fonds, University of British Columbia Archives.

45. CHO interview, 25 June 2009, Vancouver, Canada.

46. Oberlander to R. N. Squires, 1, 9 May 1972, Cornelia Hahn Oberlander estate.

47. Oberlander, "A Need for Green Streets," 36.

48. Ibid., 35.

49. Oberlander, *Playgrounds . . . a Plea for Utopia,* 2.

50. Robb, "Pram in the Hall."

51. Braham, "Vision Creates a Park for the Century," B3.

52. CHO interview, 25 June 2009, Vancouver, Canada.

53. Ibid.

54. Jacobs, *The Death and Life of Great American Cities,* 220.

55. LaFarge, *The Essential William H. Whyte,* 42.

56. Jacobs, *The Death and Life of Great American Cities,* 447.

57. Eckbo, Kiley, and Rose, "Landscape Design in the Primeval Environment," 90.

58. Church, *Gardens Are for People,* 118.

59. Halprin, *Cities,* 134.

60. Oberlander, Nadel, and Bohm, *Trees in the Cities,* 31. 61. Oberlander, "An Oasis in the City," 7.

62. Francis, "Community Design," 16.

63. See Jacobs and Appleyard, "Toward an Urban Design Manifesto."

64. See Ley, "Alternative Explanations for Inner-City Gentrification."

65. Community Arts Council of Vancouver Newsletter, July/August 1977, 2.

66. Attendance list for the official opening of the 900 Robson Block pilot project in civic improvement, Community Arts Council of Vancouver, 3 September 1964, Box 2, Special Projects, University of British Columbia Library.

67. Community Arts Council of Vancouver Minutes, 1966–69, Box 2, University of British Columbia Library.

68. Gibson, "The Meaning of Robson Square," 6.

69. Ibid.

70. Pastier, "Evaluation," 65.

71. A planted roof for Block 51, Robson Square was envisioned by Erickson from the start of the project.

72. Sarti, "49 Storeys off Bennett Tower," C2.

73. Shapiro and Windsor-Liscombe, *Arthur Erickson,* 38–39.

74. Coffin, "Court Complex Found Wanting," 2.

75. Leiren, "'Designed for Architects,'" A6.

76. Bing Thom interview with the author, 16 September 2011, Vancouver, Canada.

77. Oberlander, typed proposal, February 1974, 1, Cornelia Hahn Oberlander office files.

78. Ibid.

79. Ibid.

80. Ibid.

81. Taylor, "Mother Nature," 36.

82. Nick Milkovich interview with the author, 30 September 2011, Vancouver, Canada; and Jim Wright interview with the author, 16 September 2011, Vancouver, Canada.

83. Wright, "Vancouver Robson Square," 4.

84. Shapiro and Windsor-Liscombe, *Arthur Erickson,* 6.

85. "Vancouver's Dazzling Center," 51.

86. Harcourt, Cameron, and Rossiter, *City Making in Paradise,* 14.

87. Wright, "Vancouver Robson Square," 8.

88. Erickson, "Schematics for Robson Square," 32, August 1974, 75-023-18T, Canadian Centre for Architecture, Cornelia Hahn Oberlander Archive, 2006 Addition, Robson Square Provincial Government Complex.

89. Oberlander, "Spaces for All Seasons," 9.

90. Bentley-Mays, "Grow What You See," C1.

91. Polo, "Canadian Modern Landmarks Revisited," 44–45.

92. Erickson quoted in Aird, "The 'A' Team of Canadian Landscape Architecture," 20.

93. Lecesse, "Canadian Modern," 69.

94. CHO interview, 11 August 2010, Vancouver, Canada.

95. Oberlander quoted in Aird, "The 'A' Team of Canadian Landscape Architecture," 20.

96. Taylor, "Mother Nature," 36.

97. Oberlander, "Spaces for All Seasons," 13.

98. Oberlander, "An Oasis in the City," 9.

99. Arthur Erickson Architects, *Courthouse Renovation,* 21.

100. Glover, "Council Favors Maples over London Plane Trees," A14.
101. Arthur Erickson Architects, *Courthouse Renovation*, 18.
102. Oberlander, "An Oasis in the City," 12.
103. See the Canadian Architectural Archives, Robson Square Project, ER173510, University of Calgary.
104. Gerdes et al., *Bilder Kanadischer Landschaftsarchitektur*, 52–53.
105. Jim Wright interview with the author, 16 September 2011, Vancouver, Canada.
106. Oberlander, "An Oasis in the City," 7.
107. Gerdes et al., *Bilder Kanadischer Landschaftsarchitektur*, 56–57.
108. Shapiro and Windsor-Liscombe, *Arthur Erickson*, 38.
109. Jashemski, *The Natural History of Pompeii*.
110. Oberlander, "An Oasis in the City," 12.
111. CHO interview, 11 August 2010, Vancouver, Canada.
112. "Vancouver's Dazzling Center," 50.
113. Fairley, "Courthouse Still Leaks but Complaints Dry Up," A4.
114. Clarke, "New Heart for Vancouver Leaves Bog Questions Unanswered," 8.
115. Ibid.
116. Oberlander, "An Oasis in the City," 7.
117. Jim Wright interview with the author, 5 August 2011, Vancouver, Canada.
118. CHO interview, 11 August 2010, Vancouver, Canada.
119. Gibson, "The Meaning of Robson Square," 8.
120. Pastier, "Evaluation," 66.
121. Stephens, "Law Courts / Robson Square, Vancouver," 84.
122. Rosenberg, *The Capilano Review 40 Robson Square*, 103.
123. McCarthy, "Square Deal," 5.
124. Wilson, "Erickson Gets Burned as Block 71 Fiddled," D4.
125. CHO interview, 27 January 2010, Vancouver, Canada.
126. CHO interview, 11 August 2010, Vancouver, Canada.
127. Godfrey, "In Person: A Growing Concern," C2.
128. Bentley-Mays, "Grow What You See," C1.
129. Erickson, *Erickson 2000*.
130. Boddy, "Erickson in Washington," 25.
131. Gournay and Loeffler, "Washington and Ottawa," 488.
132. Ibid., 480.
133. Berelowitz, "Erickson," 18.
134. Oberlander, "The New Canadian Chancery," 6–7.
135. Oberlander project description, Cornelia Hahn Oberlander office files.
136. Ibid.
137. Oberlander, "The New Canadian Chancery," 6–7.
138. Gournay and Loeffler, "Washington and Ottawa," 500.
139. Ibid., 495.
140. Goldberger, "A New Embassy Mixes the Appropriate and the Awkward."

141. Hank White telephone interview with the author, 30 September 2011.

142. Lubow, "Piano Grande."

143. Oberlander and Whitelaw, "New York Times Building," 21.

144. Brown et al., "Microclimatic Design of the New York Times Tower," 14.

145. Ibid., 13.

146. Finch, "Scale, Security and the Humane," 31.

147. Hank White telephone interview with the author, 30 September 2011.

148. Lavin, *Form Follows Libido*, 140.

4 | Ecological Environment

1. Meyer, "The Post-Earth Day Conundrum," 242.

2. Newton, *An Approach to Design*, 144.

3. Nadenicek and Hastings, "Environmental Rhetoric, Environmental Sophism," 141.

4. Rome, "Give the Earth a Chance," 528.

5. Fein and Crespi, "Landscape Architecture among the Design Professions: A Survey Report," 13.

6. Ibid.

7. Nassauer, "Managing Career and Family," 31.

8. Rome, "Give the Earth a Chance," 540.

9. CHO interview, 4 July 2009, Vancouver, Canada.

10. See Herrington, "The Nature of Ian McHarg's Science."

11. See Steinitz, "Predicting the Impacts of Suburban Development."

12. Rainey, "Organic Form in the Humanized Landscape," 187.

13. See Treib, "Must Gardens Mean?"

14. See Olin, "Form, Meaning and Expression in Landscape Architecture."

15. Erickson, *The Architecture of Arthur Erickson*, 83. The museum was originally called the Museum of Man. See Banham, "Have a Good Day," 3.

16. Arnett, "Collections Come From Many Sources," 4.

17. Wachtel, "An Accessible Heritage," 8.

18. CHO interview, 4 July 2009, Vancouver, Canada.

19. Preston, "An Affinity for Natural Beauty," 19.

20. Oberlander, lecture on the Museum of Anthropology, 15, 1988, Cornelia Hahn Oberlander office files.

21. Erickson, *The Architecture of Arthur Erickson*, 83.

22. Ibid., 84–85.

23. Arnett, "Architect Reaches into B.C.'s Past for Design," 2.

24. Vastokas, "Architecture as Cultural Expression," 8.

25. CHO interview, 23 September 2009, Vancouver, Canada.

26. Lecesse, "Canadian Modern," 68.

27. Oberlander, lecture on the Museum of Anthropology, 16, 1988, Cornelia Hahn Oberlander office files.

28. "Inflation Hits Museum," 3.

29. Beardsley, "Thwarted Masterpiece," 125.
30. According to Obberlander seismic conditions had already been considered, CHO interview, 9 July 2009, Vancouver, Canada.
31. Phillips, "Apec at the Museum of Anthropology," 191.
32. Elias, "University of British Columbia Museum of Anthropology," 59.
33. Clifford, "Four Northwest Coast Museums," 218.
34. Crosby, "Construction of the Imaginary Indian," 274.
35. Hushion, "A City and Its Museums," 100.
36. CHO interview, 9 July 2009, Vancouver, Canada.
37. CHO interview, 31 July 2008, Vancouver, Canada.
38. Ord, *The National Gallery of Canada,* 16.
39. Boggs, "The Designing of a National Gallery," 204.
40. Ord, *The National Gallery of Canada,* 7–9.
41. Ibid., 5.
42. Boggs, "The Designing of a National Gallery," 201.
43. Boddy, "Critique," 45.
44. Ibid., 46.
45. Ibid.
46. Ord, *The National Gallery of Canada,* 343.
47. Safdie quoting the former prime minister Trudeau, Safdie, "The National Gallery of Canada," 8.
48. Schmertz, "Collective Significance," 120.
49. Murray and Dent, "National Gallery of Canada," 163.
50. Baele, "Northern Terrain," 39.
51. Lecesse, "Canadian Modern," 66.
52. Friedrich Oehmichen to Oberlander, 5 January 1986, Fonds 075, Folder 252351, National Gallery, 1986, Canadian Centre for Architecture, Oberlander 2008 Addition, Cornelia Hahn Oberlander Archive.
53. See Cook, "Drawing the Line."
54. Kaufmann, "Naturalizing the Nation," 685.
55. Boggs, "The Designing of a National Gallery," 205.
56. Meyer, *Minimalism,* 179.
57. Gerdes et al., *Bilder Kanadischer Landschaftsarchitektur,* 53.
58. White, "Museums and Their Buildings," 8.
59. Ord, *The National Gallery of Canada,* 23.
60. Oberdorf, "Ottawa Taiga Reveals Canada's Soul," H2.
61. Ord, *The National Gallery of Canada,* 23.
62. Rochon quoted in Gerdes et al., *Bilder Kanadischer Landschaftsarchitektur,* 18.
63. Graif, "The Paradox of Public Discourse," 21.
64. MacDonald, *A Guidebook to Contemporary Architecture in Vancouver,* 24.
65. Macaulay and McLennan, *The Ecological Engineer,* 79.
66. Graif, "The Paradox of Public Discourse," 22.

67. Oberlander to Moshe Safdie, 7 September 1991, Fonds 074, 75-2006-26T, Canadian Centre for Architecture, Cornelia Hahn Oberlander Archive.
68. Ibid.
69. Ibid.
70. Ibid.
71. Davis, "Library's Concept One for the Books," A36.
72. Ward, "And the Winner Should Be . . . ," B2.
73. McKenzie, "Mistake or Masterpiece?" 46.
74. Freedman, "Sightlines," C15.
75. Haden, "Libraries 4," 32.
76. Ledger, "Vancouver Library Competition," 22.
77. Dafoe, "Vancouver's Library Square Goes to Safdie," C1.
78. Macaulay and McLennan, *The Ecological Engineer,* 186.
79. Sullivan, "From Systems to Architecture," 104.
80. Safdie quoted in Beers, "Architect of Boom," 78.
81. Moshe Safdie to Facilities Development manager, 2 November 1992, Fonds 074, 75-2006-26T, Canadian Centre for Architecture, Cornelia Hahn Oberlander Archive.
82. Graif, "The Paradox of Public Discourse," 28.
83. Rossiter, "The Birth of a Statement," 9.
84. Beers, "Architect of Boom," 65.
85. Graif, "The Paradox of Public Discourse," 28.
86. Dudfield, "Garden in the Sky," 6.
87. Macaulay and McLennan, *The Ecological Engineer,* 179.
88. Fax from Moshe Safdie's office to Oberlander, date illegible, Fonds 074, 75-2006-26T, Canadian Centre for Architecture, Cornelia Hahn Oberlander Archive.
89. Thomas, "Canadian Collossus," 72–79.
90. Wilson, "Construction Din Fills New Library," B1.
91. Dudfield, "Garden in the Sky," 4.
92. Graif, "The Paradox of Public Discourse," 19.
93. Valpy, "Drama and Light in a Public Building," A14.
94. Graif, "The Paradox of Public Discourse," 29.
95. Ledger, "Vancouver Library Competition," 20.
96. Windsor-Liscombe, "Conditions of Modernity," 7.
97. Rybczynski, "A Sight for Sore Eyes," 82.
98. Davey, "Outrage," 21.
99. Haden, "Libraries 4," 32.
100. Boddy, "Condo Boom Pushing Out City's Creatives?" S6.
101. CHO interview, 27 January 2010, Vancouver, Canada.
102. See Johnston, McCreary, and Nelms, *Green Roofs.*
103. Dudfield, "Garden in the Sky," 4–6.
104. Jacobs, "The Greening of the City."
105. See Zeller, *Inventing Canada,* 98.

106. Newton, "An Approach to Design," 129.

107. Parsons and Carlson, *Functional Beauty*.

108. Oberlander, "CSLA 75th Anniversary Address," lecture notes, 14 August 2009, Toronto, Canada.

109. Gino Pin and Cornelia Hahn Oberlander lecture, "Designing for Extremes," University of British Columbia, Vancouver, 14 March 2009, Susan Herrington's notes.

110. Macaulay and McLennan, *The Ecological Engineer*, 201.

111. CHO interview, 30 September 2008, Vancouver, Canada.

112. Macaulay and McLennan, *The Ecological Engineer*, 203.

113. Ibid., 212.

114. Ibid., 205.

115. Grace, *Canada and the Idea of North*, 17.

116. Ironside, "Canadian Northern Settlements," 103.

117. Ibid., 106.

118. Hamilton, "Looking to the Future," 12.

119. Ibid., 13.

120. Jim Wright interview with the author, 5 August 2011, Vancouver, Canada.

121. Hamilton, "Looking to the Future," 15.

122. CHO interview, 30 September 2008, Vancouver, Canada.

123. Oberlander, "Modernism, Aesthetics and Ecology," Women and Modernism in Landscape Architecture, 18 February 2011, Graduate School of Design, Harvard University.

124. Jim Wright interview with the author, 5 August 2011, Vancouver, Canada.

125. CHO interview, 11 August 2010, Vancouver, Canada.

126. NWT Bureau of Statistics.

127. See the Canadian Great Northern Arts Festival website.

128. Kindt, *Inuvik K-12 Education Report*, 9.

129. See Beilman, Vitt, and Halsey, "Localized Permafrost Peatlands in Western Canada."

130. Walker, "Arctic Deltas," 724.

131. Gino Pin and Cornelia Hahn Oberlander lecture, "Designing for Extremes," University of British Columbia, Vancouver, 14 March 2009, Susan Herrington's notes.

132. Gagnon, "92.3 Million," 9.

133. Kindt, *Inuvik K-12 Education Report*, 9–10.

134. Ibid.

135. Ibid.

136. Ibid.

137. Gino Pin and Cornelia Hahn Oberlander lecture, "Designing for Extremes," University of British Columbia, Vancouver, 14 March 2009, Susan Herrington's notes.

138. CHO interview, 23 July 2010, Seattle, Washington.

139. Overland et al., *Arctic Report Card 2012*.

140. See Park, *The Environment*.

141. Gino Pin and Cornelia Hahn Oberlander lecture, "Designing for Extremes," University of British Columbia, Vancouver, 14 March 2009, Susan Herrington's notes.

142. Oberlander et al., "Inuvik Northwest Territories Integrating Design with a Climate of Extremes, a Fragile Ecology, and Cultural Complexities," 15.
143. Ibid.

5 | Invention

1. Ron Williams interview with the author, e-mail exchange, 13 April 2011.
2. Treib, "Axioms for a Modern Landscape Architecture," 55.
3. Oberlander, "Planning the Amenities," 28.
4. Woudstra, "The Corbusian Landscape," 149.
5. Treib, *Representing Landscape Architecture*, 113.
6. Ibid., 118.
7. CHO interview, 13 May 2008, Vancouver, Canada.
8. Michels, "The Early Drawings of Frank Lloyd Wright Reconsidered," 300.
9. Martin, *The Organizational Complex*, 5.
10. "Tick-Tack-Toe House," 16.
11. Oberlander, "Planned for Leisure Living," 11–12.
12. Oberlander, "The New Canadian Chancery," 6.
13. Simonds, *Landscape Architecture*, 287.
14. Oberlander's notes to Elisabeth Whitelaw, 19 January 1999, AP075.S1.D192, Canadian Centre for Architecture, Cornelia Hahn Oberlander Archive.
15. "Coming Up Roses," 4.
16. Behrens, "Art, Design and the Gestalt Theory," 300.
17. LeBoutillier's notes for Architectural Science 3a, p. 3, 1948 lectures. These lectures date from after Oberlander's graduation, GSD History Collection, Academic Affairs, Box 4, Design Exercises, Frances Loeb Library Special Collections, Graduate School of Design, Harvard University.
18. Ibid.
19. LeBoutillier's notes for the lecture "Point and Line," 3, October 1948, GSD History Collection, Academic Affairs, Box 4, Design Exercises, Frances Loeb Library Special Collections, Graduate School of Design, Harvard University.
20. Hamblin was an instructor for Design I, LA 8. See *The Official Register Harvard University*.
21. Halprin, *The RSVP Cycles*, 165.
22. Levitin, *This Is Your Brain on Music*, 63.
23. Huron and Ommen, "An Empirical Study of Syncopation in American Popular Music, 1890–1939," 224.
24. CHO interview, 31 July 2008, Vancouver, Canada.
25. See Maguire, "Day Trip"; and Collins, *Innisfree*.

Conclusion

1. Furedi, *Culture of Fear,* 9.
2. Lambert, *Reflections.*
3. Balfour, "Octagon," 89.

4. Ibid., 95.

5. Hamann, "Der Himmel Berlins im Mackenzie River The Mackenzie River Reflects the Berlin Sky," 67.

6. See James, "Expressionism, Relativity, and the Einstein Tower."

7. Ibid., 407.

8. See Newcomb, "Rip Rap, Form Follows Flora."

9. CHO interview, 23 April 2012, Vancouver, Canada.

BIBLIOGRAPHY

Archives

American Heritage Center, University of Wyoming, Laramie, Wyoming.
Architectural Archives, University of Pennsylvania, Philadelphia, Pennsylvania.
Canadian Architectural Archives, University of Calgary, Calgary, Alberta, Canada.
Canadian Centre for Architecture, Montreal, Quebec, Canada.
Chestnut Hill Historical Society, Philadelphia, Pennsylvania.
Collections Canada, Ottawa, Ontario, Canada.
Frances Loeb Library Special Collections, Harvard University, Cambridge,
    Massachusetts.
Harvard University Archives, Pusey Library, Cambridge, Massachusetts.
Library and Archives of Canada, Ottawa, Ontario, Canada.
National Park Service Frederick Law Olmsted National Historic Site, Brookline,
    Massachusetts.
North Carolina Department of Cultural Resources, Raleigh, North Carolina.
University of British Columbia Archives, Vancouver, British Columbia.
Vancouver Historical Society, Vancouver, British Columbia.
Walter P. Reuther Library and Archives, Wayne State University, Detroit, Michigan.

Other Sources

Adams, Annmarie. "Catherine Mary Wisnicki." *Canadian Encyclopedia.* http://www
    .thecanadianencyclopedia.com/index.cfm?PgNm=TCESearch&Params=A1.
Adolph, Karen E., with commentary by Bennett I. Bertenthal, Steven M. Boker,
    Eugene C. Goldfield, and Eleanor J. Gibson. *Learning in the Development of Infant
    Locomotion.* Chicago: University of Chicago Press, 1997.
Aird, Louise. "The 'A' Team of Canadian Landscape Architecture." *Landscape Trades*
    (1994): 12–21.
Allen of Hurtwood, Lady (Marjory Gill Allen). *Planning for Play.* Cambridge, Mass.:
    MIT Press, 1968.
Alofsin, Anthony. *The Struggle for Modernism: Architecture, Landscape Architecture,
    and City Planning at Harvard.* New York and London: W. W. Norton & Company,
    2002.
Anderson, Dorothy May. *Women, Design, and the Cambridge School.* West Lafayette,
    Ind.: PDA Publishers Corporation, 1980.
"Apartments in Philadelphia: Scissors." *The Architectural Forum* (January 1952): 108.
Archives Canada. *Justice, Webb and Vincent Landscape Architects Fonds.* http://www
    .archivescanada.ca/english/search/ItemDisplay.asp?sessionKey=999999999_142&l
    =0&lvl=1&v=0&coll=1&itm=144144&rt=1&bill=1.

Arnett, John. "Architect Reaches into B.C.'s Past for Design." *UBC Reports* 19, no. 2 (January 1973): 1–2.

———. "Collections Come from Many Sources." *UBC Reports* 19, no. 2 (January 1973): 3–4.

Arthur Erickson Architects. *Courthouse Renovation: A Study of the Potential for Accommodating Civic Uses in the Vancouver Courthouse as Part of the 51–61–71 Project.* Vancouver: Arthur Erickson Architects, 1974.

Babineau, Guy. "Erickson's Urban Waterfall." *Architecture Week* (February 2002). http://www.architectureweek.com/2002/0220/design_1–1.html.

Baele, Nancy. "Northern Terrain: National Gallery of Canada, Ottawa." *Landscape Architecture* 78, no. 8 (December 1988): 38–40.

Baeyer, Edwinna Von, and Pleasance Crawford, eds. *Garden Voices: Two Centuries of Canadian Garden Writing.* Toronto: Random House of Canada, 1995.

Balfour, Alan. "Octagon: The Persistence of the Ideal." In *Recovering Landscape: Essays in Contemporary Landscape Architecture,* ed. James Corner, 87–100. New York: Princeton Architectural Press, 1999.

Banham, Jim. "Have a Good Day." *UBC Reports* 19, no. 4 (22 February 1973): 1–12.

Bayer, Herbert, Walter Gropius, and Ise Gropius. *Bauhaus 1919–1928.* London: Allen & Unwin, 1939.

Beardsley, John. "Thwarted Masterpiece: When Do Environmentalists' Intentions Become Unreasonably Rigid?" *Landscape Architecture* 89, no. 8 (August 1999): 125, 128.

Beaudet, Marc. *The Canadian Pavilion Expo 67.* 18 min., 58 sec. Montreal: Canadian Film Board, 1967.

Beers, David. "Architect of Boom: Interview by David Beers." *Vancouver Magazine* (May/June 1995): 60–86.

Behrens, Roy R. "Art, Design and the Gestalt Theory." *Leonardo* 31, no. 4 (1998): 299–303.

Beilman, David W., Dale H. Vitt, and Linda A. Halsey. "Localized Permafrost Peatlands in Western Canada: Definition, Distributions, and Degradation." *Arctic, Antarctica, and Alpine Research* 33, no. 1 (2001): 70–77.

Bengtsson, Arvid. *Environmental Planning for Children's Play.* New York: Praeger, 1970.

Bentley-Mays, John. "Grow What You See." *The Globe and Mail,* 17 October 1992, C1–2.

Berelowitz, Lance. "Erickson: A Turning Point." *Canadian Architect* (April 1992): 18–24.

Berrizbeitia, Anita. *Daniel Urban Kiley: The Early Gardens, Landscape Views.* 2d ed., ed. William S. Saunders. New York: Princeton Architectural Press with the Harvard University Graduate School of Design, 1999.

Blossfeldt, Karl, with introduction by Karl Nierendorf. *Art Forms in Nature: Enlarged Photographs of Plant Forms.* New York: Universe Books, 1967.

Boddy, Trevor. "Condo Boom Pushing Out City's Creatives?" *The Globe and Mail,* 14 March 2008, S6.

———. "Critique: Architecture on the Fast Track." *Canadian Architect* 33, no. 6 (1988): 44–49.

———. "Erickson in Washington." *Canadian Architect* 34 (July 1989): 25–37.

Boggs, Jean Sutherland. "The Designing of a National Gallery." *The Burlington Magazine* 127, no. 985 (April 1985): 201–7, 209, 270.

Bohn, Glenn. "Women on the Move: The Place of Landscaping in the Learning Process." *The Vancouver Sun*, 11 September 1979, Sec. You, 1.

Bottomley, M. E. "Landscape Design in a Modern Manner Based on the Controls of Common Sense and Good Taste." *Landscape Architecture* 37, no. 1 (January 1947): 43–49.

Braham, Daphne. "Landscape Architect Plays Awakener Role." *The Vancouver Sun*, 21 May 2001, Lower Mainland, B3.

———. "Vision Creates a Park for the Century." *The Vancouver Sun*, 21 June 2002, B3.

Breuer, Marcel. Unpublished lecture to Yale University, 19 October 1948, Folder A004, Lectures and Writings, Breuer Files, Subseries A000. Frances Loeb Library Special Collections, Graduate School of Design, Harvard University.

Brosterman, Norman. *Inventing Kindergarten.* New York: Harry N. Abrams, 1997.

Brown, H. L. "1968 Evaluation of the Children's Creative Centre," Play, Vancouver, 1969, ARCH252382. Canadian Centre for Architecture, Cornelia Hahn Oberlander Archive, Oberlander 2008 Addition.

Brown, Robert D., Robert T. LeBlanc, Cornelia Hahn Oberlander, and Hank White. "Microclimatic Design of the New York Times Tower: Applied Landscape Research." *Landscapes/Paysages* 6, no. 1 (Winter 2004): 13–16.

Burchard, Charles. "Gropius at Harvard." *Journal of Architectural Education* 14, no. 2 (1959): 23–35.

Canada Mortgage and Housing Corporation. *To Build a Better City, Parts 1 and 2.* Vancouver: National Film Board, 1964.

Canadian Corporation for the 1967 World Exposition. "Pavilion of Canada." Information Manual, Information Services, Expo 67, S 26 1–7. Toronto: Maclean Hunter, 1967.

Canadian Great Northern Arts Festival. http://www.gnaf.org/.

Carver, Humphrey. "Reviewed Work, Habitat 1976: The Home of Man." *The Town Planning Review* 48, no. 3 (July 1977): 281–86.

Cautley, Marjorie L. Sewell. *Garden Design: The Principles of Abstract Design as Applied to Landscape Composition.* New York: Dodd, Mead & Co., 1935.

CBC Digital Archives. *Montreal Gets the Call.* 13 November 1962. http://www.archives.cbc.ca/society/celebrations/topics/100/"Montreal gets the call."

Chambers, Walter L. "Contracts and Specifications for Landscape Architects, *Landscape Architecture* 46 (October 1956): 153–56.

Church, Thomas Dolliver. *Gardens Are for People: How to Plan for Outdoor Living.* New York: Reinhold Publishing Corporation, 1955.

Clark, Doug. "A Pocket History/Histoire de poche." *Landscapes/Paysages 75 Years/ Ans Colours of the Profession/Les Couleurs de la Profession* 11, no. 2 (Spring 2009): 12–15.

Clarke, John. "New Heart for Vancouver Leaves Bog Questions Unanswered." *The Globe and Mail*, 21 October 1978, Sec. The Provinces, 8.

Clendenin, Malcolm, with an introduction by Emily T. Cooperman. "Preserve Philadelphia! Thematic Context Statement, Modernism: 1945 to 1980," 1–27. *The Preservation Alliance for Greater Philadelphia*, July 2009.

Clifford, James. "Four Northwest Coast Museums." In *Exhibiting Cultures: The Poetics and Politics of Museum Display*, ed. Steven D. Lavine and Ivan Karp, 212–54. Washington D.C.: Smithsonian Institution Press, 1991.

Coffin, Alex. "Court Complex Found Wanting." *The Province* (Vancouver), 1973, 2.

Cole, Raymond, and Sherry McKay, *Access to Architecture: Intentions and Product.* UBC School of Architecture Monographs. Vancouver: School of Architecture, University of British Columbia, 1998.

Collins, Lester. *Innisfree: An American Garden.* Portland, Ore.: Timber Press, 1983.

———. "Of Landscape Architecture." In *Landscape Architecture,* ed. Lester Collins and Thomas Gillespie, 13–14. Cambridge: Harvard University, 1951.

Collins, Lester, and Thomas Gillespie, eds. *Landscape Architecture.* Cambridge: Harvard University, 1951.

Colomina, Beatriz. *Domesticity at War.* Cambridge, Mass.: MIT Press, 2007.

"Coming Up Roses." *UBC Reports* 39, no. 7 (April 1993): 1–8.

Contosta, David R. *Suburb in the City: Chestnut Hill, Philadelphia, 1850–1990.* Columbus: Ohio State University Press, 1992.

Cook, Maria. "Drawing the Line." *The Ottawa Citizen,* 20 October 2010. http://www.ottawacitizen.com/opinion/Drawing+line/3655281/story.html.

Crosby, Marcia. "Construction of the Imaginary Indian." In *Vancouver Anthology: The Institutional Politics of Art,* ed. Stan Douglas, 266–91. Vancouver: Talon Books, 1991.

Dafoe, Christopher. "Vancouver's Library Square Goes to Safdie." The *Globe and Mail* (Toronto), 15 April 1992, Sec. The Arts Business, C1.

Davey, Peter. "Outrage." *Architectural Review* 20, no. 1199 (January 1997): 21.

Davis, Chuck. "Library's Concept One for the Books." *The Province* (Vancouver), 18 June 1992, A36.

Deforest, Lockwood. "Opportunity Knocks! This Time Will the Landscape Architect Miss the Bus?" *Landscape Architecture* 26, no. 1 (October 1945): 10.

Dev, Gita, Lisa Gelfand, and Susan Herrington. "Typology as Policy." *Architecture California* 16, no. 2 (1994): 42–48.

Dietz, Duane A. "Butler Sturtevant." In *Shaping Seattle Architecture: A Historical Guide to the Architects,* ed. Jeffrey Karl Ochsner, 234–39, reprint. Seattle: University of Washington Press, 1998.

Dingman, Jocelyn. "Expo 67." *Toronto Daily Star,* 3 July 1967, Sec. 4, 53.

Downing, Andrew Jackson. *A Treatise on the Theory and Practice of Landscape Gardening, Adapted to North America; with a View to the Improvement of Country Residences . . . with Remarks on Rural Architecture.* With a supplement by Henry Winthrop Sargent. 6th ed. New York: A. O. Moore & Co., 1859.

Dudfield, Travis. "Garden in the Sky," *Vancouver Courier,* 31 July 2009, 4–6.

Eckbo, Garrett. *Landscape for Living.* New York: F. W. Dodge Corporation, 1950.

———. *The Landscape We See.* New York: McGraw-Hill, 1969.

Eckbo, Garrett, Dan Kiley, and James Rose. "Landscape Design in the Primeval Environment." In *Modern Landscape Architecture: A Critical Review,* ed. Marc Treib, 83–87, reprint. Cambridge, Mass.: MIT Press, 1993.

Elias, P. Douglas. "University of British Columbia Museum of Anthropology: A Review." *Gazette: Quarterly of the Canadian Museums Associations* 10, no. 2 (Spring 1977): 58–62.

Ellis, Joseph. *History and Biography Panel: A Dialogue.* Lynn Hudson Parsons, Chair. American Historical Association 118th Annual Meeting, Washington, D.C., 10 January 2004. C-Span 2.

Emmons, Paul. "Diagrammatic Practices: The Office of Frederick L. Ackerman and Architectural Graphic Standards." *Journal of the Society of Architectural Historians* 64, no. 1 (March 2005): 4–21.

Erickson, Arthur. *The Architecture of Arthur Erickson.* Vancouver: Douglas & McIntyre, 1988.

———. *Erickson 2000.* http://www.arthurerickson.com/sp_mcgill.html.

———. "Progress Report: Robson Square, Vancouver, BC." *Canadian Architect* 24 (1979): 34–41.

———. "Schematics for Robson Square," 32, August 1974, 75–023–18T. Canadian Centre for Architecture, Cornelia Hahn Oberlander Archive, 2006 Addition, Robson Square Provincial Government Complex.

Erickson/Massey Architects. *A Proposal for Block 61 and the Downtown Core, Vancouver.* Vancouver: Erickson/Massey Architects, May 1966.

Fairley, Jim. "Courthouse Still Leaks but Complaints Dry Up." *The Province,* 28 December 1979, A4.

Fein, Albert, and Irving Crespi. "Landscape Architecture among the Design Professions: A Survey Report." *JAE* 31, no. 2, Research on the Profession (November 1977): 12–17.

Finch, Paul. "Scale, Security and the Humane." *Architectural Review* 223, no. 1335 (May 2008): 31.

Flanagan, Frank M. "John Amos Commenius (1592–1670) Education as a Human Right," 75–85. In *The Greatest Educators Ever.* London: Continuum, 2006.

Francis, Mark. "A Case Study Method for Landscape Architecture." *Landscape Journal* 20, no. 1 (January, 2001): 15–29.

———. "Community Design," *JAE* 37, no. 1 (Autumn 1983): 14–19.

Forty, Adrian. *Words and Buildings: A Vocabulary of Modern Architecture.* New York: Thames & Hudson, 2000.

Freedman, Adele. "Sightlines: And the Envelopes Please . . . ." *The Globe and Mail,* 14 March 1992, The Arts Column, C15.

Frost, Henry A. "School News." *Landscape Architecture* 32, no. 4 (July 1942): 166.

Furedi, Frank. *Culture of Fear: Risk-Taking and the Morality of Low Expectation.* London: Continuum, 2002.

Gagnon, Jeanne. "92.3 Million." *Northern News Service,* Monday, May 2010, 9.

Gast, Klaus-Peter. *Louis I. Kahn: Works, 1944–99.* Basel: Birkhauser, 1999.

Gerdes, Etta, Mechtild Manus, Cornelia Hahn Oberlander, Lisa Rochon, and the Canadian Centre for Architecture staff. *Bilder Kanadischer Landschaftsarchitektur: Projekte von Cornelia Hahn Oberlander Picturing Landscape Architecture: Projects of Cornelia Hahn Oberlander As Seen by Etta Gerdes.* Munich: Callwey, 2006.

Gibson, Edward M. "The Meaning of Robson Square." *West Coast Review* 15, no. 4 (1981): 5–9.

Glover, Randy. "Council Favors Maples over London Plane Trees." *The Vancouver Sun,* 11 January 1978, A14.

Godfrey, Stephen. "In Person: A Growing Concern," *The Globe and Mail,* 2 July 1988, C2.

Goff, Bruce. "Honesty in Architecture." In *Goff on Goff: Conversations and Lectures,* ed. Paul B. Welch, 111–56. Norman: University of Oklahoma Press, 1996.

Goldberger, Paul. "A New Embassy Mixes the Appropriate and the Awkward." *New York Times,* 9 July 1989. http://www.nytimes.com/1989/07/09/arts/architecture -view-a-new-embassy-mixes-the-appropriate-and-the-awkward.html?pagewanted =all.

Goldhagen, Sarah Williams. *Louis Kahn's Situated Modernism.* New Haven, Conn.: Yale University Press, 2001.

Gombrich, Ernst Hans Josef. *Art and Illusion: A Study in the Psychology of Pictorial Representation.* London: Phaidon, 1960, 1977.

Gournay, Isabelle, and Jane C. Loeffler. "Washington and Ottawa: A Tale of Two Embassies." *Journal of the Society of Architectural Historians* 61, no. 4 (December 2002): 480–507.

Grace, Sherrill. *Canada and the Idea of North.* Montreal: McGill-Queen's University Press, 2002.

Graham, Laurel D. *Managing on Her Own: Dr. Lillian Gilbreth and Women's Work in the Interwar Era.* Norcross, Ga.: Engineering & Management Press, 1998.

Graif, Linda Lewin. "The Paradox of Public Discourse: Designing Vancouver's Library Square." *Journal of the Society for the Study of Architecture in Canada* 25, no. 1 (2000) 18–32.

Gropius, Walter. "Teaching the Arts of Design." *College Art Journal* 7, no. 3 (Spring 1948): 160–64.

Gunther, Erna. *Ethnobotany of Western Washington: The Knowledge and Use of Indigenous Plants by Native Americans.* Seattle: University of Washington Press, 1945, 1973.

Gustein, Donald. *Vancouver LTD.* Toronto: Donald Gustein, 1975.

Gutheim, Frederick Albert. "Piano di transformazione della zona di Mill Creek." *Urbanistica* no. 26 (September 1956): 137–41.

Haden, Bruce. "Libraries 4: Toga Party." *Canadian Architect* 40, no. 8 (August 1995): 32–33.

Hahn, Beate. *Die Gartenfibel für Kinder, Eltern und Grosseltern* [The garden primer for children, parents and grandparents]. Zürich: Rascher, 1948.

——. *Gärten für die Jugend mit der Jugend* [Gardens for the youth with the youth]. Zürich: Rascher, 1960.

——. *Dein Garten wächst mit Dir vom Kinderbeet zum Wohngarten* [Your garden grows with your children growing from bed to a residential garden — with plan drawings by Cornelia Hahn]. Ravensburg: Otto Maier, 1952.

——. *Hurra, wir säen und ernten!* [Hooray, we sow and harvest!]. Breslau: Wilhelm Gottlieb Korn, 1935.

——. *Der Kindergarten ein Garten der Kinder — Ein Gartenbuch für Eltern, Kindergärtnerinnen und alle, die Kinder lieb haben* [The kindergarten a children's garden — A garden book for parents, kindergarten teachers, and everybody who loves children]. Zürich: Rascher, 1936.

Halprin, Lawrence. *Cities.* New York: Reinhold, 1963.

——. *The RSVP Cycles: Creative Processes in the Human Environment.* New York: G. Braziller, 1970.

Hamann, Cordula. "Der Himmel Berlins im Mackenzie River" [The Mackenzie River reflects the Berlin sky]. In *Bilder Kanadischer Landschaftsarchitektur: Projekte von Cornelia Hahn Oberlander Picturing Landscape Architecture: Projects of Cornelia Hahn Oberlander As Seen by Etta Gerdes,* Etta Gerdes, Mechtild Manus, Cornelia Hahn Oberlander, Lisa Rochon, and the Canadian Centre for Architecture staff, 65–73. Munich: Callwey, 2006.

Hamilton, David. "Looking to the Future: A New Legislative Building for the NWT." *Canadian Parliamentary Review* (Summer 1992): 12–15.

Harcourt, Mike, Ken Cameron, and Sean Rossiter. *City Making in Paradise: Nine Decisions That Saved Vancouver.* Vancouver/Toronto: Douglas & McIntyre, 2007.

Harris, Dianne. "Making Your Private World: Modern Landscape Architecture and *House Beautiful,* 1945–1965." In *The Architecture of Landscape, 1940–1960,* ed. Marc Treib, 180–205. Philadelphia: University of Pennsylvania Press, 2002.

Heller, Gregory L. "Salesman of Ideas: The Life Experiences That Shaped Edmund Bacon." In *Imagining Philadelphia, Edmund Bacon and the Future of the City,* ed. Scott Gabriel Knowles, 19–51. Philadelphia: University of Pennsylvania Press, 2009.

Herrington, Susan. "EXPO 67 Revisited." *Landscapes/Paysages* 7, no. 2 (Spring 2005): 12–14.

——. "Kindergarten: Garden Pedagogy: Romanticism to Reform." *Landscape Journal* 20, no. 1 (Spring 2001): 30–47.

——. "A Model Modern: The Landscape Architecture of Cornelia Hahn Oberlander in North America (1943–1993)." Women and Modernism in Landscape Architecture, a colloquium chaired by John Beardsley at Harvard University Graduate School of Design, 17–18 February 2011.

——. "The Nature of Ian McHarg's Science." *Landscape Journal* 29 no. 1 (January 2010): 1–20.

"High Apartments or Low." *The Architectural Forum* 96 (January 1952): 100–117.

Hill, Polly. "Children's Creative Centre at Canada's Expo 67." *Young Children* 22, no. 5 (1967): 258–63.

——. *Habitat* 13, no. 1. Ottawa: Central Mortgage and Housing Corporation, 1970.

Hopkinson, Edward. "Designation Letter Certifying Mill Creek for Redevelopment," 9 January 1948, 030 II.A.31.5. Kahn Collection, Architectural Archives, University of Pennsylvania.

Horowitz, Daniel. *Betty Friedan and the Making of "The Feminine Mystique": The American Left, the Cold War, and Modern Feminism.* Amherst: University of Massachusetts Press, 2000.

Hudnut, Joseph. *Report to the President of Harvard University on the Graduate School of Design for the Academic Year 1941–42.* http://www.oasis.lib.harvard.edu/oasis /deliver/~huao8002.

——. *Report to the President of Harvard University on the Graduate School of Design for the Academic Year 1943–44.* http://www.oasis.lib.harvard.edu/oasis /deliver/~huao8002.

——. *Report to the President of Harvard University on the Graduate School of Design for the Academic Year 1950–51.* http://www.oasis.lib.harvard.edu/oasis/deliver /~huao8002.

Huron, David, and Ann Ommen. "An Empirical Study of Syncopation in American Popular Music, 1890–1939." *Music Theory Spectrum* 28, no. 2 (Fall 2006): 211–31.

Hushion, Nancy. "A City and Its Museums." *Museum* 174, no. 2 (Paris: UNESCO, 1992): 100–102.

Iglauer, Edith. *Seven Stones: A Portrait of Arthur Erickson.* Seattle: Harbour/ University of Washington Press, 1981.

"Inflation Hits Museum." *The Ubyssey* 55, no. 28 (November 1973): 3.

Ironside, R. G. "Canadian Northern Settlements: Top-Down and Bottom-Up Influences." *Geografiska Annaler Series B, Human Geography* 82, no. 2 (2000): 103–14.

Itten, Johannes. *Design and Form: The Basic Course at the Bauhaus,* trans, John Maass. New York: Reinhold Pub. Corp., 1964.

Jacobs, Allan, and Donald Appleyard. "Toward an Urban Design Manifesto." In *The City Reader,* ed. Richard T. LeGates and Frederic Stout, 164–75. London: Routledge, 1996.

Jacobs, Jane. *The Death and Life of Great American Cities.* New York: Vintage Books, 1961.

——. "The Greening of the City." *New York Times Magazine,* 16 May 2004. http:// www.nytimes.com/2004/05/16/magazine/16ESSAY.html?pagewanted=all.

Jacques, David. "Art and Instinct: Modernist Landscape Theory." *Garden History* 28, no. 1 (Summer 2000): 88–101.

Jacques, David, and Jan Woudstra. *Landscape Modernism Renounced: The Career of Christopher Tunnard (1910–1979).* New York: Routledge, 2009.

James, Kathleen. "Expressionism, Relativity, and the Einstein Tower." *Journal of the Society of Architectural Historians* 53, no. 4 (December 1994): 392–413.

Jarzombek, Mark. *The Psychologizing of Modernity: Art, Architecture, and History.* New York: Cambridge University Press, 2000.

Jashemski, Wilhelmina Feemster. *The Natural History of Pompeii.* Cambridge: Cambridge University Press, 2002.

Jellicoe, Sir Geoffrey. "Jung and the Art of Landscape: A Personal Experience." In *Denatured Visions Landscape and Culture in the Twentieth Century,* ed. Stuart Wrede and William Howard Adams, 124–28. New York: Museum of Modern Art, 1991.

Jellicoe, Sir Geoffrey, and Susan Jellicoe. *The Landscape of Man: Shaping the Environment from Prehistory to the Present Day.* New York: Viking Press, 1975.

Johnson, Jory, with photographs by Felice Frankel. *Modern Landscape Architecture: Redefining the Garden.* New York: Abbeville Press Publishers, 1991.

Johnston, Chris, Kathryn McCreary, and Cheryl Nelms. *Green Roofs.* http://www.kwl.bc.ca/docs/GreenRoofPaper04–0430final.pdf.

Kahn, Louis I. *Mill Creek Redevelopment Area Plan.* Philadelphia: City Planning Commission, 1954.

———. "Toward a Plan for Midtown Philadelphia." *Perspecta* 2 (1953): 10–27.

Kassler, Elizabeth (Mock) Bauer. *Modern Gardens and the Landscape.* New York: Museum of Modern Art, 1964.

Kaufmann, Eric. "Naturalizing the Nation: The Rise of Naturalistic Nationalism in the United States and Canada." *Comparative Studies in Society and History* 40, no. 4 (October 1998): 666–95.

Keatinge, M. W. *Great Didactic of Comenius.* Whitefish, Mont.: Kessinger Publishing, 1992.

Kiley, Dan, and Jane Amidon. *Dan Kiley in His Own Words: The Complete Works of America's Master Landscape Architect.* New York: Thames & Hudson, 1999.

Kindt, Don. *Inuvik K-12 Education Report: Educational Planning for SAM and SHSS.* http://www.ece.gov.nt.ca/divisions/kindergarten_g12/Education%20Plans/Inuvik%20K-12%20Education%20Report%20Educational%20Planning%20for%20SAMS%20and%20SHSS.pdf.

Koss, Juliet. "On the Limits of Empathy." *The Art Bulletin* 88, no. 1 (March 2006): 139–57.

Kozlovsky, Roy. "Adventure Playgrounds and Postwar Reconstruction." In *Designing Modern Childhoods: History, Space, and the Material Culture of Children,* ed. Marta Gutman and Ning De Coninck-Smith, 171–90. New Brunswick, N.J.: Rutgers University Press, 2008.

LaFarge, Albert. *The Essential William H. Whyte.* 2d ed. New York: Fordham University Press, 2000.

Lambert, Phyllis. *Reflections.* March 2011. http://www.docs.google.com/viewer?a=v&q=cache:nljm4aVcdkMJ:tclf.org/sites/default/files/pioneers/oberlander/videos/pdf/PhyllisLambet.pdf.

Laqueur, Walter. *Generation Exodus: The Fate of Young Jewish Refugees from Nazi Germany.* Hanover, N.H.: Brandeis University Press, University Press of New England, 2004.

Larivée, Francine. "City Art: Placing Private Visions in Public Places." *City Woman* 1, no. 1 (September/October 1978): 26.

Lavin, Sylvia. *Form Follows Libido: Architecture and Richard Neutra in a Psychoanalytic Culture.* Cambridge, Mass.: MIT Press, 2004.

Lay, Charles Downing. "Space Composition." *Landscape Architecture* 8 (January 1918): 77–86.

LeBoutillier, George Tyrrell. Architectural Science 3a Lectures, Lecture Notes, 1948, Folder BC003, GSD History Collection, Academic Affairs: An Inventory. Frances Loeb Library Special Collections, Graduate School of Design, Harvard University.

Lecesse, Michael. "Canadian Modern." *Landscape Architecture* 70, no. 10 (December 1989): 64–69.

Ledermann, Alfred, and Alfred Trachsel. *Creative Playgrounds and Recreation Centers.* New York: Frederick A. Praeger, 1959.

Ledger, Bronwen. "Vancouver Library Competition: A Public Affair." *Canadian Architect* 37, no. 7 (July 1992): 20–27.

Leiren, Hall. "'Designed for Architects' Says Council: Civic Square Plan Attacked." *The Vancouver Sun,* 20 July 1973, A6.

Levitin, Daniel J. *This Is Your Brain on Music.* New York: Dutton, 2006.

Ley, David. "Alternative Explanations for Inner-City Gentrification: A Canadian Assessment." *Annals of the American Association of Geographers* 76, no. 4 (December 1986): 521–35.

Lubow, Arthur. "Piano Grande." *Departures* (January 2004). http://www.departures.com/2008/0514/design 2–1.htm.

Luxton, Donald. "The Rise and Fall of West Coast Modernism in Greater Vancouver, British Columbia." *APT Bulletin* 31, no. 2/3 (2000): 55–61.

Macaulay, David R., and Jason F. McLennan. *The Ecological Engineer.* Vancouver: Ecotone, 2006.

MacDonald, Chris. *A Guidebook to Contemporary Architecture in Vancouver.* Vancouver: Douglas & McIntyre, 2010.

McLeod, Mary. "Undressing Architecture: Fashion, Gender, and Modernity." In *Back from Utopia: The Challenge of the Modern Movement,* ed. Hubert-Jan Henket and Hilde Heynen, 312–25. Rotterdam: 010 Publishers, 2002.

Maguire, Ellen. "Day Trip: In the Garden of Yin, Yang and Yeats." *The New York Times,* 1 July 2005. http://www.travel.nytimes.com/2005/07/01/travel/escapes/01trip.html?pagewanted=print.

Mallgrave, Harry Francis. *Modern Architectural Theory: A Historical Survey, 1673–1968.* Cambridge, Mass.:Cambridge University Press, 2005.

Marcuse, Herbert. *Eros and Civilization: A Philosophical Inquiry into Freud.* Boston: Beacon Press, 1955, 1966.

Martin, Reinhold, *The Organizational Complex: Architecture, Media, and Corporate Space.* Cambridge, Mass.: MIT Press, 2003.

McCarthy, Michael. "Square Deal." *Vancouver Courier,* 5 August 1998, 1, 4–5.

McHarg, Ian L. *Quest for Life: An Autobiography.* New York: John Wiley & Sons, 1996.

McKay, Sherry. "Urban Housekeeping and Keeping the Modern House." *BC Studies Domestic Spaces* no. 140 (Winter 2003/4): 11–38.

McKenzie, Sandra. "Mistake or Masterpiece?" *Vancouver Magazine* (February–March 1993): 43–50.

Meyer, Elizabeth K. "The Post-Earth Day Conundrum: Translating Environmental Values into Landscape Design." In *Environmentalism in Landscape Architecture,* ed. Michel Conan, 187–244. Washington, D.C.: Dumbarton Oaks, 2000.

———. "Kiley and the Spaces of Landscape Modernism." In *Dan Kiley Landscapes: The Poetry of Space,* ed. Ruben M. Rainey and Marc Treib, 117–43. San Franscico: William Stout Books, 2009.

Meyer, James. *Minimalism: Art and Polemics in the Sixties.* New Haven, Conn.: Yale University Press, 2001.

Michels, Eileen. "The Early Drawings of Frank Lloyd Wright Reconsidered." *Journal of the Society of Architectural Historians* 30, no. 4 (December 1971): 294–303.

Moir, Nikki. "Sculptured in the Play of Tomorrow's Child, Landscaper Begins at Home." *The Province,* 7 April 1962, Sec. Women's News, 23.

Morgan, David. "The Enchantment of Art: Abstraction and Empathy from German Romanticism to Expressionism." *Journal of the History of Ideas* 57, no. 2 (April 1996): 317–41.

Morris, Meaghan, and Naoki Sakai. "Modern." In *New Keywords: A Revised Vocabulary of Culture and Society,* ed. Tony Bennett, Lawrence Grossberg, and Meaghan Morris, 219–24. Malden, Mass.: Blackwell, 2005.

Mumford, Eric. "The 'Tower in the Park' in America: Theory and Practice, 1920–1960." *Planning Perspectives* 10, no. 1 (1995): 17–41.

Murray, Irena Żantovská, and Laura E. Dent, eds. "National Gallery of Canada," 163. *Moshe Safdie: Buildings and Projects, 1967–1992.* Canadian Architectural Collection, Blackader-Lauterman Library of Architecture and Art, McGill University. Montreal: McGill-Queen's University Press, 1997.

Museum of Modern Art. "Modern Gardens and the Landscape." Press Release, 1–2. Friday, 11 December 1964. http://www.moma.org/docs/press_archives/3356/releases/MOMA_1964_0143_1964–12–11_95.pdf?2010.

Nadenicek, Daniel, and Catherine M. Hastings. "Environmental Rhetoric, Environmental Sophism: The Words and Work of Landscape Architecture." In *Environmentalism in Landscape Architecture,* ed. Michel Conan, 133–61. Washington, D.C.: Dumbarton Oaks, 2000.

Nairn, Janet. "Vancouver's Grand New Government Center." *Architectural Record* 168, no. 8 (1980): 65–75.

Nassauer, Joan Iverson. "Managing Career and Family: The Experience of Women Landscape Architects." *Landscape Journal* 4, no. 1 (Spring 1985): 31–38.

———. "Messy Ecosystems, Orderly Frames." *Landscape Journal* 14, no. 2 (Fall 1995): 161–70.

Neutra, Richard. *Mystery and Realities of the Site.* Scarsdale, N.Y.: Morgan & Morgan, 1951.

Newcombe, Tim, with Linda McIntyre, ed. "Rip Rap, Form Follows Flora." *Landscape Architecture* 100, no. 9 (September 2010): 34.

Newton, Norman T. *An Approach to Design.* Cambridge, Mass.: Addison-Wesley Press, 1951.

———. *Design on the Land: The Development of Landscape Architecture.* Cambridge, Mass: Belknap Press of Harvard University Press, 1971.

NWT Bureau of Statistics. 2010. http://www.stats.gov.nt.ca/.

Oberdorf, Charles. "Ottawa Taiga Reveals Canada's Soul." *The Toronto Star,* 6 July 1996, Sec. Life, H2.

Oberlander, Cornelia Hahn. "Book Review of *Neue Gärten* [New gardens] by Ernst Baumann." *Landscape Architecture* 46, no. 3 (April 1956): 174–78.

———. "Good Land Use + Good Architecture = Long Earning Life." *House and Home* (February 1956): 162–67.

———. "Housing and Landscape Architecture." *Ontario Housing* 10, no. 6 (December 1964): 12–15.

———. "Landscaping the Single Family House." *Canadian Architect* (June 1956): 21–25.

———. "Modernism, Aesthetics and Ecology." Women and Modernism in Landscape Architecture, a colloquium chaired by John Beardsley at Harvard University Graduate School of Design, 17–18 February 2011.

———. "A Need for Green Streets." *Canadian Architect* 19 (1974): 34–37.

———. "The New Canadian Chancery: 501 Pennsylvania Avenue, Washington, D.C." *Landscape Architectural Review* 11, no. 4 (October 1990): 6–7.

———. "An Oasis in the City: Robson Square and the Law Courts." *Landscape Architectural Review* 2, no. 2 (June/July 1981): 6–15.

———. "Parks, Playgrounds and Landscape Architecture." *Community Planning Review/Revue Canadienne D'Urbanisme* 6, no. 1 (March 1956): 4–12.

———. "Planned for Leisure Living: The UBC Home of Dr. and Mrs. Sydney M. Friedman." *Western Homes and Living* (1955): 11–15.

———. "Planning the Amenities." *Houses for All: Proceedings of the Vancouver Housing Authority.* Vancouver: Hotel Vancouver, 19–29 January 1954.

———. *Playgrounds . . . a Plea for Utopia or the Recycled Empty Lot.* 2d ed. Ottawa: Department of National Health and Welfare, Canada, 1974.

———. "Spaces for All Seasons," 1–13. Public Lecture Notes Given to Columbia University, 9 March 1988.

———. "Women and the Idea of LEISURE," Lecture Notes, Landscape Architecture Education, ARCH252362. Canadian Centre for Architecture, Cornelia Hahn Oberlander Archive, Oberlander 2008 Addition.

Oberlander, Cornelia Hahn, Ira Bruce Nadel, and Lesley R. Bohm. *Trees in the Cities.* New York: Pergamon Press, 1977.

Oberlander, Cornelia Hahn, and H. Peter Oberlander. "The Spirit of Architecture in the Canadian Northwest." *Progressive Architecture* (February 1958): 120–32.

Oberlander, Cornelia Hahn, and Elisabeth Whitelaw. "New York Times Building: A Garden At Its Heart." *Landscapes/Paysages* 10, no. 2 (2008): 20–22.

Oberlander, Cornelia Hahn, Elisabeth Whitelaw, and Beryl Allen. "Inuvik Northwest Territories Integrating Design with a Climate of Extremes, a Fragile Ecology, and Cultural Complexities." *Sitelines* (February 2010): 14–15.

Oehmichen, Friedrich. Letter to Cornelia Hahn Oberlander, 5 January 1986, National Gallery, ARCH252351. Canadian Centre for Architecture, Cornelia Hahn Oberlander Archive, Oberlander 2008 Addition.

Offen, Karen M. *European Feminisms, 1700–1950: A Political History.* Stanford, Calif.: Stanford University Press, 2000.

The Official Register Harvard University 43, no. 24 (September 1946): Design I, LA 8. Harvard University Archives, Pusey Library.

Olin, Laurie. "Form, Meaning and Expression in Landscape Architecture." *Landscape Journal* 7, no. 2 (Fall 1988): 149–68.

Ord, Douglas. *The National Gallery of Canada: Ideas, Art, Architecture.* Montreal: McGill-Queen's University Press, 2003.

Orland, H. P. "Book Review of *Architectural Graphic Standards* by Charles G. Ramsey and Harold R. Sleeper." *Sewage and Industrial Wastes* 23, no. 9 (September 1951): 1218.

Overland, J., J. Key, B. M. Kim, S. J. Kim, Y. Liu, J. Walsh, M. Wang, and U. Bhatt. 2012. "Air Temperature, Atmospheric Circulation and Clouds," 13–21. *Arctic Report Card 2012.* http://www.arctic.noaa.gov/reportcard.

Park, Chris. *The Environment: Principles and Applications.* New York: Routledge, 2001.

Parsons, Glenn, and Allen Carlson. *Functional Beauty.* Oxford University Press, 2008.

Passantino, Ericka D. "Adventure Playgrounds for Learning and Socialization." *The Phi Delta Kappan* 56, no. 5, Special Issue on Curriculum (January 1975): 329–33.

Pastier, John. "Evaluation: Skyscraper on Its Side." *Architecture* 78 (1989): 64–67.

Pearlman, Jill. *Inventing American Modernism: Joseph Hudnut, Walter Gropius, and the Bauhaus Legacy at Harvard.* Charlottesville: University of Virginia Press, 2007.

Perez-Gomez, Alberto, and Louise Pelletier. *Architecture Representation and the Perspective Hinge.* Cambridge, Mass.: MIT Press, 1997.

Phillips, Ruth B. "Apec at the Museum of Anthropology: The Politics of Site and the Poetics of Sight Bite." *ETHNOS* 65, no. 2 (2000): 172–94.

Pollock-Ellwand, Nancy. "Gréber's Plan and the 'Washington of the North': Finding a Canadian Capital in the Face of Republican Dreams." *Landscape Journal* 20, no. 1: (January 2001): 48–61.

Polo, Marco. "Canadian Modern Landmarks Revisited: Robson Square and Law Courts." *Canadian Architect* 39 (1994): 40–45.

Pond, Bremer W. "Book Review of *Topiary: An Historical Diversion.*" *Landscape Architecture* 46, no. 3 (April 1956): 176.

———. "50 Years in Retrospect: A Brief Account of the Origins and Development of the ASLA." *Landscape Architecture* 40, no. 2 (January 1950): 59–66.

———. "Foreword." In *Landscape Architecture*, ed. Lester Collins and Thomas Gillespie, 5. Cambridge: Harvard University, 1951.

Portland Hotel Society. *Shared Learnings on Homelessness.* 2003. http://www.shared learnings.org/index.cfm?fuseaction=Prof.dspProfileFull&profilesid=18131194 -83ff-4f31-aea0-37e8756b3d0e.

Preston, Brian. "An Affinity for Natural Beauty." *Imperial Oil Review* (1994): 18–21.

Proctor, Robert. "The Architect's Intention: Interpreting Post-War Modernism through the Architect Interview." *Journal of Design History* 19, no. 4 (Winter 2006): 295–307.

Rainey, Reuben M. "Organic Form in the Humanized Landscape: Garrett Eckbo's 'Landscape for Living.'" In *Modern Landscape Architecture: A Critical Review,* ed. Marc Treib, 180–205. Cambridge, Mass.: MIT Press, 1993.

"Related Design Fields: Neighborhood Playground." *Progressive Architecture* 36 (December 1955): 102–3.

Ricoeur, Paul. *Freud & Philosophy: An Essay on Interpretation,* trans. Denis Savage. 4th ed. New Haven, Conn.: Yale University Press, 1977.

Riley, Robert. "Book Review of *Landscape for Living* by Garrett Eckbo." *Harvard Design Magazine* 6 (Fall 1998): 76–78.

Robb, Stephanie. "Pram in the Hall: Interview with Cornelia Hahn Oberlander." Architectural Institute of British Columbia. aibc.ca/pram interviews/cornelia ,html.

Robinson, William. *The Parks, Promenades and Gardens of Paris, Described and Considered in Relation to the Wants of Our Own Cities.* London: John Murray, 1869.

Roeckelein, Jon E. *Elsevier's Dictionary of Theories, Laws, and Concepts in Psychology.* Amsterdam, The Netherlands: Elsevier, 2006.

Rome, Adam. "Give the Earth a Chance: The Environmental Movement and the Sixties." *The Journal of American History* 90, no. 3 (September 2003): 525–54.

Rosenberg, Ann. *The Capilano Review 40 Robson Square.* North Vancouver, B.C.: Capilano College, 1986.

Rossiter, Sean. "The Birth of a Statement: The New Library as an Instant Landmark, But Is It Our Landmark?" *The Georgia Straight* (26 May–2 June 1995): 9–11.

Ruskin, John. *The Seven Lamps of Architecture.* London: Smith, Elder, and Co., 1849.

Rybczynski, Witold. "A Sight for Sore Eyes." *Saturday Night* 111, no. 2 (March 1996): 82.

Safdie, Moshe. Office fax transmittal to Oberlander, 11 December 1992, 75–009–03T. Canadian Centre for Architecture, Cornelia Hahn Oberlander Archive, 2006 Addition, Library Square.

———. "The National Gallery of Canada." *Architecture & Urbanism* 9, no. 240 (September 1990): 3–36.

———. Undated letter to City of Vancouver, 75–009–03T. Canadian Centre for Architecture, Cornelia Hahn Oberlander Archive, 2006 Addition, Library Square.

Sarti, Robert. "49 Storeys off Bennett Tower: 'Civic Park' Complex Unveiled." *The Vancouver Sun,* 14 March 1973, C2.

Scarry, Elaine. *On Beauty and Being Just.* Princeton, N.J.: Princeton University Press, 1999.

Schenker, Heath. "Feminist Interventions in the Histories of Landscape Architecture." *Landscape Journal* 13, no. 2 (Fall 1994): 107–12.

Schmertz, Mildred F. "Collective Significance." *Architectural Record* 176, no. 12 (October 1988): 120–29.

School History. Frances Loeb Library Special Collections, Graduate School of Design, Harvard University.

Shanken, Andrew M. *194X: Architecture, Planning, and Consumer Culture on the American Home Front.* Minneapolis: University of Minnesota Press, 2009.

Shapiro, Barbara E., and Rhodri Windsor-Liscombe. *Arthur Erickson: Selected Projects, 1971–1985.* New York: Center for Inter-American Relations, 1985.

Simonds, John Ormsbee. *Landscape Architecture: A Manual of Site Planning and Design.* 2d ed. New York: McGraw-Hill Book Company, 1983.

Sketchley, Dale A., and Ronald M. Clowes. "A Gravity Survey of the Igneous Body at Little Mountain, Vancouver, B.C." *Canadian Journal of Exploration Geophysics* 12, no. 1 (December 1976): 64–74.

Smiley, David. "Making the Modified Modern." *Perspecta, Resurfacing Modernism* 32 (2001) 38–54.

Spencer-Wood, Suzanne M. "Turn of the Century Women's Organizations, Urban Design, and the Origin of the American Playground Movement." *Landscape Journal* 13, no. 2 (1994): 124–37.

Spirn, Anne Whiston. "Restoring Mill Creek: Landscape Literacy, Environmental Justice and City Planning and Design." *Landscape Research* 30, no. 3 (July 2005): 395–413.

Stanton, Jeffrey. *Expo 67—Architecture.* http://www.westland.net/expo67/map-docs/architecture.htm.

Steinitz, Carl. "Predicting the Impacts of Suburban Development upon an Historically Valuable Landscape, the Boston Region South Shore." *Environmental Review* 4, no. 3 (1980): 2–23.

Stephens, Suzanne. "Law Courts / Robson Square, Vancouver." *Progressive Architecture* 62 (1981): 82–87.

Stevenson, Markley. "A Transitional Year: Annual Report of the President of the American Society of Landscape Architects." *Landscape Architecture* 37, no. 4 (1947): 123–27.

Stinson, Kathy. *Love Every Leaf: The Life of Landscape Architect Cornelia Hahn Oberlander.* Toronto: Tundra Books, 2008.

Stonorov, Oskar, and Louis I. Kahn. *Why City Planning Is Your Responsibility.* New York: Revere Copper and Brass, 1943.

———. *You and Your Neighborhood: A Primer for Neighborhood Planning.* New York: Revere Copper and Brass, 1944.

Storrer, William Allin. *The Architecture of Frank Lloyd Wright: A Complete Catalog.* 3d ed. Chicago: University of Chicago Press, 2002.

Sullivan, Ann C. "From Systems to Architecture." *Architecture* 84, no. 10 (October 1995): 101–5.

Taylor, Timothy. "Mother Nature." *Vancouver Magazine* (2007): 34–38.

Tentori, Francisco, Edmund Bacon, Arthur Row, and David Wallace. "Il piano regola-tore di Philadelphia." *Casabella*, no. 260 (February 1962): 4–25.

Thomas, Christopher. "Canadian Collossus." *Architecture* (October 1995): 72–79.

Thompson, Ian. *Rethinking Landscape: A Critical Reader.* London: Routledge, 2009.

"Tick-Tack-Toe House." *Western Homes and Living* (April 1959): 14–18.

Treib, Marc, ed. *The Architecture of Landscape, 1940–1960.* Philadelphia: University of Pennsylvania Press Studies in Landscape Architecture, 2002.

———. "Axioms for a Modern Landscape Architecture." In *Modern Landscape Architecture: A Critical Review*, ed. Marc Treib, 36–67. Cambridge, Mass.: MIT Press, 1993.

———. "Meaning in Landscape Architecture: Looking Backward and Forward." Panel discussion with Laurie Olin, Marc Treib, Jane Gillette, and Susan Herrington at the Council of Educators in Landscape Architecture Annual Meeting, January 2009, Tucson, Arizona.

———. "Must Gardens Mean?" *Landscape Journal* 14, no. 1 (Spring 1995).

———. *Representing Landscape Architecture.* London: Taylor & Francis, 2008.

———. *Thomas Church, Landscape Architect: Designing a Modern California Landscape.* San Francisco: William Stout, 2003.

Treib, Marc, and Dorothée Imbert, with an afterword by Garrett Eckbo. *Garrett Eckbo: Modern Landscapes for Living.* Berkeley: University of California Press, 1997.

Treib, Marc, and Ruben M. Rainey, eds. *Dan Kiley Landscapes: The Poetry of Space.* San Franscico: William Stout Books, 2009.

Tunnard, Christopher. *Gardens in the Modern Landscape.* London: The Architectural Press, 1938, 1948.

———. "Modern Gardens for Modern Houses: Reflections on Current Trends in Land-scape Design." *Landscape Architecture* 32, no. 2 (January 1942): 57–68.

———. "What Is Happening to Modern Architecture? A Symposium at the Museum of Modern Art." *The Bulletin of the Museum of Modern Art* 15, no. 3 (Spring 1948): 4–20.

Tyng, Anne. "Number Is Form and Form Is Number." Interview 11 and 13 November 2003 by Robert Kirkbride. *Nexus Network Journal* 7, no. 1 (Spring 2005): 127–38.

"Up, Down, and Over: Philadelphia's Children Get Exciting Set of Playgrounds." *LIFE* (13 September 1954): 118–20.

Valpy, Michael. "Drama and Light in a Public Building." *The Globe and Mail*, 3 November 1998, A14.

"Vancouver's Dazzling Center: Arthur Erickson Designs an Airy, Elegant Master-piece." *TIME* 114, no. 14 (October 1979): 50–51.

Vastokas, Joan M. "Architecture as Cultural Expression." *Artscanada* (October/November 1976): 1–15.

"The Viewpoint Early Childhood Education Child Study Centre Faculty of Education." *University of British Columbia* 4, no. 4 (December 1969): 1–12.

Virtual Museum Canada. http://www.virtualmuseum.ca/Exhibitions/Billreidpole/english/resources/moa_village.html.

Wachtel, Eleanor. "An Accessible Heritage." *UBC Alumni Chronicle* 31, no. 2 (1977): 8–13.

Walker, H. Jesse. "Arctic Deltas." *Journal of Coastal Research* 14, no. 3 (Summer 1998): 718–38.

Walker, Peter, and Melanie Simo. *Invisible Gardens: The Search for Modernism in the American Landscape.* Cambridge, Mass.: MIT Press 1994.

Walpole, Horace. *Essays on Modern Gardening.* Canton, Penn.: Kirgate Press, 1904. http://www.archive.org/details/essayonmoderngaoowalpgoog.

Ward, Robin. "And the Winner Should Be . . . ." *The Vancouver Sun,* 21 March 1992, B2.

Way, Thaïsa. "Social Agendas of Early Women Landscape Architects." *Landscape Journal* 25, no. 2 (Fall 2006): 187–204.

———. *Unbounded Practice: Women and Landscape Architecture in the Early Twentieth Century.* Charlottesville: University of Virginia Press, 2009.

Waymark, Janet. *Thomas Mawson: Life, Gardens and Landscape.* London: Frances Lincoln, 2009.

Wellwood, John. "Making Top Grades." *National Post Saturday,* 24 July 1999, Weekend Post, Sec. Homes and Gardens, 21.

White, Stephanie. "Museums and Their Buildings: Our National Galleries." *Vanguard* (1985): 8–12.

Whyte, William H. *The Social Life of Small Urban Spaces.* New York: The Conservation Foundation, 1980.

Williams, Ron. *Landscape Architecture in Canada.* Montreal: McGill-Queen's University Press, in press.

Wilson, Peter. "Construction Din Fills New Library." *The Vancouver Sun,* 16 November 1995, B1.

———. "Erickson Gets Burned as Block 71 Fiddled." *The Vancouver Sun,* 14 March 1992, D4.

Windsor-Liscombe, Rhodri. "Conditions of Modernity: Sightings from Vancouver." *Journal of the Society for the Study of Architecture* 25, no. 1 (2000): 3–17.

———. *Historic Context Statement Post-1940 Register Update and Statements of Significance.* Vancouver: MacDonald Barman, Cook, Birmingham & Wood, Windsor-Liscombe, 2006.

———. *The New Spirit: Modern Architecture in Vancouver, 1938–1963.* Vancouver: Douglas & McIntyre, 1997.

Woudstra, Jan. "The Corbusian Landscape: Arcadia or No Man's Land?" *Garden History* 28, no. 1, Reviewing the Twentieth-Century Landscape (Summer 2000): 135–51.

———. "Danish Landscape Design in the Modern Era (1920–1970)." *Garden Design* 23, no. 2 (Winter 1995): 222–41.

Wright, Jim. "Vancouver Robson Square: Redefining Architecture and Landscape." Unpublished Report, 2004.

Zeller, Suzanne. *Inventing Canada: Early Victorian Science and the Idea of a Transcontinental Nation.* Toronto: University of Toronto Press, 1987.

INDEX

Italicized page numbers refer to illustrations.

abstraction: and empathy, 76–77; in modern landscape architecture, 2, 6, 35–36; in Oberlander's design, 4, 6, 11, 26–27, 207–9; and Wright residence (Highlands), 84
Action Society for Children (Vancouver), 114
"adventure playgrounds," xi, 97, 102
aesthetic changes in landscape architecture, 181–83
affective functions, 37
affordable housing, 34, 61
AGO (Art Gallery of Ontario), 92
Ahlson, Frederick T., 68
Aklavik (ancestral settlement), 192
Allen, Marjory, 102
Almonte Day Care Centre (Ontario), 112
Alofsin, Anthony, 21
American Institute of Architects: Committee on the Environment recognizing C. K. Choi building, 186; Gold Medal for Canadian Chancery (Washington, D.C.), 141
American Society of Landscape Architects (ASLA), 34, 151; President's Award of Excellence for Robson Square, 137
American vs. Canadian landscape architecture, 4–5, 233n98
Andre, Carl, 167
Appleyard, Donald, 121
Approach to Design, An (Newton), 29, 36, 150
Architectural Forum, on Mill Creek landscape, 48
Architectural Graphic Standards, 32
architectural historians, 99
Architectural Institute of British Columbia, 173
Architectural Review, on Library Square (Vancouver), 178
Architecture as Space: How to Look at Architecture (Zevi), 99
Arctic Circle, 192, 193, 198
Arctic Report Card, 195–96
Arnheim, Rudolf, 210
Art and Illusion: A Study in the Psychology of Pictorial Representation (Gombrich), 75
Art Gallery of Ontario (AGO), 92
Asian influence in modern

landscape architecture, 91–92, 216. *See also* Japanese influences
Asia-Pacific Economic Cooperation leaders' summit (1997), 161
asymmetry, 76, 205
Atwood, Margaret, 4
Austria, 223

Babylon's hanging gardens, 141
Bachelard, Gaston, 99
Bacon, Edmund, 41
Bainbridge Island, 84
Balfour, Alan, 222
Balkind, Alvin, 57
Barnes, Elizabeth Bird, 23
Barry Downs Architects, 74
Basic Design studio (course at GSD), 25–26, 29; LeBoutillier's lecture notes, 25
Bauer, Catherine, 119
Bauhaus: design methods, 207; and Gestalt theory, 210; influence of, 2; Vorkurs (Preliminary Course), 25, 26
Baumann, Ernst, 59
Beardsley, John, 160
Beaudet, Marc, 108
Beaufort Sea, 192, 193
beauty's importance in human life, 6
behaviorist models in urban design, 147
Behrens, Peter, 210
Bejach house (Berlin), 12, 224
Bennett, Bill, 126
Bennett, W. A. C., 123
Bennett Building, 123
bentonite, application of, 200
Berlin, 12, 13, 139, 222–24; Wall, 222–23
Bertelsen, John, 102
biodiversity, 3
Bloedel, Prentice, 84
Bloedel Reserve, 84
Blom, Holger, x
Blossfeldt, Karl, 224
Boddy, Trevor, 164, 178
Boggs, Jean Sutherland, 164, 165, 170
Bohm, Lesley R., 120
Borden, Alice, 105
Borden, Charles, 157
Boston Herald, on women's admission to Graduate School of Design (GSD), 22
Bottomley, M. E., 36
Bourgeois, Louise, 171

Breuer, Marcel, 2, 26, 210
Brink, Vernon "Bert," 158
Britain: adventure playgrounds, 102; eighteenth-century landscape gardens in, 5
British Columbia, as leader in children's play and development, 114. *See also specific cities and areas by name*
British Columbia Institute of Technology Discovery Parks, 200
Brosterman, Norman, 26
Brown, Robert, 145
Bruegger, Willy, 134
Brundtland Commission, 182
Bryant Park (New York City), 144
Bunyan's Chess (di Suvero), 85
Busby, Perkins + Will Architects, 224

Calgary, 59
California, orange trees from, 135
Cambridge School of Architecture and Landscape Architecture, 16, 22
Cameron, Underwood McKinley, 62
Campbell, Gordon, 117
Canada: burning of Canadian forests, 180; climate change awareness in, 180; early churches in, 169; environmental legislation of, 153; landscape architecture, history of, ix, xii, 4–5, 233n98; Vietnam War era in, 122. *See also specific regions and cities by name*
Canada Mortgage and Housing Corporation (CMHC), 61, 62, 64
Canadian Architect: Oberlander article in (1956), 59, 75, 82; Oberlander article in (1974), 118; residential projects of Oberlander featured in, 72; review of Library Square (Vancouver) in, 173–74, 178
Canadian Centre for Architecture (CCA), 222; Cornelia Hahn Oberlander Archive, 7, 164, 203; exhibit of Oberlander's landscapes at, 223
Canadian Chancery (Washington, D.C.), 118, 140–43, 164, 205

Canadian Council of Children and Youth, 114
Canadian Embassy (Berlin), 222–23
Canadian Embassy (Washington, D.C.). See Canadian Chancery (Washington, D.C.)
Canadian Film Board, 108
Canadian Museum Construction Corporation, 163–64, 165
Canadian Pavilion, The (Canadian Film Board), 108
Canadian Shield, 166, 189
Canadian Society of Landscape Architects: Award of Merit for North Shore Neighbourhood House play environment, 111; International Citation Award for Canadian Chancery (Washington, D.C.), 141; membership demographics for, 58–59; Oberlander address to (1955), 60; Oberlander address to (2009), 182; Oberlander as environmental chair of, 152; Oberlander as president of, 152; Regional and National Award for National Gallery (Ottawa), 169
"carbon neutral," 181
Carlson, Allen, 182
Carroll, Grisdale & Van Allen Architects, 200
Carson, Rachel, 150
Carter, Anthony Lawrence, 157
case studies, 7
"Case Study Method for Landscape Architecture, A" (Francis), 7
Caulfield (West Vancouver), 201–2
Caulfield gneiss, 202
Cautley, Marjorie L. Sewell, 20
CCCP. See Citizens' Council on City Planning (CCCP)
Centre for India and South Asia Research, 183. See also C. K. Choi building (University of British Columbia)
Chakraborty, Kathleen James, 223–24
Chambers, Walter L., 2, 29, 30
Cherokee Village project (Philadelphia), 30, 50–52, 72, 87–88, 202
children: gardening programs for, 13–15, 112; imagination, challenge, and spontaneous exploration of, 108. See also developmental psychology; playgrounds
Children's Creative Centre

(Expo 67), 103–9, 107. See also Expo 67 (Montreal)
Children's Garden Project (Child Study Centre), 105
Children's Play Resource Centre, 114
Child Study Centre (University of British Columbia), 105
China, 62
Chinatown (Vancouver), 62, 63, 126
Chinese influences, 88, 90, 216
Chrétien, Jean, 192
Chris Spencer Foundation, 109
Church, Thomas Dolliver, 32, 34, 72, 74–75, 83, 84, 120
circles, 37, 62, 76
cities. See urban landscapes
Citizens' Council on City Planning (CCCP), 2, 40–41, 42, 44, 52, 69, 121, 204; Oberlander's work for, 42, 43
citizens' participation. See community participation
City Beautiful movement, 33–34
City Planning Commission (Philadelphia), 41, 47, 50, 52
C. K. Choi building (University of British Columbia), 179, 183–87; design process of, 183–84; infrastructure and water system of, 185; landscape strategy of, 184–86; Matsuzaki as collaborator on, 189; reception of, 186–87; recycling at, 184–86; water filtration trench of, 184, 186, 187
classical references. See historical context of modern landscape
Clendenin, Malcolm, 52
Cleve, Erwin C., 62; McLean Park Rental Housing project, 66; Skeena Terrace Housing project, 64
climate change, 180, 187, 193
CMHC. See Canada Mortgage and Housing Corporation (CMHC)
collaborative nature of work, 29–30, 183–84. See also cross-disciplinary collaborations
Collins, Lester, 2, 29, 37, 89, 211, 216
Colomina, Beatriz, 71, 77
Colosseum (Rome), 173, 177
Columbia University's School of Architecture, 40
Columbushaus (Berlin), 222
Comenius, John Amos, 14
Community Arts Council (CAC, Vancouver), 57, 122–23

community participation: Oberlander's view of landscape architect's role, 60, 121, 187; in Philadelphia, 41; in urban planning, 40
Community Planning Association (Vancouver), 57
Community Planning Review, 29–30, 54
Conical Depression (Webster), 85
Conway, Jill Ker, 109
Cook residence (Alberta), 205, 206
Coriolis force, 196
Council of Educators in Landscape Architecture, 199
courthouse design. See Robson Square (Vancouver)
Cranmer, Doug, 159
Creative Playthings, 232n81
creativity: in Children's Creative Centre (Expo 67), 103–4, 108; Eckbo on, 101; and play environments, 101–3, 114, 118
crime and vandalism, 65, 102
cross-disciplinary collaborations, 2, 11, 118
Crowe, Sylvia, 100
cultural practices. See First Nation peoples

Daniel Solomon ETC Architects, 68
Dattner, Richard, 103
Day, Kenneth, 47
Death and Life of Great American Cities, The (Jacobs), 119
Deforest, Lockwood, 35
de Graaff, Jan, 231n31
Denmark, 101–2
Desaulniers, Robert, 223
Design on the Land (Newton), 99–100
Design with Nature (McHarg), 147–48
Desmond Muirhead & Associates, 59
Deutsches Architektur Zentrum (Berlin), 223
developmental psychology, 97, 104, 109
disappearance, xii–xiii
di Suvero, Mark, 85
D. K. Consulting, 194
Dodge, Donald, 51
Downing, Andrew Jackson, 36
Downs/Archambault & Partners, 150, 173, 174
drafting skills, 27–28, 202–4, 203, 204
drip irrigation, 127
Dudfield, Travis, 178

D. W. Graham and Associates of Ottawa, 105

East Three School (Inuvik), 192–98; community involvement in design of, 197; cultural learning and references, 194, 198; design process of, 194–95; and drifting snow, 196; landscape strategy of, 195–97, 196, 211; and permafrost, 193–95; playground of, 194, 197, 211; reception of, 197–98; tree plantings and replantings at, 197, 198, 211, 212; "V" plan of, 195; and wind, 195–97

Eckbo, Garrett: on architect as psychoanalyst, 75; architectural influences on, 35; and child development, 99; on creativity, 101; drafting style of, 204; egalitarian views of, 36; Farm Security Administration work of, x, 34; and Goldfinger's diagram of space, 98; on Gropius, 26; on historical context, 87; on human need for contact with nature, 120; in Landscape Architecture exhibit catalog (1951), 32; on landscape design, 154; Oberlander seeking job with, 39; Oberlander's opinion on, 23; on organization as goal for landscape architecture, 80; postwar modern landscape architecture, effect on, 5–6; on quality of movement, 76

Eckbo, Dean, Austin and Williams (EDAW), 19

École des Beaux-Arts tradition, 4, 20, 21, 36, 92, 134–35, 200

ecological concerns, 149–98; and aesthetic changes, 181–83; climate change, 180, 187, 193; conservation of old-growth forests, 96; effect on landscape architecture, 3, 4, 147–53, 180–81, 225; green rating systems, 181; Kiley teaching Oberlander about, 45; linguistic and communicative properties, 153–55; social forces coalescing to raise, 151; suburban sprawl, 180; in urban landscapes, xii, 3, 4, 127, 180–98. See also recycling

"ecological footprint," 181

Edmonton plantings used in Yellowknife, 190

18th and Bigler Street Playground (South Philadelphia), 52–56, 53, 55, 104, 106, 220,

227n19, 232n81; featured in Life magazine (Sept. 1954), 28; in The Province article on Oberlanders, 71; sculptures in, 62

Einstein Tower (Potsdam), 223–24

electrical lines, burying from view, 51

Ellis, Joseph, 2, 4

Emdrup (Copenhagen), 101–2

empathy, 75–76, 98

"environ" concept. See human environment

Environmental Design Research Association, 121

environmental movement. See ecological concerns

Environment for Creative Play and Learning, 97, 103, 114

equality and agency, 6, 36

Equinox Festival (Vancouver), 118

Erickson, Arthur: Canadian Chancery (Washington, D.C.), 140–43, 205; collaboration with Oberlander, 3, 30, 92, 118, 125, 139–40, 142, 156, 201; collaborative approach of, 183; Hwang residence, 89–91, 90, 91; meeting Oberlander in Vancouver, 58; on modern landscape architecture, 44; Monteverdi Estates (West Vancouver), 202; Museum of Anthropology (UCB), 155–56, 158, 160, 161, 162; on Oberlander's special ability with plants, 19; Oberlander's view of, 139; Portland Hotel, 66–67; Robson Square, ix, 123–34, 127, 130, 131, 132, 133, 137; UBC Faculty Club and Social Centre water feature, 207, 210; Waterfall Building, 143; Wright residence, 83–86, 86, 87, 192

Erickson Massey Architects, 123, 125

Eros and Civilization: A Philosophical Inquiry into Freud (Marcuse), 100

Essays on Modern Gardening (Walpole), 5

ethnobotanical gardens, 157, 163

Ethnobotany of Western Washington: The Knowledge and Use of Indigenous Plants by Native Americans (Gunther), 158

European adventure playgrounds, 101–3

European influences, 44, 92, 101, 166

European modernism, 5

Evans, Liz, 67

Everett, Jim, 115

Evergreen Building (Vancouver), 118, 139

Experiments in the Environment workshops (1960s), 213

Expo 67 (Montreal), 3, 97, 103–9, 122; design process of, 104–5; landscape strategy of, 105–7, 220; Op-Art Wall at, 107, 108; Pan-a-bode interlocking logs at, 106, 107; reception of, 107–9; Rockcliffe Park Elementary School Playground (Ottawa) compared to, 112

Farm Security Administration, x, 34

Farrand, Beatrix Jones, 20

Fein, Albert, 151

female landscape architects, history of, 3, 20–21

Feminine Mystique, The (Friedan), 18

feminist movement, 17–18, 22, 228n14

Ferguson Simek Clark Engineers, 189; Northwest Territories Legislative Assembly building, 191

First Nation peoples: Canadian treatment of, 155; earliest settlements of, 176, 192; ecological influences on Oberlander, 149; Inuvik population, 192, 194; and Museum of Anthropology (MOA), 8, 154–61. See also Musqueam First Nations people

Fix Up events (Philadelphia), 41

Forbes, Gordon, 206

"Form, Meaning and Express in Landscape Architecture" (Olin), 154

Forty, Adrian, 36

Fox & Fowle, 144; New York Times Building, 145

Frame Lake (Yellowknife), 189; Geological Trail, 191

Francis, Mark, 7, 121

Frankel, Felice, 85

Frank Stella Garden, 92

Fraser River, 176

French influence, 92

Freud, Sigmund, 100

Friedan, Betty, 17–18, 228n14

Friedberg, M. Paul, 103

Friedman residence (Vancouver), 77, 78, 83, 205, 221

Froebel, Friedrich, 13–15, 26, 207

Frost, Henry A., 16, 22–23, 27

Frost, Jeanette, 183, 184

Fuller, Buckminster, 103
functionality, 33–34; and abstraction, 36; affective functions, 37; Assigned functions, 37; in landscape architecture, 36–37; linked to appreciation, 37, 39; linked to honesty, 38; in modern architecture vs. landscape architecture, 35; vs. style, 36; use functions, 37, 230n19
Furedi, Frank, 220
Furnell, Scoop, 28

Gardens Are for People (Church), 75
Gardens in the Modern Landscape (Tunnard), 23, 35, 75, 76, 86–87
Gastown (Vancouver), 185
Gastown Riots of 1971 (Vancouver), 122
gender. See women's role
"Generation Exodus," 11–12
geometric design of 18th and Bigler Street Playground, 53, 53–54
Gerdes, Etta, 223
German influences, x, 222–23
German Jews, 11–12, 15
Germantown Gardens Exploration Trip (Philadelphia), 41
Germany, 2, 60, 222–23
Gerrard, Diana, 68
Gerson, Wolfgang, 59
Gestalt theory, 209–10
Gibson, W. C., 135
Giedion, Sigfried, 99
Gilbreth, Lillian Moller, 13, 16, 18–19
gingko trees, 184
Glemme, Erik, x
global thinking of Oberlander, xiii
Goat Mountain (Oberlander sculpture), 54, 55, 55
Goethe Institute, 223
Goldberger, Paul, 142
Goldfinger, Erno, 98, 99
Goldhagen, Sarah Williams, 88
Gombrich, Ernst Hans Josef, 75
"Good Land Use + Good Architecture = Long Earning Life" (Oberlander article), 30
Gore, Al, 180
Gothic Revival, 165
Gould, Glenn, 188
Grace, Sherrill, 188
Graduate School of Design (GSD). See Harvard University, Graduate School of Design (GSD)

Granville Island (Vancouver), 103, 142
Great Neck (Long Island), Rose's show garden, 39–40
Great Northern Arts Festival (Inuvik), 192
green rating systems, 181
Green Roofs (Oberlander, Whitelaw, and Matsuzaki), 182
Grohs, Edwin, 68
Gropius, Walter, 2, 21, 23–26, 36, 58
Group of Seven, 166, 170
GSD. See Harvard University, Graduate School of Design (GSD)
Gunther, Erna, 158
Gwaii Haanas National Park Reserve and Haida Heritage Site, 152

Haag, Richard, 45, 84
habitat areas, 149
Habitat 67 (Safdie), 103
Hadrian's villa, 141
Hahn, Albert (great-grandfather), 228n18
Hahn, Beate (mother), 9, 12–15, 17, 18, 26; Oberlander's plan view for Der Kindergarten ein Garten der Kinder, 15
Hahn, Franz (father), 12–13, 16
Hahn, Kurt (uncle), 15–16, 228n18
Haida grass mix, 182
Haida Gwaii (formerly Queen Charlotte Islands), 141, 152, 156, 157
Haida Nation, 141, 152, 155, 156, 157, 159, 161; village and totem poles, 162
Halprin, Anna, 213
Halprin, Lawrence, 4, 24, 32, 72, 120, 204, 213, 229n42
Hamann, Cordula, 223
Hamblin, Stephen F., 211
Harland Bartholomew and Associates, 56
Harmon, Jack, 171
Harris, Dianne, 72, 79, 83
Harvard University, Graduate School of Design (GSD), x, 2, 11, 22–26, 28–30, 89, 153, 210–11, 228n35; Oberlander's plan views in Landscape Architecture exhibit catalog, 33; Peter Oberlander's Ph.D. from, 56
Haws, Frank, 87–88
Hawthorn, Audrey, 155–56, 161
Hawthorn, Harry, 155, 161
Heidegger, Martin, 99
Henriquez, Richard, 171

Henry, Sallie and Charles Wolcott, 51
Herd, Elizabeth, 39
Highlands, The. See Wright, Bagley and Virginia: residence (The Highlands, Seattle)
Hill, Polly, 104–5, 108, 109
Hisho, Sensai, 216
historical context of modern landscape, 1, 3–4, 86–93; and Canadian Chancery (Washington, D.C.), 140–41; and Chinese influences in Hwang house, 89–90, 90, 91; clients' preference for, 88; and Japanese influences in residence, 88–89, 89; Kiley's vs. Oberlander's use of, 88; and Library Square (Vancouver), 174–75, 176; and National Gallery (Ottawa), 169–70; Oberlander's references to, 154–55, 170; and Residence Y (Vancouver), 88–89; and Robson Square (Vancouver), 134–35
HIV/AIDS, 67–68, 137
HM White Site Architects, 118, 144; New York Times Building, 145
Hol, Norm, 197
homeless and recovering drug addicts, housing for, 67
Homer Street (Vancouver), 172, 176
honesty: linked to function, 38; in modern architecture vs. modern landscape architecture, 35; Oberlander's desire for honest expression, 38–39
horizontal relationships, 77, 126
Horowitz, Daniel, 228n14
House and Home magazine (1956), 30
House Beautiful: garden articles in, 72; on landscaping for privacy, 79
house's relationship to garden, 77, 78
Hudnut, Joseph, 23, 228n35
human environment, 97–148; cities, 119–48; Oberlander's design for, 211–16, 225; philosophical meditation linked to, 235n4; play spaces, xi, 52–56, 62, 97–118. See also playgrounds; urban landscapes
humanist conception of environment, 4
human rights protests, 122
human scale in Oberlander's work, 4

Hurra, wir säen und ernten! (Hooray, we sow and harvest!; B. Hahn), 13
Husserl, Edmund, 99
Hutcheson, Martha Brookes, 20
hutong (U-shaped courtyard), 88
Hwang (Paul and Josephine) residence (Vancouver), 89–90, *90, 91*

Idea of North, The (Gould documentary), 188
Innisfree landscape (Millbrook, New York), 216
Institute of Asian Research, 183. *See also* C. K. Choi building (University of British Columbia)
Institute of Design (Chicago), 23
Intersection (film), 161
Inuvik, 192–95; Community Greenhouse, 193; community involvement in design, 197; light and prolonged days in, 193; and permafrost, 193–95. *See also* East Three School (Inuvik)
inventions and design solutions of Oberlander, 199–217; abstraction, use of, 207–9; designing and drafting, 202–4; fit of structure and land, 200–202; green roof projects, 200; grid method for application of bentonite, 200; logic of the module, 204–7; modern methods, 200; playground apparatus, 200, *201;* reinforced-concrete flowerpots, 200; syncopation, use of, 216–17; tree layout, 209–11
"invisible mending" technique, 190
irrigation systems, 127, 147
Itten, Johannes, 26

Jackson, A. Y., 166, 170
Jacobs, Jane, 49, 119, 122, 179
James (Chakraborty), Kathleen, 223–24
Janis Gallery (New York), 84
Japanese influences, 87, 88–89, *89,* 91–92, 205, 216
Jarzombek, Mark, 76
Jashemski, Wilhelmina Feemster, 135
Jastrow, Anna Seligmann (grandmother), 18
Jastrow, Elizabeth (aunt), 18
Jastrow, Ignaz (grandfather), 18, 228n18
Jeanne Mance housing complex (Montreal), 64

Jellicoe, Geoffrey and Susan, 100
Jensen, Jens, 42; trees planted by, at Solidarity House, *43*
Jericho Beach (Vancouver), 58
Jews in Germany, 11–12, 15
Jim Everett Memorial Park (Vancouver), 98, 114–18, *117;* design process of, 115–16, 211; reception of, 117–18
Jim Koe Park (Inuvik), 195
John Hay Neighborhood Association (Philadelphia), 41–42, *43*
John Marshall Place Park (Washington, D.C.), 140–41
John Parkin and Associates, 164
Johnson, Carol L., 140–41
Johnson, James, 28
Johnson, Jory, 85
Jones, John Paul, 68
Journal of Archibald Menzies, The (Menzies), 224
Judd, Donald, 167
Jung, Carl, 100
Junior League of Vancouver, 109
junk playgrounds, 101–2
Justice, Clive, 59

Kahn, Louis I., 2, 40, 42, 46, 47–48, 50, 88, 125
Kahn, McAllister, Braik, & Day, 47
Kantian genius in postwar design, 20
Kassler, Elizabeth Bauer (Mock), 21
Keevil, Dr. and Mrs. Norman, Sr., 79; residence, *80, 81*
Kiley, Daniel U.: on Gropius, 26; on human need for contact with nature, 120; influence of, 2, 88, 191; in *Landscape Architecture* exhibit catalog (1951), 32; Mill Creek Public Housing, 49; Oberlander seeking job with, 39; Oberlander's opinion of, 23; Oberlander working with, 31, 44–48, 69; public housing work of, 34, 46, *46*
kindergarten: Froebel's pedagogy on, 26; German ban of, 227n6 (ch. 1); Hahn's model of, 13–14, 26
Kindergarten ein Garten der Kinder, Der—Ein Gartenbuch für Eltern, Kindergärtnerinnen und alle, die Kinder lieb haben (The kindergarten a children's garden; B. Hahn), 14, *15*
Koe, Jim, 195
Koerner, Leon J. and Thea, 207

Koerner, Marianne and Walter, 155
Koss, Juliet, 98
Kuwabara, Payne, McKenna, Blumberg Architects, 222
Kwakwaka'wakw artifacts, 155

Ladies' Home Journal, 39–40
Lambert, Phyllis, 222
landscape architecture: aesthetic changes in, 181–83; as agent for social change, 6, 33–34; ecological concerns of, 3, 4, 147–53, 180–81, 225; evolution to modern conception of, 32–34; Fein on future of, 151; as invisible profession, ix, xiv; for middle-class housing, 72; promotion to women's groups, 60; psychological nature of, 69, 74–75, 100–101; university training in Canada, 59. *See also* inventions and design solutions of Oberlander; "site," understanding of
Landscape Architecture (exhibit catalog), 31–34, *33*
Landscape Architecture (magazine), 22, 35, 36, 39, 59
Landscape Architecture: A Manual of Site Planning and Design (Simonds), 98
Landscape for Living (Eckbo), 5–6, 35, 76, 80, 87
Landscape of Man, The (Jellicoe and Jellicoe), 100
Landscape We See, The (Eckbo), 75
Laqueur, Walter, 11–12
Lasserre, Fred, 58, 59, 77, 207, 221; Friedman residence, *78*
Lavin, Sylvia, 75, 147
Law Courts (Robson Square). *See* Provincial Law Courts (Vancouver)
Lawrence, Alexander, 15–16
Laxton Building (Vancouver), 139
LeBlanc, Robert, 145
LeBoutillier, George Tyrrell, 26, 210–11; lecture notes, *25*
Le Corbusier, 35, 36, 201
Ledermann, Alfred, 54
Lee, Harry, 73, 88
LEED, 181
Leipziger Platz (Berlin), 222–23
Lenne, Peter Joseph, 222
Le Nôtre as influence, 88
Leopold, Aldo, 150
Lewin, Kurt, 210
Lewis, Martin, 64
Library Square (Vancouver), xii, 150, 172–79; Block 56,

172; compared to Canadian Embassy (Berlin), 223; controversy over roof garden of, 175, 220; design process of, xii, 172–74; overall concept of, 174–75; Proposal A or B, 173; Proposal C, 173–75; reception of, 177–78; redesign of roof garden of, 175–76; secret roof garden of, 178
Life and Death of Great American Cities, The (Jacobs), 49
Life magazine, 28, 54
light and shade, 25, 37, 88, 123, 145, 178, 193, 211
Little Mountain (Vancouver), 72
Living Building Challenge, 181
Livingston, Bill, 58
Lutheran Settlement House (Philadelphia), 204, *204*
Lyle, John, 92; Residence X, *93*, *94, 95*

MacDonald, Chris, 172
MacDonald, Clair, 123
Mackenzie River and Mackenzie River Delta, 193, 194, 197, 223
male dominance of landscape architecture, 20–21
Mallgrave, Harry Francis, 76
Maman (Bourgeois), 171
"Man and His World" (Expo 67), 103
Mann, Frederic R., 54
Manning, Warren, 46
Marcuse, Herbert, 100, 122
Marxism, 154
Massachusetts Emergency and Hygiene Association, 41
Matsuzaki, Eva, 139, 182, 183–84, 189, 201, 202
Matsuzaki/Wright Architects, 183, 189; C. K. Choi building, *185, 187*; Northwest Territories Legislative Assembly building, *191*
Mawson, Thomas, 59
Mayer, Albert, 28
McAllister, Louis E., 47
McCall's magazine funding of play space, 102
McHarg, Ian L., 4, 32, 51, 56, 147–48, 152–53, 180, 199
McKim, Mead, and White, 25, 51
McLean Park Rental Housing project (Vancouver), 61–66, *66*, 104
McLeod, Mary, 21
McNab, Duncan, 73; Wong residence, *73*
McTavish, Bruce, 190
Mead, Margaret, 160

Mendelsohn, Erich, 12, 222, 223–24
Mendham (New Jersey), 40
Menzies, Archibald, 224
Merleau-Ponty, Maurice, 99
Messel, Alfred, 222
Messier, Olivier, 26
"Messy Ecosystems, Orderly Frames" (Nassauer), 181
Meyer, Elizabeth K., 4, 149
Michels, Eileen, 204
Migge, Leberecht, x
Mile of History, The (Ottawa), 163, 165
Milkovich, Nick, 66–67, 125, 142, 221; Waterfall Building, *143*
Millbrook (New York), 216
Mill Creek Public Housing project (West Philadelphia), 47–50, 51; crime and vandalism at, 65; design process of, 47–48; landscape strategy of, 19, 48–49, *49*; Phase One, 46, 47–48, 49; plans for, 31, *203*; reception of, 49–50
Miller, James Marshall, 40
Minneapolis, 102, 120
mixed-use development, 172
modern architecture: influence on modern landscape architecture, 35, 65; module's role in, 204–5; in private residences, 71–72
modern art, 35–36, 169
Modern Gardens and the Landscape (Kassler), 21
modernism, 60, 69, 100
modern landscape architecture: GSD training on, 23; Oberlander's role in, 5–6, 11, 60, 69, 72, 219; style of, 21
module, rubric of, 204–7
Moeller-Nielsen, Egon, 54, 55
Moir, Nikki, 64, 71
Mondawmin Shopping Center (Baltimore), 45
Monteverdi housing estates (West Vancouver), 201–2
Montreal, 64, 103. *See also* Expo 67 (Montreal)
Moresby Island, 152
Morgan, David, 82
movement: in architectural space, 98, 213; and asymmetry, 76; in modern design, 211; in urban environment, 147
multidisciplinary teams. *See* cross-disciplinary collaborations
Mumford, Eric, 44, 49
Mumford, Lewis, 119
Museum of Anthropology

(MOA, University of British Columbia), 149, 154, 155–63, *162*; Audrey and Harry Hawthorn Library and Archives, 161; Centre for Cultural Research, 161; design process of, 156–58; expansion of (2009–10), 161–63; gun emplacements of, *157*, 158; Haida grass care at, 182; landscape strategy of, 159–60; Oberlander's involvement over time, 182, 221; overall concept of, 158; as paternalistic toward First Nations cultures, 160–61; reception of, 160–61; and syncopation, 217; visible storage in museum, 156; water feature of, 160, 161–62, *162*, 200; Yosef Wosk Reflecting Pool, 162, *162*
Museum of Modern Art (New York City), 21, 87
Musqueam First Nations people, 156, 161–63
Mysteries and Realities of the Site (Neutra), 75

Nadel, Ira Bruce, 120
Nassauer, Joan Iverson, 151, 181
National Capital Commission, 166
National Defense Housing projects, 29
National Gallery of Canada (Ottawa), 150, 163–71, *167, 168*; design process of, 164–65; fast-track method at, 190; landscape strategy of, 165–69; Library Square (Vancouver) compared to, 173; Minimalist Courtyard, 166–67; Northwest Territories Legislative Assembly Building (Yellowknife) compared to, 189, 190; Op-Art Path, 167, *169*, 171; overall concept of, 165; postconstruction, 170–71; reception of, 169–70; Rideau Chapel, 169; sculpture at, 171; Taiga Garden, 165–66, *167*, 170, 171
National Organization for Women (NOW), 18
National Post article (1999), 18
National Socialists, 2, 12–13
National Task Force on Children's Play, 114
National War Museum (Ottawa), 163, 167
native plants, 3, 117, 181, 224. *See also* First Nation peoples
natural function, 37

"Natur and Kind" (Nature and Child) diagrams in B. Hahn's book, 14
Nazi Germany, 2, 12–13
"Need for Green Streets, A" (Oberlander), 118
Neill, John, 60, 156
Nemetz, Sonny, 135
Nepean Point (Ottawa), 163, 167, 171
Neue Gärten (New gardens; Baumann), 59
Neutra, Richard, 36, 58, 75
Newbrun, Emiel, 28
New Brunswick, 180
New Democratic Party (NDP), 123
New Design Gallery (Vancouver), 57
New Holly Park Phase III (South Beacon Hill, Washington), 68–70, 70
New Rochelle (New York), 16
Newton, Norman T., 29, 36–37, 99–100, 150, 181; demonstration of definition of function in Residence Y landscape design, *38*
new urban building typology, 2
New Urbanism, 180
New York City, 31, 56, 93, 119, 139, 143–44; Oberlander jobs in, 27–29; Theater District redevelopment, 144. *See also* New York Times Building
New Yorker, The, praising Robson Square (Vancouver), 136
New York Evening Post on burning Canadian forests (1862), 180
New York Regional Plan Association, 40–41
New York Times Building, 118, 143–48, *145,* 220
New York Times Magazine article on Vancouver, 179
New York Times, praising Robson Square (Vancouver), 136
Nick Milkovich Architects, 66
Nitobe Garden, 184
Noguchi, Isamu, 54
Norberg-Schulz, Christian, 235n4
North America: environmental legislation in, 153; houses based on ancient temple architecture in, 36; multidisciplinary firms in, 120; Oberlander in ranks of landscape architects, x–xi; playgrounds, 102, 114, 220; pollution concerns in, 150; raising buildings on pillars in, 201;

and social good, x; subsidized housing design in, 67; Vancouver as fastest growing urban housing in, 126
Northern Canada, 179, 187–88. *See also* Arctic Circle; Inuvik
North Shore Neighbourhood House (North Vancouver), 109–11, *110, 111*
Northwest Territories, xiii, 188
Northwest Territories Legislative Assembly Building (Yellowknife), 179, 187–92; boardwalk system of, 191; "cookie tray technique" at, 190–91, *191;* design process of, 189; fast-track method at, 190; "invisible mending" technique, 190; landscape strategy of, 190–91; peat bog, 189–92; reception of, 192
Notre-Dame Island, 103
Nunavut, 188

Oakland Museum, 124
Oberdord, Charles, 170
Oberlander, Cornelia Hahn, *12, 14, 16, 17, 24, 221;* atelier-style small office of, 19–20, 202; birth of, 11; brief biography of, x, 2–3; children of, 105; choice of profession, 21–22; college years at Smith, 16–18; direct management style of, 19–20; drafting skills of, 27–28; early gardening efforts of, 13; and ecological environment, 148, 179, 182–83; fearlessness of, 220; and feminism, 17–19; first architectural job, 27–28; first solo public housing project (18th and Bigler Street Playground), 52–56; "fit between land and structure," 200–202; Graduate School of Design (GSD) training and graduation, x, 23–26, 28–30; hearing impairment of, 13; hiring landscape architects to work in her office, 164; innate curiosity of, xii; interviews with, 7–8; inventions of, 199–217; marriage of, 2, 19, 28–29, 56, 71; as modern landscape architect, 5–6, 225; move from Germany to America, 12–16; move to Ottawa, 112; move to Vancouver, 2–3, 56–61; mumps during McLean Park Housing project, 62; National Task Force on Children's Play, member of, 114; Order of Canada

given to (1990), 182; parents of, 12–13; perseverance of, 222; practice of working in an architect's office, 46; professional recognition of, 20, 111, 137, 141, 143, 169, 182, 186; public housing career of (*see* public housing work); sculpture by, 54–55, *55;* Tick-Tack-Toe House design by, 73–74, *74,* 83, 205; travel to Germany, 223–24. *See also* inventions and design solutions of Oberlander; playgrounds; public housing work; rooftop landscapes; *and specific projects by name*
Oberlander, H. Peter (husband), *29;* background of, 28, 223, 229n59; and Brundtland Commission report, 182; graduation and award of Wheelwright Traveling Fellowship, 30; marriage of, 2, 19, 28–29, 56, 71; meeting Wrights, 83–84; Ph.D. at Harvard, 56; and Robson Square planning, 126; Secretary to the Ministry of State for Urban Affairs, appointment as, 112; similar views to Cornelia, 28–29; and Skeena Terrace opposition, 63; Tick-Tack-Toe House design of, 73, *74,* 205; travel to Germany, 223–24; University of British Columbia, School of Community and Regional Planning, 41; Vancouver connections of, 58
Oberlander, Judy (daughter), 105, 200
Oberlander, Tim (son), 105
Oberlander, Wendy (daughter), 105
occult balance, 207
Oehmichen, Friedrich, 166
Offen, Karen M., 18
"Of Landscape Architecture" (Collins), 37
Olin, Laurie, 154
Olmsted, Frederick Law, ix
Olmsted Brothers, 16, 51, 83
Olympic and Paralympic Games (Vancouver 2010), 138–40
Olympic Sculpture Park (Seattle), 85
One Hundred Foot Line (Paine sculpture), 171
Ontario, 92, 112
Ontario Housing, 34
Operation Fix Up (Philadelphia), 41
Ord, Douglas, 163, 170

Order of Canada given to Oberlander (1990), 182
organizational needs of homeowners, 79–80
originality: as male purview, 20; in playground elements, xi
otosclerosis, 13
Ottawa: City Hall, 171; The Mile of History, 163, 165; Oberlanders' move to, 112; River, 163, 169, 171; UN Peacekeeping Memorial, 171. *See also* National Gallery of Canada (Ottawa)
overlay mapping method, 153

Pacific Spirit Regional Park (Vancouver), 115
Paine, Roxy, 171
Pan-a-bode interlocking logs, 106, *107*
Panofsky, Erwin, 154
Parc des Buttes Chaumont (Paris), 38
Parsons, Glenn, 182
partnerships of male landscape architects, 19
Pastier, John, 137
Pearlman, Jill, 24
peat bog (Yellowknife), 189–92
Pelletier, Louise, 202
Pencil Points, 23
Pennsylvania Avenue Development Corporation (PADC), 140, 141
people with special needs, 6
Perez-Gomez, Alberto, 202
permafrost, 193–95
"Perpetual Holiday is a Good Working Definition of Hell, A" (Shaw), 22
phenomenology, 99, 167, 198
Philadelphia: International Airport, 200; Lutheran Settlement House, 204, *204;* public housing, 31, 65–66; and urbanism, 40; Vancouver public housing compared to, 5, 65–66. *See also* Citizens' Council on City Planning (CCCP); City Planning Commission (Philadelphia); 18th and Bigler Street Playground (South Philadelphia); Schuylkill Falls Public Housing project (Philadelphia)
Piano, Renzo, 144, 146; New York Times Building, *145*
Picasso, Pablo, 164
picturesque theories of eighteenth and early nineteenth centuries, 76
Pin, Gino, 189, 194, 196

Pin/Matthews Architects, 189; Northwest Territories Legislative Assembly building, *191*
Pin Taylor Architects, East Three School, *196, 198*
"Planning and Living in Your Garden" (Oberlander lecture), 80
Planning Board of Township of Mendham, New Jersey, 40
Planning for Play (Allen), 102
planting: aesthetic changes in, 181–83; Edmonton plantings used in Yellowknife, 190; empathy in choice of plants, 76; "invisible mending" technique, 190; new techniques for Robson Square, 128–29; new techniques for Yellowknife and Inuvik, 190, 197; plans, 21, 45–46, *46,* 62–63; purpose of, 37; research on First Nation use of plants, 158; research on plants to filter runoff, 184; species selection for Taiga Garden, 166. *See also* rooftop landscapes *and* landscape strategy *under specific projects*
playgrounds, xi, 52–56, 62, 97–118; "adventure playgrounds," xi, 97, 102; apparatus invented by Oberlander for, 200, *201;* change in North American views on, 114, 220; compared to Royston, xi; creative environments for play, 101–3; diagrams of Oberlander for, 99; Jim Everett Memorial Park (Vancouver), 114–18, *117;* junk playgrounds, 101–2; Lutheran Settlement House (Philadelphia), 204, *204;* Oberlander's beliefs about, 101, 211–13, 220; Ottawa and Toronto, 112; policy development by Oberlander, 113–14; safety-approved equipment for, 114; Space for Creative Play (North Shore Neighbourhood House, Vancouver), 109–11, *110, 111;* and syncopation, 216; Vancouver, 109–18; "vertical climbing tree," 200. *See also* 18th and Bigler Street Playground (South Philadelphia); Expo 67 (Montreal)
Playgrounds . . . a Plea for Utopia or the Recycled Empty Lot (Oberlander), 113
Pliny, 141
political mobilization of Canadians in 1960s, 122

political values of Oberlander, 6, 55–56
pollution. *See* ecological concerns
Polo, Marco, 127
Pond, Bremer W., 27, 30, 32, 59
popular culture, 76
Portland Hotel (Vancouver), 66–68
Portland Hotel Society, 67
postmodernism, 5, 154
Potsdam, 223
Pratt, Ned, 206
precautionary principle, 220
prefabricated materials, 12, 72, 205
privacy, 67, 79
private residences, 3, 70–96; historic references in, 86–93; and human control of nature, 82–83; intimate nature of designing for, 74–75; key garden features of, 72–83; Oberlander's involvement over time with, 221–22. *See also* names *of homeowners*
Proctor, Robert, 7–8
Progressive Architecture, 54, 60, 137. See also *Pencil Points*
promenade architecturale, 48
Province, The, 64, 71
Provincial Law Courts (Vancouver), 127, *127,* 128, 130, *130, 131, 132;* classical references in, 135; as landmark project of Oberlander, ix–x, xi; opening of, 135; planning for, 124; reception of, 137; and revitalizing of neighborhood, ix, xi; waterfalls in, 132–33, *133. See also* Robson Square (Vancouver)
psychological nature of landscape architecture design, 69, 74–75, 100–101, 209–10
public housing work, 2–3, 32–39; negative forces dooming, 50; neglected in landscape architecture history, 44; Oberlander's continuing commitment to, 6, 68; Oberlander's drafting skills honed on, 28; Philadelphia compared to Vancouver, 5, 65–66; tower form, 44, 50; Vancouver, 171. *See also specific projects by name*
Public Works and Government Services Canada, 182
Puget Sound, 84–86
Pullan, Selwyn, 71

Quadra Island, 96
Quayle, Moira, 121

Queen Charlotte Islands. See Haida Gwaii (formerly Queen Charlotte Islands)
Queens Botanical Garden, 144

racial segregation, 50
Radburn planned community, 20
Rankin, Harry, 124
Rattenbury, F. M., 127, 129
Raven and the First Men (Reid), 160
Ravine House (Oberlanders' home), 74, 201
Reciprocal Research Network, 162
recycling, xii, 3, 14, 181, 184–86
redevelopment projects. See public housing work
refugees, from pre–World War II Germany, 12, 15
Regent Park South (Toronto), 64
Regional Plan Association of New York (RPA), 40–41
Reid, Bill, 141, 156, 159, 160
relational feminism, 18–19
renewable energy, xii
Renzo Piano Building Workshop, 18
Representing Landscape Architecture (Treib), 202
research-intensive approach of Oberlander, 30, 202
research methods of author, 6–8
Residence X (Toronto), 92–93, 93, 94, 95
Residence Y (Vancouver), 37, 38, 77, 79, 88, 89
residential gardens. See private residences
Rice, Norman, 82; Home Design Competition, 82
Robillard, Raoul, 127, 129
Robinson, William, 38, 202–3
Robson, John, 135
Robson Square (Vancouver), 122–38, 127, 130, 131, 132, 133, 221; Block 51, 123–24, 128, 133, 135, 136, 138, 215; Block 61, 123–24, 126, 128, 129–30, 131, 132, 133–39, 177, 213, 215, 216; Block 71, 123–24, 128, 130, 132, 133, 135, 137, 215; Canadian Chancery (Washington, D.C.) compared to, 140; Centennial Fountain, 122, 126; changes since completion of, xi, 137–38, 221; design process of, 125–26, 213–16; Erickson collaboration on, 3, 20, 118, 123–34; historical references in, 134–35; Jacobs commending nature's use in, 179; as landmark project of Oberlander,

ix, xi; landscape strategy of, 128–35; level matrix of, 213–16, 214–15; Library Square (Vancouver) compared to, 172, 176, 177; Matsuzaki collaborating on, 183; Oberlander asked to participate, 124–25; and Olympic and Paralympic Games (2010), 138–40; outdoor furnishings of, 134; overall concept of, 126–27; pavers, 133–34; planters, 129–31, 130; railings installed, 138; reception of, 135–38; Restaurant Courtyard level, 213; stramps connecting terraced spaces, 134, 216; subsequent rehirings of Oberlander, 221; and syncopation, 216; tree removal, 19, 138; VanDusen Botanical Gardens Visitor Centre compared to, 225; waterfalls, 132–33, 133; Wright as collaborator, 189
Robson Street (Vancouver), 137, 172. See also Robson Square (Vancouver)
Rochon, Lisa, 170
Rockcliffe Park Elementary School Playground (Ottawa), 112
Rockefeller Research Project in Landscape Architecture, 56
Rogatnick, Abraham, 57, 134
Rome, Adam, 151–52
roofing membranes, xii, 128–29, 138, 176, 221
rooftop landscapes: Canadian Embassy (Berlin), 223; inventions by Oberlander for, 200; Library Square (Vancouver), 150, 173, 175, 178–79; New York Times building, 144–45, 147; as Oberlander signature, 1, 182; Portland Hotel, 67–68; Robson Square (Vancouver), 123–24, 127, 139; VanDusen Botanical Gardens Visitor Centre (Vancouver), 224–25; Waterfall Building (Vancouver), 143; Wong summer residence (Quadra Island), 96
Rose, James, 19, 23, 26, 39–40, 72, 120
Rouse, James, 45
Rowland, André, 206
Royal Canadian Mounted Police, 192
Royston, Robert, xi
Ruskin, John, 38
Rybczynski, Witold, 177

Safdie, Moshe: Gothic Revival style used by, 165; Habitat

67 at Expo 67, 103; Library Square (Vancouver), 150, 172–73, 175–77; National Gallery of Art (Ottawa), 164, 167, 168, 169, 169; Ottawa City Hall, 171
St. Ann's Hill House, 39
Saint Helen's Island, 103
Sakuteiki (Sensai Hisho), 216
Samuel Hearne Secondary School (SHSS, Inuvik), 194
Sand County Almanac, A (Leopold), 150
San Francisco, 65, 120
Sartre, Jean-Paul, 99
Sasaki, Hideo, 32
Sasaki, Walker and Associates (SWA), 19
Scarry, Elaine, 6
Schenker, Heath, 3
Schinkel, Frederick Karl, 222
Schuylkill Falls Public Housing project (Philadelphia), 31, 44–46, 46, 50, 65
Schwab, Erasmus, 14
sculptures: 18th and Bigler Street Playground, 54–55, 55; National Gallery of Canada (Ottawa), 170–71; Residence X, 93, 94; Skeena Terrace, 54–55; UN Peacekeeping Memorial, 171
Seattle, 68–70, 120; Art Museum, 85; Housing Authority, 68–69
Semmens & Simpson, 65, 172
senior housing, 64–65
Seven Lamps of Architecture, The (Ruskin), 38
Shanken, Andrew M., 40
Shapiro residence (Vancouver), 206
Sharp and Diamond Landscape Architects, 224
Sharp, Thompson, Berwick & Pratt, 206
Shaw, G. B., 22
Shipman, Ellen Biddle, 20
show gardens, 39–40
Silent Spring (Carlson), 150
Simard, Jean-Francois, 199
Simonds, John Ormsbee, 32, 98–99, 205, 216
simplicity, 140
Sir Alexander Mackenzie School (SAM, Inuvik), 194–95
"site," understanding of, xii, xiii, 37, 183–84, 199–202. See also design process under specific projects
Sixty Years of Living Architecture (exhibit), 44
Skeena Terrace Housing project

(Vancouver), 61, 63–66, *64,* 104
Skidmore Owings and Merrill (SOM), 27–28
Smith, Gordon, 107
Smith, Tony, 85
Smith College, 2, 16–18, 22; Medal awarded to Oberlander, 109
Social Credit Party, 125–26
social good: and ecological concerns, 151; in landscape architecture, x, 31, 33–34; as Oberlander theme, x, 67. *See also* public housing work
social justice, linked to beauty, 6
Social Life of Small Urban Spaces, The (Whyte film), 119
social transformation, modernism in terms of, 5–6
Society for Children and Youth (Vancouver), 114
Society of Beaux-Arts Architects, 92
socioeconomic geography of urban areas, 121–22
Solidarity House (Detroit), 42, 43
Sørensen, Carl-Theodor, xi, 101–2
South Beacon Hill (Washington). *See* New Holly Park Phase III (South Beacon Hill, Washington)
South Boston GSD projects, 29
South Moresby Island, 152
space, use of, 35, 82, 96, 98; in historical landscapes, 99–100; in playgrounds, 118
Space for Creative Play (North Shore Neighbourhood House, Vancouver), 109–11, *110, 111*
Space, Time and Architecture (Giedion), 99
specifications, 45, 49
"Spirit of Architecture in the Canadian Northwest, The" (Oberlander and Oberlander), 60
Spirit of Haida Gwaii, The (Reid sculpture), 141
Spirn, Anne Whiston, 47, 50
spontaneous exploration, 108–9
Stanley Park (Vancouver), 57, 59
Steinitz, Carl, 153
Stephens, Suzanne, 137
Stewart, Cecil, 59
Stonorov, Oskar: Cherokee Village, 50–52, 202; historical references in work of, 87–88; as inspiration to Oberlander, 125; Oberlander and Kiley working for, 46; as

public housing architect, 2; Schuylkill Falls Public Housing, 44–46; Solidarity House, 42, 43
Stonorov & Haws, 50
Strait of Georgia, 96, 156
Strathcona area (Vancouver), 61, 62. *See also* McLean Park Rental Housing Project (Vancounver)
Street Life Project, The (New York City), 119
Stuart residence (Vancouver), 221
Sturtevant, Butler, 68–69
Styrofoam use, 125, 128–29
subconscious, access of, 100–101
suburban sprawl, 180
Sullivan and Adler, 204
sun/shade analysis. *See* light and shade
Sussex Drive (Ottawa), 166–67
Suzhou (China), 90–91
syncopation, use of, 216–17

Taiga Plains, 188, 193
Taiga Shield, 166
Taoism, 100
Terre Sauvage (Jackson), 166, 170
Thiry, Paul, 68
This is Haida (Carter), 157
Thom, Bing, 124, 139
Thompson, Ian, 37
Thompson, Berwick, Pratt, and Partners, Residence Y, *79*
Tick-Tack-Toe House (Oberlanders' home), 71, 73, *74,* 83, 205
time, role of, 221–22
Time magazine praising Robson Square (Vancouver), 136
Times Square (New York City), 144
To Build a Better City (CMHC film), 61
Todd, Frederick, 57, 103
topiary, 27
Topiary: An Historical Diversion (Stewart), 59
Toronto, 64, 68, 93, 112. *See also* Residence X (Toronto)
Toronto Daily Star review of Expo 67 children's playground, 107
Toronto Star review of National Gallery, 170
Townsend, Mark, 67
Trachsel, Alfred, 54
transparency, 144, 146, 172, 174, 177
trees: Canadian Chancery (Washington, D.C.), 205; Cherokee Village

(Philadelphia), 51; C. K. Choi building (University of British Columbia), 183–84; East Three School (Inuvik), 197, *198,* 211, *212;* 18th and Bigler Street playground (South Philadelphia), 54–55; formula to determine number for open space, 45; gingko, 184; Jim Everett Memorial Park (Vancouver), 115; McLean Park Housing (Vancouver), 62; Mill Creek (West Philadelphia), 48; National Gallery of Canada (Ottawa), 166–67; New York Times building, 145–47; Oberlander's layout of, 209–11, *212;* Portland Hotel (Vancouver), 67; Robson Square (Vancouver), 129–32, *132,* 135; Skeena Terrace (Vancouver), 63, *64;* Taiga Shield, 166; typology of, 45
Trees in the Cities (Oberlander, Nadel, and Bohm), 120
Treib, Marc, 5–6, 7, 199, 202
Trudeau, Pierre, 160, 163, 164, 165
Tunnard, Christopher, 2, 23–24, 32, 35, 38–39, 75–76, 86–87, 91–92, 216
Turner, Nancy, 158
Tyng, Anne G., 47

Unbounded Practice: Women and Landscape Architecture in the Early Twentieth Century (Way), 3
Underwood, McKinley, Cameron, Wilson & Smith, Architects, 63; Skeena Terrace Housing project, *64*
UNESCO, 161
unity, 77, *78, 79,* 207
Universal and International Exposition of 1967. *See* Expo 67 (Montreal)
University of British Columbia (UBC): Acadia Married Student Housing complex, 112, *113;* Child Study Centre, 105; Faculty Club and Social Centre, 207–8, *208–9, 210;* female audience at Oberlander's lecture, 60; landscape architecture program at, 59; Oberlander's contribution to, xiv; Robson Square, use of, 138; Rose Garden, 208–9; School of Architecture and Landscape Architecture, 60, 121; School of Community and Regional Planning, 41;

University of British Columbia (UBC) (*continued*) University Endowment Lands (UEL), 74, 115, 116; University Village, 115–16. *See also* C. K. Choi building (University of British Columbia); Museum of Anthropology (MOA, University of British Columbia)

University of California, Berkeley, 121

University of Guelph lectures by Jellicoe, 100–101

University of Pennsylvania, 41, 153

UN Peacekeeping Memorial (Ottawa), 171

Urban Design Panel (Vancouver), 57

urbanism, 40, 150

urban landscapes, 119–48; citizens' participation in, 40; ecological infrastructure in, 3, 147–48, 180–98; of National Defense Housing projects, 29; New York Times Building, 118, 143–48, *145*; trends in 1970s, 3. *See also* Canadian Chancery (Washington, D.C.); community participation; Robson Square (Vancouver)

urban renewal, 118, 119, 140, 144. *See also* Robson Square (Vancouver)

Urformen der Kunst (Art forms in nature; Blossfeldt), 224

use functions, 37, 230n19

Vancouver: city planning for, 61, 126; description of, 56–57; European modernism's influence on, 5; Gastown Riots (1971), 122; as Hollywood North, 142; housing expansion in, 126; landscape architecture's history in, 5; Oberlander as environmental advocate in, 152; Oberlander continuing to work while living in Ottawa, 112; Oberlanders' move to, 2–3, 56–61; Philadelphia public housing compared to, 5, 65–66; playgrounds in, 109–18; population boom post–World War II, 70; public housing in, 34, 61–66, 171; senior population in, 61; Southeast False Creek area, abandoned buildings in, 122; wood as favored building material in, 138, 205. *See also* Library Square (Vancouver);

Robson Square (Vancouver); University of British Columbia (UBC)

Vancouver Art Gallery, 80, 123, 136–37

Vancouver City Council, 124, 174, 175

Vancouver Foundation, 109

Vancouver Housing Association, 57

Vancouver Housing Authority's Houses for All conference (1954), 200

"Vancouverism," 171

Vancouver Magazine, on Library Square rooftop garden, 175

Vancouver Public Library Board, 172

Vancouver School (architects' group), 65

Vancouver School Board, 112

vandalism. *See* crime and vandalism

van der Rohe, Mies, 35

VanDusen Botanical Gardens Visitor Centre (Vancouver), 224–25

Venturi, Robert, 50, 51

vertical relationships, 77

Vietnam War and draft evaders from United States, 122

visible storage in museum, 156

Wagner, Martin, 24, 222

Wallace McHarg Roberts & Todd (WMRT), 19

Walpole, Horace, 5

Wandering Rocks (Smith), 85

Warhol, Andy, 164

Washington, D.C., 120. *See also* Canadian Chancery (Washington, D.C.)

watercolors, 27

water conservation, xii, 3, 127, 176, 181, 184, 186, *185*, *187*

Waterfall Building (Vancouver), 142–43, *143*, 220

Way, Thaïsa, 3

Webb, Harry J., 59

Webster, Meg, 85

Weimar Germany, 11–12, 21, 223–24

Wellesley Central Place (Toronto), 68

West End (Vancouver), 61

Western Homes and Living, 72, 205

W. Georgia Street (Vancouver), 136, 172, 176, 178

"What Is Happening to Modern Architecture?" (MOMA symposium 1948), 87

Wheelwright Traveling Fellowship, 30

White, Hank, 144

Whitelaw, Elisabeth, 19, 67, 164, 182, 202, 206–7; drawing by, *70*

Whittlesey, Julian, 28

Whole Art of Teaching, The (Comenius), 14

Whyte, William H., 119

wilderness design, xi

Williams, Ron, 4, 60, 121, 199

Windsor-Liscombe, Rhodri, 5, 57, 58, 63–64, 177

Wisnicki, Catherine, 58

Wittkower, Rudolf, 154

Wolfeboro (New Hampshire), 16, *17*

Wolverton, Bill, 184

women's role, 17–19; admission to Harvard's Graduate School of Design, 22; in landscape architecture, 20–21, 60, 151, 220; traditional, 219; working in community, 41, 57. *See also* feminist movement

Wong, Milton and Fei, 72–73, 88, 96; residence (Vancouver), 72–73, *73*, 88, 200; summer residence (Quadra Island), 96

"Working with Children and Communities in the Planning Process" (Oberlander workshop), 121

World's Fair (1967). *See* Expo 67 (Montreal)

World's Largest Tea Party (Robson Square, Vancouver), 136

World War II, 11, 34

Wosk, Yosef, 179

Woudstra, Jan, 101–2, 201

Wright, Bagley and Virginia, 83–86; residence (The Highlands, Seattle), 83–86, *86*, *87*, 192; —, design process, 83–84; —, landscape strategy, 84–85; —, reception, 85–86

Wright, Frank Lloyd, 44, 204

Wright, Jim, 19–20, 125, 126, 139, 189

Yellowknife, xii, 188–89. *See also* Northwest Territories Legislative Assembly Building (Yellowknife)

Yorke, Linda, 206

Yukon, 188

Zennaro, Alberto, 134

Zevi, Bruno, 99

Zion, Beatrice L., 32

Zion, Robert L., 32